After Khomeini

For Iran the years since Ayatollah Khomeini's death have been dominated by the need for political consolidation and economic reconstruction.

The book assesses the critical dilemmas of the regime both previous to and since the demise of its first spiritual leader. The vital issues of political succession and constitutional reform are addressed, contributing to an analysis of the structures and politics of power. How these have reflected upon economic policy is considered, with close attention being given to the reform policies of Rafsanjani. Foreign policy and security issues are discussed in both regional and global terms and include a study of Iranian defence strategy and its controversial rearmament drive.

At the heart of this study is the belief that the Islamic regime has, since the cease-fire with Iraq, but more specifically since Ayatollah Khomeini's death, passed into a new stage of development, referred to in the book as the 'Second Republic'. Students of this vitally important Middle Eastern state will find the book an invaluable guide to its changing internal political scene and its role in the region.

Anoushiravan Ehteshami is Senior Lecturer in Middle East Politics and Director of Postgraduate Studies at CMEIS, the University of Durham.

After Khomeini
The Iranian Second Republic

Anoushiravan Ehteshami

London and New York

First published 1995
by Routledge
11 New Fetter Lane, London EC4P 4EE

Simultaneously published in the USA and Canada
by Routledge
29 West 35th Street, New York, NY 10001

Typeset in Times by
Michael Mepham, Frome, Somerset.

Printed and bound in Great Britain by
Mackays of Chatham PLC, Kent

British Library Cataloguing in Publication Data
A catalogue record for this book is available from the British Library

Library of Congress Cataloging in Publication Data
A catalogue record for this book has been requested

ISBN 0–415–10878–0 (hbk)
ISBN 0–415–10879–9 (pbk)

To my wife, Emma, and in memory of my mother

Contents

List of tables

Acknowledgements

Although the name of only one individual appears on the cover of this book, like most projects of this nature it would never have reached fruition if it was not for the generous support and encouragement of a small army of friends and colleagues, and the readiness of very many good listeners to criticise and comment on parts and earlier drafts of this book. Chief among them I count my dear wife, who has been a tower of strength and support to me. To say that her help at every stage of research, development of ideas and formulation of my findings was crucial would probably not do justice to her efforts.

As the idea of writing this book emerged back in 1990, inevitably many individuals have since passed through the revolving door of dialogue with me. Three in particular need a special mention, Tim Niblock, Kamran Mofid and Gerd Nonneman, who were involved from the earliest stages. Other colleagues and friends without whose advice and comments the book would have been much poorer in content I must name Fred Halliday, Roy Hinnebusch and Eric Hooglund. In the course of developing my ideas for the book, I used many colleagues as sounding boards. Their insights and comments on different aspects of the arguments in the book proved invaluable. Colleagues at the PHP Research Institute of Japan, the Japan Institute of Middle Eastern Economies and the Institute of Developing Economies of Japan need a special mention for their help in sharpening my ideas.

No one but myself, of course, is responsible for the arguments presented in this book and its shortcomings.

Introduction

No revolution in recent years has gained as much international political commentary and media attention as the Iranian revolution which culminated in the establishment of the Islamic Republic of Iran in 1979. The profoundly Islamic character of the new regime sent ripples of unease through the Middle East region and the wider world as representatives of an unknown quantity, led by the apparently uncompromising and forceful figure of Ayatollah Ruhollah Khomeini, set about building an Islamic state at home and spreading its influence throughout the Middle East.

Under his often apparently very personal guidance, Iran steered a course marked by policies of fervent non-alignment, total integration of the executive and legislature with clerical authority, and broadly populist economic redirection. The policies were often somewhat eclectic and unco-ordinated, reflecting both the chaotic residue of the revolutionary process itself, and the unpreparedness of the theological establishment to actually wield the reins of power, in both practical and ideological terms. For the greater part of the era of his rule, Ayatollah Khomeini's Iran was further engaged in a prolonged and bloody war with neighbouring Iraq, and was subject to political, diplomatic and economic conditions which were to severely test the strategic potential of the young republic. Khomeini himself was to die in June 1989, leaving a gaping hole in terms of ideological authority and personal leadership. Yet, contrary to the expectations of many commentators, no succession crisis appeared to threaten the republic's progress along the Islamic path. Several years later, and in spite of grave economic difficulties and outward isolation, Islamic government remains in place.

Since the patriarch's death, however, the pace of reform in the republic has accelerated, encompassing virually all aspects of life in the country and its foreign relations. These reforms, moreover, should be seen in the context of the Thermidor of the Iranian revolution, by which I mean when the revolutionary process ends and 'the beginning of the definitive establishment of the new regime' (Mozaffari 1993: 611) is in sight. As will be argued in this book, Thermidor has been the most revolutionary change that could have affected the Islamic Republic. Although there is little consensus as to the date of the Thermidor of the Islamic revolution, most analysts seem to agree that the process may have accelerated with Iran's acceptance of a cease-fire in the Iran–Iraq war and gathered momentum after Ayatollah Khomeini's death a year later. Abrahamian argues that the process had begun as long ago as 1983, but he too acknowledges that it was not until Ayatollah Khomeini's death that the Khomeini era was finally over (Abrahamian 1993). But what has replaced the revolutionary regime? On this issue there still exists much controversy and debate.

It was through the search for some answers to the above question that this book was born. It attempts to accomplish two complementary tasks: to account for the basis of the Thermidor of the Iranian revolution on the one hand, and to try and explain the nature, outlook and policies of the political regime which has succeeded Ayatollah Khomeini on the other. To denote the changes in the formal distribution of power in Iran since Ayatollah Khomeini's death, the constitutional changes of 1989, the leadership style of Ayatollah Khomeini's heirs, the content of the policies of the post-Khomeini leadership and the ways in which their policies differ from those of the Khomeini era, I have adopted the term the Second Republic. This is my shorthand for separating the two periods in Iran's recent experience of republicanism. The term Second Republic does not imply a break with the past. On the contrary, in many ways the Second Republic is a direct product of the Khomeini order, and post-Khomeini leaders owe their positions to the republican form and nature of the regime that the leader of the revolution founded.

It is, therefore, in examining the nature of the post-Khomeini leadership in Iran, changes in the structure and formal distribution of power therein, and the economic, political, foreign and defence and security policies pursued by Ayatollah Khomeini's lieutenants, that one finds reason to refer to the emergence of a 'new' republic whose *modus operandi* can be said to be different from that of the original, First Republic, and thus allows one to use the phrase the Second Republic.

The question of leadership has been, and remains, central to the debate about Iran, and is therefore the key to understanding the nature of power under Iran's Faqih-based system. Hence this book starts with a discussion of political succession in Iran and continues, in chapter 2, with an examination of the changes that the constitutional amendments of 1989 have brought about. Chapter 3 is a study of the distribution of power in post-Khomeini Iran and the power base of the key players in the country. It also analyses in some detail the politics (and outcome) of general elections in the Second Republic and draws some conclusions by looking at the relationship between elections and political power in post-Khomeini Iran. Chapters 5 to 8 focus on the policy content of the Islamic Republic, and through comparisons of the First and the Second attempts to shed some light on the latter's policy objectives and orientation. Chapter 9 is a reflective concluding chapter which puts the Iranian revolution in broader context. Having argued that the Thermidor has well and truly set in, and that post-Khomeini Iran is 'an ordinary state' now, it was only fitting to ask, what, if anything, can be learned from the Iranian revolutionary experience.

1 Political succession in republican Iran

> The February revolution was a surprise attack, it took the old society unawares . . . it is no longer the monarchy that appears to have been overthrown but the liberal concessions extracted from it by a century of struggle. Instead of society conquering a new content for itself, it only seems that the state has returned to its most ancient form, the unashamedly simple rule of the military sabre and the clerical cowl.
>
> Karl Marx, *Surveys from Exile* (II)

Since the defeat of Mohammad Mossadeq's bid for political power in 1953, the question of the political continuity of leadership in Iran has been fraught with uncertainties. Although the rule of Mohammad Reza Shah Pahlavi was uninterrupted from 1953 until 1979, his reign was not to be unchallenged (not least by Ayatollah Khomeini himself during the mid-1960s) (Abrahamian 1982: 473–9). The monarch's consequent preoccupation with control of the Iranian elite, coupled with his concerns over dissension from the traditional ruling classes or the armed forces, ensured that he would not accord the question of succession priority lest it might help to undermine his position as the governing monarch. In a formal sense the issue of succession had resolved itself with the birth of a male heir, Reza Pahlavi, in 1960 and it was not until 1978 and the advent of the revolutionary movement that the issue of succession became a serious political factor in the considerations of the opposition and the loyalists alike. The rapid erosion of support for the Pahlavi monarchy, coupled with the steady deterioration in the regime's ability to confront the revolutionaries, accelerated the collapse of the whole system, leaving little prospect of the Shah abdicating in favour of his son in order to provide for the continuity of the Pahlavi dynasty.

Similarly, the question of succession has since been an important political factor in revolutionary Iran. The revolution of 1979 gave birth to a new (ruling) political elite which, during the first two years of the Islamic Republic, remained a coalition between the Shah's secular and religious opponents. After 1981, the clerical forces gained the upper hand and, under the guidance of Ayatollah Ruhollah Khomeini (the Supreme Leader), formed the backbone of the republic's political leadership. After 1989, however, important changes in the political leadership occurred, giving rise to the consolidation of the position of some of Ayatollah Khomeini's more junior trusted allies at the top of the power pyramid. They solved the issue of succession to their own advantage by gaining the upper hand in the contest for the control of the state and its constituent parts. In so doing, they seemed to have put an end to the problem of political continuity in modern Iran, as defined by the absence of a peaceful transfer of power, which had always threatened to undermine the position of the ruler in Iran's post-1945 history. This is perhaps the most important demonstration of a much altered political structure and attendant policies which emerged during and since the period of Ayatollah Khomeini's demise and which merit the use of the term Second Republic. The problems of succession and political continuity are at the heart of the progression of the Islamic Republic from a state the authority of which is ultimately in the hands of one man to a constitutionally more solid and institutionally based distribution of power.

If one is to look for political continuity in republican Iran, one has to accept that the seeds of the Second Republic were sown during the infant years of the republican regime and the unfolding drama surrounding the balance of forces therein. It was almost inevitable that the system would change after Ayatollah Khomeini's death, although it was never certain in just what manner. Less clear still was whether the Islamic Republic as a system would survive the death of its founder. As the years wore on, it became apparent that even if the system survived Ayatollah Khomeini's death it would inevitably have to change in order to adapt to new realities.

The problems of political continuity after Khomeini's death were evident from the earliest days of the revolution, in some ways reflecting a concern inherited from the Pahlavi regime along with the structures of power. Not least of the worries of the revolutionary forces was the advanced age of Ayatollah Khomeini, the undisputed leader of the revolution after October 1978, and the knowledge that a resolution of the succession dilemma would have to come sooner rather than later.

The Iran–Iraq war provided the main backdrop to the internal debates of the ruling elite about the succession. Any successor, it was assumed, would have to have the necessary skills to lead the country's war effort, maintain cohesion amongst the ruling factions, and provide guidance for the masses. A tall order indeed. It is not surprising, therefore, that no single individual with the required qualities emerged in the early years of the republic. The leadership problem was compounded by in-fighting and factionalism at the national political level and the opposition of a number of the leading Shii clerics (Ayatollahs and Grand Ayatollahs) to the Faqih doctrine of Ayatollah Khomeini and his followers in the Shii hierarchy. The peculiarities of the Islamic Republican system and the constitutional pronouncements on the qualities of the Faqih – he had to be of high (Iranian) Shii Islamic standing, and a recognised leader in the field of Islamic scholarship – made the prospects of a 'natural' leader emerging that much harder (Abrahamian 1993).

The doctrine of the Velayat-e Faqih as enunciated by the late Imam caused some serious difficulties for his political and politico-religious successors, who were by and large of a more junior religious rank and status. Indeed, this was the case largely because the concept clearly assigned the responsibility of leading the nation to the Marja'a-e Taqlid (source of emulation in Shiism), and not to the junior clerics themselves. 'The just fuqaha', wrote Khomeini, 'must be the leaders and rulers, implementing divine ordinance and establishing the institution of Islam' (Algar 1982: 79). As Irfani points out, the 'just fuqaha are none other than the Marja'a-e Taqlid' (Irfani 1986: 35). Omid also stresses the plurality of (religious) leadership in Ayatollah Khomeini's conceptualisation of an Islamic government. In his writings, Ayatollah Khomeini normally referred to the 'Fuqaha' (religious leaders) and not the 'Faqih' (religious leader) (Omid 1992). Milani notes that the framers of the 1979 constitution deliberately established an organic relationship between the institution of the Faqih and the Marja'aiyat (Milani 1992). In 1989, therefore, when Khomeini's death resulted in the post of Faqih being transferred to his successor, the question was left open as to when the new Faqih, only recently promoted to the rank of Ayatollah, might become a Marja'a. This has since become a highly controversial political issue and a source of great tension within the system, being exacerbated by the passing away of the established Ayatollah Ozmas (Grand Ayatollahs) in recent years (Jahanpour 1994).

As it was, a number of senior Ayatollahs opposed the concept of the Faqih. At least one Grand Ayatollah raised objections to the whole process of the religious establishment's drive to monopolise political power. Grand Ayatollah Hassan Tabataba'i Qomi's comments stand as a testimony to the depth of the opposition among the orthodox Shii establishment to the fundamentalist Islamic republicans' rush for power:

I told Ayatollah Khomeini that the IRP [Islamic Republican Party] was corrupt and rotten, and it was for him not to permit these filthy laws to come into force nor allow a bunch of corrupt, irrelevant, and unqualified 'experts' to go ahead and constitute authority.

(Irfani 1983: 221)

Qomi went as far as declaring the new constitution 'no good' because a number of its articles were un-Islamic, in his view.

Another aspect of Ayatollah Khomeini's rule with a bearing on the succession issue was his style and leadership. In general Ayatollah Khomeini himself did not engage in factional politics until the latter part of the 1980s, when a crisis of institutional competition demanded it of him. Although his subordinates were selected or elected to run the Islamic state, the centrality of his role as the Supreme Leader often meant that he would exercise his power by passing judgement on major issues of the day. His pronouncements, however, were usually open to interpretation and his interventions non-strategic; they did not end a line of thought, but merely helped to weaken it against others. By intervening to bolster the position of an individual, an institution or a line of thought against others, he in fact tended to fuel the factionalism and competitive nature of elite politics in the Islamic Republic (Schahgaldian 1989). A by-product of this method of rule was the way in which it allowed the development of diverse interpretations of his views that crystallised into ideological factions among the politicised clergy. Khomeini's style of leadership has had significant implications for his successors because some of them, including perhaps the current Faqih, may not have the temperament, acumen or charisma to forge compromises among the factions as Khomeini himself managed to do so successfully.

CONTINUITY AND CHANGE IN IRAN'S POLITICAL POWER STRUCTURES

If the issue of succession has dogged the Islamic Republic since its early years, so too have the structures of Pahlavi society, many of which have remained in place, sometimes essential to the new republic and at other times appearing to haunt it. For many observers of (and participants in) the 1979 anti-Shah revolution, the movement fell well short of a social transformation of society by forcibly limiting the boundaries of change to the political level. Moaddel argues that:

> The initial years of the post-revolutionary period were punctuated by events favouring a major structural change directed against the landowners and capitalists. However, a reverse trend soon gained momentum. At first, it was able to halt the move toward social revolution. Then it began to undo what had been done in [the] previous phase.
>
> (Moaddel 1991: 319)

Although the social structure of the Islamic Republic did change sufficiently to reflect Iran's new political realities (in terms of the overthrow of the Shah and the departure and/or alienation of the '*comprador*' social groups allied to his regime), the view persisted that the emergence of the Islamic Republic signified an exercise in the violent circulation of Iran's political elite and not a revolutionary transformation of its social structure (Ja'far and Tabari 1984). As such, therefore, it was argued that the new elite not only did not 'revolutionise' the centralised state machinery (its monopoly of legitimacy, administration and violence), but went only so far as to fine-tune it and to add new appendages to the government machinery as hallmarks of the Islamic Republic's life.

There is considerable evidence to suggest that the social relations of 'production, circulation and exchange' created by the Shah remained very much intact under the new system. Later chapters will deal at some length with the economic structures of the Islamic Republic. It is sufficient to say here that at the socio-economic level capitalism was not eradicated with the end of the 'dependent capitalist system' of the post-1953 Pahlavi period. Its political appearances changed, however, to reflect Iran's new class realities. If the Shah had come to represent the pinnacle of the socio-economic pyramid of Iran, the republican leadership reflected the ascendancy of lower social strata; they in fact came to signify the medium and upper layers of the new 'flat-top' socio-economic pyramid. Despite Ayatollah Khomeini's efforts to institutionalise a new pinnacle (substituting the Faqih for the Shah), the newly liberated 'flat-top' elites of the pyramid had already begun their competition for political power (and for control of the state as the enabling instrument of power), the essential condition for perpetuating their own social existence.

The revolution neither eliminated the political challenge of the former elites nor ended the challenge of the politically active non-elites to the preserved and newly established vestiges of power. Despite their physical and intellectual presence, however, many of the Islamic Republic of Iran (IRI), opponents be they monarchist or republican, failed to mount an effective challenge. Part of the reason for this failure lay in the opposition's inability to account correctly for the nature of the theocratic regime. Many elements within the leftist movements, for instance, limited their analytical tools to a prescribed set of conditions said to have existed during the Shah's era. They continued to identify the players and forces of the clergy-led movement – and regime – with the so-called 'dependent capitalist' socio-economic model. According to this view, if the entire Iranian system was, and continued to be, dependent capitalist then its ruling class(es) must also be, or eventually become, *comprador* bourgeois (this view was particularly prevalent amongst those leftists who had been influenced by the views and theories of the Fadayin Organisation) (Moghadam 1987). Furthermore, the state machinery was said to continue to operate according to the governing laws of the capitalist system which dominated Iran before the revolution and *vis-à-vis* the world capitalist system. The latter enabled the former to gain some autonomy from the ruling classes in order to fulfil its own historical function of preserving the interests of dependent capitalism in the long term. The recommended solution of the leftists was therefore the destruction of the entire system.

The left Islamic Mojahedin movement based its analysis of the IRI system on the character and personality of the Ayatollah himself. In the early days of the revolution they viewed him as a progressive cleric. By 1981, however, they had revised their opinion, comparing his socio-economic position to that of the Shah. They saw in Ayatollah Khomeini the symbol of an Islamic Republican dependent system, little different from the capitalist-dependent system of the Pahlavis save in its Islamic accessories. Their failure to recognise the relationship between Khomeini himself and the character of the Islamic Republic was reflected in their choice of strategic slogans. The continuing belief that without Khomeini the Islamic Republic could indeed abandon its capitalist-dependent status led them to call for 'Death to Khomeini' along with 'Death to the Shah', reflecting the desire to attain a tactical goal, i.e. to create a change in the regime through removing the republic's leading figure(s) but preserving the post-Pahlavi structures. A fissure existed, then, between leftist secular groups – who called for an end to the Islamic Republican structures ('Death to the Islamic Republic') – and the Mojahedin – who sought only an end to Khomeini's personal rule. This confusion over strategy and differences over the choice of correct slogans served to distance the Mojahedin from their potential allies on the left at the height of the struggle between the regime and its opponents. Divided and confronted by overwhelming popular support for the regime, the opposition fell!

The monarchist and pro-monarchist forces, on the other hand, were likewise unable to analyse the nature of the revolutionary changes in Iran. Convinced of the Pahlavi regime's integrity, they constantly looked beyond Iran to find exogenous causes of the revolution, such as 'international communism'. The conspiracy to overthrow the Shah, in the eyes of the pro-Pahlavi groups, did not end with communist interference, however. Their assessment was very wide in scope, ranging from accusing the PLO of having organised and armed the militant Islamic groups, attacking President Carter for his human rights campaigns (seen to have helped to undermine the Iranian monarch's authority at home), and condemning the Carter administration for not rushing to the aid of the Shah in his hour of need. The monarchical forces failed to understand the configuration of forces which had come to make up the political elite of the Islamic Republic. The Paris-based National Movement of Iranian Resistance (NAMIR), headed by the late Shahpour Bakhtiar (the Shah's last Prime Minister), for instance, continued to identify the leading clerics of the republic with the Soviet Union and the 'sinister aims of World Communism'. In adopting such positions he and his contemporaries failed to appreciate the socio-economic dimensions of the regime's suppression of the leftist-radical and reformist movements in Iran, in the process missing the opportunity to organise an effective united front-type structure with some of the domestic opposition forces.

Both republican and monarchist camps were divided over how to deal with the burning issues of the day: social philosophy, the national economic development strategy, land reform, taxation, whether to expand the public sector or free the economy to market forces, foreign policy, the role of clergy in politics, and the status of the expatriates. Lack of clear-cut policies on these issues added to the confusion over the future development of Iran and the country's place in the international community.

Thus it is fair to say that, during the crucial first two years after the revolution, the clerics were able to build upon continuities in the political and socio-economic realms to consolidate their own power, while the contenders for that power were emasculated by failure to comprehend the nature of those continuities and their own positions within the new republic. If one is to ask at this point where the succession issue comes into this, it is in the realisation by the republican Islamic regime that, to hold on to that power and to continue to defy the efforts of the opposition to seize it from them, they must recreate the existing system to allow for a peaceful transfer of power from one generation of Islamic leadership to another without exposing fragilities which could be exploited for their downfall.

At this point, it is useful to identify the various factions and political groupings which were competing for power in the early post-revolution years and to assess their respective impacts upon the succession issue within the Islamic Republic. This can provide us with essential clues as to why the Islamic regime was able to manage its peaceful transfer of power as and when it did.

THE REPUBLICAN CONTENDERS

The republican camp can be divided into three distinct groups: the fundamentalist Islamic republicans (FIR), the liberal Islamic republicans (LIR) and the secular republicans (SR). It was the first two of these groups which were ultimately to capture the reins of power at the expense of the third.

It is within the first category that the Islamic Republic's internal feuds have been fermenting. Most observers have divided the factions in the FIR camp into three or four competing groups. Until the official demise of the Hojatieh Society, the on-going power struggle within the FIR camp had centered around the two main axes of the Hojatieh and the 'Followers of the Imam's Line' (also known as the Maktabis). While formally everyone involved with the governing and administering of the state adhered to the

Imam's Line, clear and distinguishable differences over the interpretation of its content began to emerge soon after the revolution. From the ranks of the 'Followers of the Imam's Line' were drawn the so-called 'radicals', those who from the period prior to the death of Ayatollah Khomeini were associated with anti-Western foreign policy, favouring the continuation of the war with Iraq, the export of the 'Islamic revolution' by any means, state control of the economy and strict imposition of the Islamic social and legal system.

Many Western analysts at this time regarded Ali Khamenei, Mir Hussein Moussavi, Ali Akbar Hashemi Rafsanjani and Ayotolloh Hussein Ali Montazeri (all key figures in the Islamic Republic) as Maktabis (or Towhidis), all being committed to the reform of Iran's economy in a more populist direction (full land reform, high taxation, subsidised goods and services for the poor and needy, anti-foreign capital investment policies, nationalisation of foreign trade, etc.). James Bill, for instance, has classified both Khamenei and Rafsanjani as 'political extremists' (Bill 1982: 36). According to a *Financial Times* report, 'on the one side there are social reformers, represented by the President [Khamenei] . . . the Prime Minister [Moussavi], and . . . Speaker of the Parliament [Rafsanjani] [who are] . . . eager to push through land reform laws and the nationalisation of foreign trade' (6 May 1983). Others, Akhavi (1987), Schahgaldian (1989), Behrooz (1991) and Abrahamian (1993) among them, found a much more differentiated elite structure in post-Pahlavi Iran.

It is clear that while there was consensus over certain issues, social policy in particular, unanimity was certainly not detectable in other fields, notably economic policy and regional and international policies. 'Differences of opinion', as the regime's propagandists liked to call the divisions within the governing camp, began to emerge even in areas such as social and cultural policy, where some consensus had previously been in evidence (Siavoshi 1992). After the official demise of the Hojatieh Society (which believed strongly in free enterprise), for instance, many of the prominent radicals began to express support for the strengthening of the private sector. Ayatollah Khomeini himself was explicit in his endorsement of the private sector and the bazaar: 'The things which the government is not able to do, the government should not do. But do not prevent the bazaar from doing the things which it can do' (*The Middle East*, October 1984: 23). He also said to the economic exiles, 'return home and work and we promise that as long as there is Islam there will be free enterprise' (*The Sunday Times*, 10 January 1983).

Compared with the Imam's Line faction, the Hojatieh had a longer history and tradition, with crystal-clear objectives. Formed in the 1950s as an anti-Bahai organisation, this secretive society played an important role in the shaping of the Islamic Republic. Many of it members came to hold important posts and executive office after the victory of the revolution. In a broad sense, the Hojatieh was vehemently anti-communist, passionately free-marketeer (in both trade and industry) and emphatically traditionalist on social issues (Schahgaldian 1989). The Hojatieh has interpreted Quranic judgements on private property advocating an unfettered free market and non-government intervention in economic affairs, going so far as to question even the Islamic legal basis of the notion of a 'social market' system. The main criticisms levied against the Hojatieh by followers of the Imam's Line were of the latter's economic doctrine, summed up by the Prime Minister of the time as follows: 'here is a line of thought that believes in the capitalism of the 18th and 19th centuries' (Moussavi, quoted in *The Middle East* April 1985: 52–3).

The Society's best known government members, Habibollah Asgharou-ladi and Ahmad Tavakoli, were both ousted from the Cabinet in 1983, largely as a result of concerted attacks by the Maktabi-dominated Majlis and the rest of the Cabinet. Their dismissal marked the decline of the Society's influence at the formal level of government. Simultaneously with the two Ministers' departure from the Cabinet, a host of other high-ranking Hojatieh adminis-trators were also sacked, including eight of the republic's 27 provincial governors, the head of the politically sensitive State Grain Organisation, and the head of the Foundation of the Affairs of War Victims. Despite these setbacks, however, the Hojatieh continued to hold its own in bodies such as the Council of Experts, the Majlis, the Council of Guardians and the Pasdaran, as well as in the lower echelons of clerical bureaucratic power (Schahgaldian 1989; *MEED* 21 October 1983 and 5 September 1983). The Hojatieh's influence was such that Asgharouladi was appointed as a member of the Imam Khomeini Relief Fund only months after his resignation as the Minister of Commerce. Ten years later Tavakoli re-emerged to pose the greatest chal-lenge to President Rafsanjani as his main rival in the 1993 Presidential elections.

In addition to the bureaucratic rivalry between the Maktabis and the Hojatieh factions, doctrinal differences militated against a *rapprochement* between the two. The Hojatieh continued to question the concept of the Faqih, the cornerstone of the republic's constitution and the very basis of the regime's (theocratic) power structures, believing instead in the infallibility of the 'Twelfth Imamism' (that only the twelfth 'absent' Imam of the Shiis can claim power in the name of Islam). Based on this ideological objection to the existing Islamic Republic, and in co-operation with many senior clerics who did not agree with Ayatollah Khomeini's thesis but chose silent oppo-sition rather than open confrontation of the Faqih system, the Hojatieh maintained the potential to activate its forces to subvert the regime and undermine the power of Ayatollah Khomeini's successors.

Other important factions within the FIR category included Behzad Nabavi's Mojahedin of the Islamic Revolution (MIR). In the early 1980s it boasted an organisation of several thousand armed members. MIR members were very active in the quashing of the leftist forces during the 1981 mini-civil war and in the purges of the regular armed forces. As one of the few *kolahi* (non-clerical religious groups or individuals within the Islamic Republic) organisations with an independent armed organisation, MIR was expected to play an active part in the struggle for power after the patriarch's death. To this end, many of the MIR's followers joined the Pasdaran, but kept their ties to the original organisation (Schahgaldian 1989). Coupled with his strategic post of Minister of Heavy Industry in the Moussavi government, Nabavi's role was seen as crucial by the various FIR factions in charting a new economic strategy after the war.

Another small but influential organisation in the FIR category was the Fadayin Islam, whose leadership included Ayatollah Sadeq Khalkhali (an important figure during the revolution and in the early years of the republic, and a leading parliamentarian) and Navab Safavi (an active figure in organising revolutionary Islamic organisations). This group remained loyal to the Faqih doctrine, the Maktabi agenda, and to the person of Ayatollah Khomeini.

The second movement in the republican camp was that of the liberal Islamic republicans. Many individuals from this group have at one time or another held important posts in Iran's post-revolution governments, particularly during the 1979–81 period. Some of the leaders of the LIR forces were at the forefront of the struggle against the Shah, providing the 'moderate' liberalist Islamist intellectual spirit of the revolutionary drive against the Shah. Mehdi Bazargan's National Liberation Movement of Iran (Nehzat-e Azadi) dominated the first (provisional) government of the republic. Ex-President Abolhassan Bani-Sadr, the late Foreign Minister Sadeq Qotbzadeh, Admiral Madani (one of the armed forces' most senior personnel) and many middle-ranking and senior clerics were also part of the LIR. Noted religious figures who could be said to have belonged to the LIR tendency included Grand Ayatollah Kazem Shariatmadari (who was 'defrocked' by the Faqih and died in isolation in 1986). Shariatmadari led the Muslim People's Republican Party (MPRP) which dominated the Azerbaijani provinces in opposition to the regime's Islamic Republican Party (IRP). His movement was not in favour of the clergy's participation in, let alone domination of, the government, supporting instead the basic principle of an independent (even secular) government within the context of an Islamic Republic.

For our purposes, largely due to its ideology, the Mojahedin Iranian People's Organisation (MIPO) can also be characterised as an LIR movement. The MIPO collaborated extensively with the *kolahi* elements of the liberal Islamic groups, particularly during its legal and semi-legal existence (1979–81). Before 1981 a number of non-ruling clerics (either openly or clandestinely) identified themselves with the LIR agenda. The most prominent amongst these were Ayatollah Eshraqi (Khomeini's son-in-law), Ayatollah Qomi, Ayatollah Shirazi, Ayatollah Zanjani, Ayatollah Mara'ashi, Ayatollah Lahouti and Ayatollah Bahaedin Mahallati. Of all the leading factions in the LIR category, Bazargan's Nehzat movement survived the longest through the traumas of the IRI's internal feudings; Bani-Sadr and Madani chose exile, Qotbzadeh was executed in Iran, and Shariatmadari was defrocked and his MPRP suppressed in the early years of the republic. The price paid by the Nehzat movement has been high (including harsh treatment and jail sentences), but nonetheless they remained the only domestic-based 'secular' LIR force tolerated by the regime.

The third group in the republican camp, the secular republicans (SR), enjoyed least representation in the Islamic Republic. Technically, the regular armed forces could also be regarded as SR. But their negative role in the revolution, coupled with their systematic 'de-ideologisation' and numerous purges since 1979, makes the armed forces an unknown quantity. The armed forces' ambivalence on the important issues of the day also raises the question as to whether one can regard them as an effective political force, even if one acknowledges their influence in society.

Not unlike many of the LIR, the SR forces enthusiastically welcomed the anti-Shah revolution. But no notable group or individual from the SR category has held any office or position of responsibility in the Islamic Republic, apart from the few secularists who were involved in the Bazargan government. The last SR groups which fell prey to the theocracy were the rather influential Tudeh (Communist) party and the 'majority' wing of the Organisation of Iranian People's Fadayin (OIPF). The OIPFG, which was formed a decade before the revolution, split into two – Majority (Aksariat) and Minority (Aghaliat) – factions in 1980, the Majority faction becoming known as the OIPF and dropping 'Guerrilla' from its title. The Majority allied itself closely with the Tudeh party and followed the latter's political line on domestic matters and international affairs. Both parties believed that the theocracy was 'progressive' in objective terms because it confronted US imperialism in Iran and throughout the region (Alaolmolki 1987). The Tudeh and the OIPF maintained that the class base of the regime was to be found in the (largely traditional but also modern) *petit bourgeoisie*. These groups believed that the (anti-revolutionary) bourgeois factions in the revolutionary coalition were to be found in the ranks of the 'liberals' of the provisional government, the forces around Bani-Sadr, and their clerical allies. The Tudeh and OIPF forces played a critical role in support of the government camp during the mini-civil war that accompanied the impeachment of the republic's first President, Bani-Sadr.

Many of the SR groups tried to form a common programme against the regime, but their ideological and organisational differences, lack of grass-roots support for their doctrinaire positions, particularly those attached to Marxism–Leninism platforms, and endemic factionalism militated against a single alliance emerging in time to fight the FIR forces before elements from the latter moved to monopolise power in their own hands. Nevertheless some common platforms were formed. The National Council of Resistance (NCR), formed in exile in 1981, largely by an alliance between the MIPO and Bani-Sadr, is an example of a drive towards forming anti-regime common platforms. Through its wide membership the NCR could, in its heyday (1981–3), boast of representing a cross-section of Iranian political opinion as well as a politico-military organisation. Its membership included the Kurdish Democratic Party (KDP) (the largest and most powerful organisation in Iranian Kurdistan), the National Democratic Front (Jebhe-e Demokratik-e Melli) (a splinter of the Union of National Front Forces), over 80 respected nationalists and independent socialists (including Sheikh Ezzedin Husseini, a prominent Kurdish religious figure), some splinter groups from the OIPFG (Minority), the Union of Iranian Communists organisation and the pro-Albanian Toofan organisation (later reorganised into the Workers' and Peasants' party).

At the same time, however, considerable SR and leftist effort was devoted to fighting the NCR. Groups of different sizes, such as the OIPFG, Peykar, Organisation of Communist Unity (Sazeman-e Vahdat-e Komonisti), Workers' Way (Rah-e Karegar), Toilers' Party (Hezb-e Ranjbaran), Komeleh (Kurdish-based Marxist–Leninist organisation) remained in opposition to the ruling regime as well as to coalitions like the NCR where the Marxist–Leninists did not play a 'leading' role. These differences ensured that the SR forces could not unite to pose a serious political challenge to the position of the ruling FIR. Even the NCR began to fall apart after 1985. By 1987 the KDP, Toofan and many other smaller groups had left the NCR, and Bani-Sadr's departure effectively ended the organisation's ambitions to offer a viable national alternative to the Islamic Republic. In the NCR's scheme of things for post-Khomeini Iran, Bani-Sadr was to be the interim President of the post-Velayat-e Faqih system of the 'Democratic Islamic Republic of Iran'. Indeed, Bani-Sadr continues to claim to be the only legitimate President of the republic: 'I am the only one who has real legitimacy in Iran because I took part in the revolution from the beginning and because I was the first elected President in Iran's history' (Lahoud 1992: 26).

Prior to the banning of the Tudeh party in 1983 four main positions towards the Islamic regime were discernible among the Iranian secular republican left:

1 To support the Islamic Republic unconditionally and attempt to strengthen the position of the anti-imperialist forces within the regime.
2 To offer the regime conditional support.
3 To join the NCR and radicalise it from within.
4 To oppose the bourgeois and *petit-bourgeois* alternatives in Iran and aim to establish a united Marxist–Leninist front against the FIR, the LIR and the monarchists.

By the time of Ayatollah Khomeini's death no clear synthesis of these positions had emerged. In general terms, well established organisations of the left had effectively been suppressed or disbanded, and the newer groupings simply did not have the expertise and the organisational resources to regroup and 'hibernate' until better political conditions presented themselves. The Communist Party of Iran, for instance, formed in 1983 by the amalgamation of three organisations (Komeleh, the Unity of Militant Communists and Sahand), expanded rapidly in the early years of its existence, mainly because many of its new members came from the other failing communist and leftist organisations. But by 1989 the second post-revolution communist party formed in Iran had effectively ceased to exist, its forces scattered and dissipated. It is worth noting that the first CP after the revolution was formed in early 1979 and led by Mr Azaryun, who himself had split from the Tudeh party.

On another front, the OIPFG tried to act as a magnet for the disparate leftists, forming the Organisation of Revolutionary Workers of Iran (Sazeman-e Kargaran-e Enghelabi-e Iran, or ORWI) in the mid-1980s as a way of expanding the presence of the left in national affairs. In anticipation of Ayatollah Khomeini's death and the ensuing confusion, ORWI aimed to assist in organising secret worker and peasant committees to facilitate organised labour's participation in any power structure that might follow. Its priority, therefore, was to establish and develop links with workplaces and seek frameworks for organic structural linkages with workers' movements and left-wing political coalitions. The ORWI's limited resources and lack of experienced cadres peripherised this organisation soon after its foundation.

Besides the KDP, the small but high-profile National Democratic Front (NDF; led by Mossadeq's grandson, Hedayatollah Matindaftari) was the only other notable SR force not espousing a left-wing or Marxist ideology. The Front, which had been alienated from the Islamic regime soon after the end of the Provisional Government, collaborated closely with the NCR, accruing considerable prestige to the latter while the alliance lasted. As the NDF was prominent largely because of its leading personalities, it was in no position to affect the political balance of power among the SR forces in any one direction. It enjoyed, in other words, a narrow social base. Moreover its influence over the power struggle within the ruling FIR factions was practically non-existent. That said, such groups are by no means dead and buried. They maintain contacts with the modern middle classes which, under more democratic conditions and in spite of their otherwise narrow social base, could lead to them rapidly increasing their influence if the scope of political freedom were to be extended. Their role would become particularly important if a more balanced mix of secular and Islamic leadership were ever to emerge in Iran.

In 1983 Hassan Nazih, former Chairman of the National Iranian Oil Company, set up yet another SR organisation in exile, known as the Front for the National Sovereignty of Iran (FNSI). This described itself as a 'middle national alternative to the extremist leftist and rightist opposition groups' (*MEED* 4 November 1983). Aiming to be a consensus-based movement, it strove to unite the liberal SR and LIR forces within a single front-type organisation. The strategic aim of the FNSI was to offer an easily recognisable alternative to the 'extremists' of FIR, the hard left and the monarchist groups still bent on reinstating the Pahlavi dynasty. Like all other foreign-based organisations, however, its impact on the domestic political scene in Iran and its influence over the succession issue were negligible.

None of the SR groups and organisations was therefore in a position to challenge the regime after Ayatollah Khomeini's death, nor were they able to present themselves as viable alternatives to the Islamic Republic. By the time of Ayatollah Khomeini's death the only non-FIR group of any substance in the Islamic Republic was Bazargan's Nehzat-e Azadi movement. It too came under severe pressure after 1988 and its voice was effectively silenced during the crucial days in June and July 1989 when a new leadership was emerging to replace Ayatollah Khomeini.

THE MONARCHIST CONTENDERS

The monarchist contenders for power in Iran can be divided into a number of categories, based on leadership, political programme, and closeness to the *ancien régime*. The fundamentalist monarchists (FM) constituted that faction of the monarchist camp that believed in a strong, independent and powerful Shah at the helm of the state. Total loyalty to this father figure forms a central plank of the FM's outlook. The FM leadership, mainly in exile, includes Mohammad Reza Shah's own sister (Princess Ashraf Pahlavi), many of his former military commanders, many members of the Imperial Guard, and high and middle-ranking leaders of the state security organisation, SAVAK.

Soon after the overthrow of the Shah, leading military figures, such as Generals Ariyana, Oveissi and Palizban, established military-style organisations abroad, with secret links with some of Iran's officer corps and national minorities. General Ariyana's Iran Liberation Army (Azadegan) was the most prominent of FM entities. The strength of these groups was at its greatest in the early years of the Islamic Republic. According to exile sources in Europe, elements from this group routinely co-operated with General Oveissi's military organisation and former Prime Minister Bakhtiar's (assassinated in Paris in August 1991) NAMIR organisation. Confidential reports indicate that in the early days of the Iraqi invasion of Iran in 1980 a Bakhtiar–Oveissi alliance mobilised its joint military forces from the Iraqi and Turkish borders with the intention of overthrowing the Tehran government and replacing it with a military–civilian government of 'national unity' under the premiership of Shahpour Bakhtiar (based on conversations with a number of army colonels, undertaken in Los Angeles, April 1987). Their military attacks were halted when the armed gang encountered logistical difficulties on the Turkish border; the chain of command broke down and the group failed to gain Western and large-scale Turkish support for this operation.

The Free Iran (Iran Azad) group, led by Princess Ashraf's daughter (Azadeh Shafiq), constituted the only civilian link of the FM organisations. The combination of its leaders' family heritage and its civilian character placed the Free Iran group in a position to work closely with the groups and personalities of both the FM and what can be termed the constitutional monarchists.

The constitutional monarchist (CM) forces draw inspiration from the democratic 1906 constitution of Iran for their preferred political system, which also reserves a special (supervisory) role for the Islamic hierarchy. Before his assassination, Bakhtiar headed the largest and best organised of the CM groups. Founded soon after Bakhtiar's departure from Iran in 1979, NAMIR claimed to have a popular base in Iran's bureaucratic and military circles. The organisation's declared intention was to lead 'a coalition of democratic forces including intellectuals, middle class liberals, army officers, tribesmen and working classes to replace the Ayatollah's regime with a just and constitutional government', with 'the young Shah . . . as [its] constitutional monarch' (Bakhtiar's speech at the Royal Institute of International Affairs, *Voice of Iran* 13, July–August 1984: 7).

To this end, NAMIR and former Prime Minister Ali Amini's Iran Liberation Front (ILF), the only other significant CM faction, signed an agreement in July 1983 calling for the return of a constitutional monarchy with Reza Shah II as the new monarch. By 1984, however, personality clashes and differences over policy had reduced the influence of this alliance among the monarchist groups. With Bakhtiar's untimely departure from the scene little prospect for the success of the alliance remained.

Despite their well financed and impressive organisational networks in exile, in the absence of substantial apparent support among the masses and at the grass-roots bureaucratic level, the monarchists could not contemplate a return to power in Iran without the unreserved support of the armed forces. As Houshang Nahavandi, one of the late Shah's close advisers has put it, 'The [monarchist] politicians without the support of the military and the confidence of the Iranian armed forces have no role, in my opinion, in the immediate future of Iran' (quoted by Renner 1982: 9).

By contrast, many of the LIR forces rejected a political role for the armed services. Many of the LIR and SR forces remained sceptical of the contribution that the armed forces could make, either to assist in the overthrow of the ruling regime or in constructing a new democratic government in post-Khomeini Iran. Bani-Sadr's position is revealing in this context: 'I think that the bulk of the army is on my side. But I am not at all in favour of the army going into political action . . . To remake, re-establish, a military regime in Iran would be to recommence an experiment that has already failed' (ibid.).

Paradoxically, therefore, in order to recover his crown, the 'liberal' Crown Prince himself had no option but to support the FM groups. This relationship had a direct impact on the prospects of a return of the Pahlavi monarchy to Iran. This was so because even though his personal preferences reflected a desire to return to Iran as a constitutional monarch, so long as he remained surrounded by the discredited functionaries of his father he could not claim to represent a democratic future for Iran based on the slogan 'The Shah must reign and not rule'. The absence of such commitments in the monarchist camp prevented the emergence of a broad support base for the institution of the monarchy in republican Iran.

THE SIGNIFICANCE OF THE STATE

It has been clear that, despite the distinct platforms of the individual entities, organisations, groups and personalities already discussed, one factor provided a notable element of commonality: the role of the state in making their visions realisable. According to Hamza Alavi, the state in post-colonial countries is an 'overdeveloped bureaucratic-military apparatus' that manages and administers the ruling 'national elite' of landlords and a small indigenous and powerful *comprador* bourgeoisie (Alavi 1979). Alavi's rather simplistic 'tripartite' elite analysis notwithstanding, the focus on the 'system' highlights the indispensable function of the bureaucratic-military state to the survival of most, if not all, the capitalistic and 'socialist-oriented' Third World elites. Iran is no exception to this rule, but a recognition of the role of the *petit bourgeoisie* (traditional and modern) at the leadership level is also vital to an understanding of the First and Second Iranian Islamic Republics.

When the equilibrium of forces (formed around certain class interests) alluded to by Alavi is disturbed then the state becomes both the end and the means to a new balance of forces. In pre- and post-revolution Iran, control of the state machinery has enabled a particular class to control virtually all aspects of national life – economic, political, ideological, cultural and social. Indeed, it can be argued that the swift transfer of political power and of the nation's identity in the ideological, cultural and social spheres helped, more than any other process, to camouflage the non-transformability of the existing national economic relations.

To put it simply, by taking control of the substantial assets of the royal family and its class allies, the new elite in post-revolution Iran expanded the role of the state. Since it had itself assumed control over the state it at once both consolidated and increased its own power. In this sense the role of the Iranian state became even more central to its political masters than would be suggested by the Alavi model: control of the state having a direct bearing on the competition for political power. Moreover, it is in the interests of the state itself to encourage the return of stability to the country, hence its apparent readiness to swing its support behind the most effective faction in the power struggle.

One associated aspect of the continuity to be found in the strategy of the republican regime which may be said to have existed under its predecessor was that, despite its clear popular base amongst the 'deprived' classes, the new elite showed sufficient pragmatism to court also the domestic private sector and thus to encourage the emergence of a new 'bourgeois' stratum which (as had been the case under the Pahlavi regime) might come to owe its livelihood and legitimacy to the longevity and consent of the elite in control of the state. After the defeat of the LIR factions in 1981, the ruling elite gave enough economic leverage to the traditional merchant class (largely but not exclusively bazaar-based) to ensure the latter's continued support for the government.

THE CRISIS OF SUCCESSION

The complexities of Iranian political leadership and relation among the FIR ruling forces themselves led some to conclude, prior to Ayatollah Khomeini's death, that the tensions between the various factions within the theocratic 'ruling class' would lead to the FIR's downfall after the departure of the Islamic Republic's only cohesive force. One observer was to state categorically that the system would not survive for long:

the clergy have failed either to establish a cohesive and enduring polity or to address imaginatively and forcefully Iran's economic problems let alone rise to the aspirations of the Iranian people . . . [*sic*] the growing challenge to theocratic rule ... would not fail to ultimately undermine the clerical regime's hold on power. The gathering storm is too powerful for the debilitated clerical regime to effectively weather and survive ... the end of the clergy is not far in sight.

(Kadhim 1983: 66)

In retrospect, however, attention should be paid to the emerging balance of power within the FIR camp in the course of and after Iran's acceptance of the cease-fire resolution SCR 598 in 1988. One faction of the FIR category, which became known as the 'realists' or 'pragmatists', formed an alliance with the social conservatives and was increasingly able to dominate the state machinery. In doing so, it progressively marginalised the influence of the Maktabi forces in the Islamic and secular national institutions of power.

Much of the analysis of this process has, however, misunderstood the dynamics of the process involved. The anonymous author of a booklet published before Ayatollah Khomeini's death was to say, for example:

it is clear today that the supporters of the privatisation of trade and industry led by the technocrats like Rafsanjani, Khamenei and Moussavi are in control of the instruments of power, and the principle opposition factions, the Imam's Line and Hojatieh, have been removed from the political scene and from control of the state.

(*Baresieh-e Siasy-ijtemayi-e Rejeem-e Jomhouri Eslami Iran*: 12)

This view underplays the purely political differences in the ruling elite and looks for structural factors in order to offer an understanding of the real motives behind the rivalries that beset the FIL forces. In doing so, it first of all seeks to separate the 'pragmatic' influences in the regime from the two main factions of FIR (Imam's Line and Hojateih). Secondly, it completes the separation by introducing a new category to the FIR, attributing autonomous life to a set of influential actors, the so-called (clerical – Rafsanjani and Khamenei, and *kolahi* – Moussavi) technocrats in the Islamic Republic.

I would argue that the presence of a technocratic coalition had been in evidence since the mid-1980s. However, the technocrats themselves were not in any sense a homogeneous and cohesive force in the republic; nor did they entertain a common set of principles and unbending objectives. By definition, their pragmatism in dealing with matters of the state necessitated extensive alliance building with other influential actors and groups, however tactical and short-term. While such alliances helped to deflect attacks by other factions of the FIR, the uncertainties arising from such fluid relationships led to a sense of insecurity among the governing ranks of the republic, which in turn bred opportunism within the elite.

Inevitably, there was much behind-the-scenes negotiation. In search of power the various factions sought to extend their influence to the institutional levers of such power, including the newly created instruments of the Islamic state. Consolidation of power bases was also the order of the day as the news of the Ayatollah's worsening health condition became common knowledge after 1987. Institutions of power, therefore, were in danger of being irredeemably divided along factional lines. The competition continued regardless of the fact that Ayatollah Montazeri had already been selected by the Council of Experts to succeed Ayatollah Khomeini. A symptom of the institutionally based rivalry was the announcement in February 1988 that Ayatollah Khomeini had appointed a number of the senior clergy to serve on a new state body empowered to resolve the increasingly intractable differences over policy, legislation, and the interpretation of the law. The Council for the Determination of Expediency (or 'what to do for the best') was established to try to resolve the profound differences between the Council of Guardians (the 'upper chamber' in a loose sense), the Majlis, and the executive. Such differences in the end came down to the competition between two 'politico-ideological schools of thought', one bent on continuing the domestic and foreign policies of the war years, and the other urging the reform of the entire system.

The battle between the two FIR camps became violent in the mid-1980s, when the armed bodies of the Islamic regime fought the battles of local clerics in the major Iranian towns and cities of Isfahan, Shiraz, Mashad and Kerman (Akhavi 1987). The end of the Iran–Iraq war meant that the leaders of the republic were forced to address the country's problems in a more immediate and tangible manner, exacerbating the hostilities between the factions. In the context of the Expediency Council's inability to resolve the differences within the FIR, largely because the council itself mirrored the same patterns of rivalry, Ayatollah Khomeini, who for the most part had assiduously kept aloof from the in-fighting among his clerical lieutenants and had intervened only as the final arbiter, was forced to intervene.

To force the issue, a ranking member of the clergy sent a letter to the Ayatollah (dated 21 October 1988) pleading with him to intervene before the whole system became threatened with extinction. Hojjatoleslam Mohammad Ansari Kermani wrote his note in a guarded manner, but his criticism of Ayatollah Khomeini's vacillation was ill concealed:

> two politico-ideological schools of thought, both affiliated to the revolution and defenders of Islam, with a huge following, including important personages, have embarked on serious competition against each other today. This rivalry is not confined to theoretical issues alone; it has appeared on the political, social and economic scenes. The more it pro-

gresses, the greater the rivalries . . . I see that many members of the two factions enjoy the support of Your Eminence; that whenever Your Eminence has expressed your support for one faction, an endorsement of the other has followed. There are numerous examples, when the Society of Theological Teachers or the Publicity Organisation is endorsed, immediately the staff of the Publicity Office are given support; on the one hand the honourable Council of Guardians is endorsed, and the Council of Expediency on the other; the Tehran Struggling Clerical Society on the one hand, and the Struggling Clergy on the other; Mr Mohtashemi and the Prime Minister on the one hand, and Messrs Nateq and Azari on the other.
(Hojjatoleslam Ansari Kermani's letter to Ayatollah Khomeini, *Kayhan*
16 November 1988)

The letter ended with the following plea: 'To Your Eminence . . . the issue is clear, but unfortunately we have not been able to understand it . . . I feel that this problem . . . can only be solved by Your Eminence's instructions and views'.

Bearing in mind the crisis of leadership which was by now engulfing the republic, and the stark differences over preferred policy for the future development of the Islamic Republic, Ayatollah Khomeini's reply (dated 1 November 1988) left much to be desired. One particularly disturbing feature was that for the first time he publicly raised doubts regarding the suitability of Ayatollah Montazeri (his own chosen successor) for the position of the Faqih:

There should always be jurisconsults in Islamic governments. The revolution and the system always allow the expressing of theological and jurisprudential views, even if they contradict one another. No one has the right or the authority to prevent this . . . Unity of action and ideas is necessary. Jurisprudence at seminary level is not sufficient. If a person is extremely knowledgeable in matters concerning seminaries, but cannot determine what is good for society, or cannot distinguish between suitable and unsuitable persons, or in general lacks the necessary wisdom in social and political issues, that person is not a jurisconsult [or Faqih], as far as social and governmental matters are concerned. He cannot rule the society . . . Clearly, if there are differences between the various personalities and factions of the revolution, they are purely political, even if they appear to be ideological because they all share common principles; that is why I approve of them. They are faithful to Islam, the Quran and the revolution. They each have their own plans for the advancement of Islam and the services of Muslims [*sic*] . . . it is clear to me that both factions have faith in God and serve the public . . . I reiterate that since our country is in the reconstruction stage, it needs unity and camaraderie.

(The Echo of Iran 1 December 1988: 23)

Ayatollah Khomeini's reply not only failed to propel one or other faction unequivocally into dominance within government, but it also undermined the one element of certainty regarding the continuity of the regime in terms of succession to his own rule. Thus at a time when a pronouncement was vital that would secure the regime from the destructive impact of factionalism, he was actually contributing to the existing fissures.

In attempting to take advantage of the regime's apparent disarray, the opposition groups chose this time to step up their campaigns. Many of the monarchist groups, the Mojahedin and some LIR forces sought to enlist elements of the officer corps in their plots to topple the regime. Despite the military's three or so coup attempts in the 1979–87 period, there was little evidence available to support the contention that the armed forces had been sufficiently politicised by the war and the excesses of the revolution to make a concerted bid for power. The attempted coups, in any case, were all guided by a civilian political leadership; the armed forces were not acting independently. The military establishment was certainly an 'elite in itself' but not 'an elite for itself'. Therefore, to win the support of this institution, the opposition forces were devoting considerable resources to secret recruitment among the officer corps. Sepehr Zabih's analysis of the Mojahedin's policy towards the armed forces is every bit as applicable to the strategy of the other opposition forces in the LIR category, the FM and some forces of the left. He states that:

the Mojahedeen have now been concentrating on recruiting army officers. Rajavi [the leader of the MIPO] seems to be convinced that as long as Khomeini is alive the Pasdaran will remain loyal to him because they owe their very existence to him. The Army, on the other hand, has very few reasons to display irreversible loyalty to the Ayatollahs.

(Zabih 1982: 107)

Concrete evidence of the success of this strategy is to be found in the number of officers who, in exile, declared their allegiance to the various opposition camps. For example, Captain Firouz Behseresht (naval officer), Colonel Abbas Abedi (deputy commander of the air force), Colonel Ismail Talayeh, and Colonel Ali Akbar Eskandari (military attaché of IRI in India) joined NAMIR, and Captains Mohammad Ali Aryafar and Bahram Afzali (commander of the navy) joined the MIPO and the Tudeh party respectively (all data obtained from interviews with West European-based opposition sources).

Although the military personnel opposed to the Islamic Republic posed less of a threat, being based as they were outside Iran, it remained a preoccupation of the regime to uncover the networks and the secret cells which might remain intact within. Despite the periodic purges, execution and exile of many military personnel the regime continued to doubt the allegiance of the armed forces to the ruling FIR. To appease the military, therefore, the pragmatists chose to align themselves with the regular armed forces and went as far as to suggest that the defeats and reversals on the war fronts were largely due to the incompetence of the Pasdaran commanders and their troops rather than to that of the regular armed forces.

Taking the longer view, it can be said that the inter-elite, intra-elite and non-elite confrontations of the 1979–89 period took their toll of all the parties concerned. On the FIR side the losses were significant. In 1981 alone the regime lost over 100 of its high- and middle-ranking officials and personalities. The more significant losses of the regime included Ayatollah Beheshti (the head of the Supreme Court and the leader of the IRP), the majority of the IRP's central committee, four Cabinet Ministers, five Deputy Ministers, one Prime Minister (Hojjatoleslam Bahonar), one President (Rajaii), more than 20 MPs, Hassan Ayat (the regime's leading ideologue), Gilan Province Governor Ali Ansari, Hojjatoleslam Ali Qodousi (the Revolutionary Prosecutor-General), Hojjatoleslam Abdulkarim Hashemi Nejad (Secretary-General of the IRP), Ayatollah Asadolah Madani (Ayatollah Khomeini's representative in Tabriz), Ayatollah Abdul-Hussein Dastghaib (a senior Khomeini aide), a number of Friday prayer leaders, Defence Minister Colonel Namjou, and Air Force Commander Colonel Javad Fakouri (data compiled from *Jomhouri Eslami*, *Kayhan*, *Keesing's Contemporary Archives*, *Mojahed*, *Kar*, and the 1980–1, 1981–2, 1982–3, 1983–4 editions of *Middle East Contemporary Survey*).

The opposition's losses were also great. The MIPO lost some 30,000 of its members and supporters in the first few years of the republic, including three of its most senior leaders (Khiabani, Sa'adati and Kazem Rajavi – the brother of MIPO's leader). The OIPFG lost hundreds of its forces and at least two of its leaders, Sultanpour and a military leader known only as Eskandar. Peykar Organisation lost much of its central committee (such as Rouhani, Ashtiani and Haqshenas) in addition to scores of its members and supporters. The Tudeh party also did not escape the wrath of the regime: Kianouri, Tabari and Eskandari of the central committee and over 2,000 of its members were either executed or imprisoned. The KDP, CPI and other leftist groups sheltering in Kurdistan continued to lose cadres in their confrontations with the Pasdaran and the military in Kurdistan. The leader of the KDP, Dr Abdulrahman Ghasemlou, was assassinated in Vienna in 1989. Many of the monarchist movements' leadership were lost through assassinations, including Shahriar Shafiq (founder of Iran Azad), General Oveissi, Ali Akbar Tabataba'i and Bijan Fazeli. Although the death of General Ariayna of the Azadegan FM group was not instigated by the regime, according to Azadegan sources, as many as 12 other military officers may have been assassinated abroad by agents of the regime (*Mednews* 3 December 1990).

Clearly the struggle for power, both between republicans and their opposition as well as within the regime itself, was a costly business. The regime was weakened in its first decade by its efforts to fend off competitors for power, as well as by the internal struggles which resulted from uncertainties surrounding the whole issue of succession. In this connection it should be remembered that succession was not simply a question of which personality or personalities should assume the titles of power after Khomeini's death. It was an elemental battle between strands of ideology and policy which had evolved through the revolutionary process, each of which now sought to mark the revolution as its own. As if these confrontations were not enough for so young a regime, they took place at least until July 1988 within the context of the Iran–Iraq war, which itself debilitated and infected the republic with its own damaging impositions.

IRAN'S ACCEPTANCE OF SCR 598 AND ITS CONSEQUENCES

Within the ruling elite, the issue of the war was inextricably linked with the question of the export of the revolution. The 'internationalists' regarded the war as the best conduit for the export of the revolution, whereas the 'Stalinists' on the war issue advocated consolidation at home as the best strategy for the republic's future progress. Mozaffari argues that, like its Russian counterpart, which eventually became 'revolution in one country', 'the Islamic revolution has also evolved from the Umma revolution to the Iranian Islamic revolution' (Mozaffari 1993: 614).

The war had already been condemned as 'un-Islamic' by some senior Islamic figures. Grand Ayatollah Tabataba'i Qomi, for instance, had issued a *fatwa* against continuing the war in 1985. It read as follows: 'The war between Iran and Iraq is completely *haram* [forbidden by the Sacred Law] . . . Large sums of money are wasted. Towns and villages are destroyed. Women are widowed and children are orphaned' (*Voice of Iran* 17, March–April 1985: 17). This *fatwa* appeared at the time when Ayatollah Khomeini and his FIR followers were preaching that the war was a 'blessing' for the Islamic Republic.

The end of the war, furthermore, produced difficulties of its own for the regime. After some years of absence the armed forces would be reintegrated with civil society, particularly through their involvement in the economic reconstruction effort of the government, a prospect which carried with it the possibility of their renewed politicisation. Moreover, with the war emergency conditions over, the opposition groups would be in a better position to reactivate their remaining forces against the regime. The MIPO was the only opposition force which had been preparing in a systematic way to challenge the regime from exile. Enjoying considerable Iraqi hospitality, it set about creating a substantial military force, known as the National Liberation Army of Iran (NLA), in Iraq. By 1987 the NLA was ready to take on the Islamic Republic on the battlefield. It could field as many as 15,000 troops by 1988 (*Jane's Defence Weekly* 18 April 1987; *Middle East International* 9 January 1988; *The Washington Post* 10 January 1988). The NLA launched a number of military offensives against Iranian regular and Pasdaran forces in 1988 and 1989, but was not successful in holding any territory or translating its military operations into any political gains. Its similar operations in 1992 and 1993 were equally unsuccessful.

To secure their position against these threats, the key personalities at the highest echelons of power moved swiftly to put into operation the mechanisms of succession shortly after the end of military hostilities with Iraq. However, Ayatollah Khomeini was still pursuing his line of personal intervention, much as he had since the early days of the revolution. He maintained his role as the ultimate power broker and his practice of selecting or designating his trusted allies for sensitive posts. It should be noted that Ayatollah Khomeini's office used to select the Friday prayer leaders of the provinces and appoint six of the 12 members of the influential Council of Guardians. He had personal representatives on the Supreme Defence Council and on all other revolutionary and Islamic organs, including the regular armed forces and the Pasdaran. It was Ayatollah Khomeini who appointed Hojjatoleslam Rafsanjani as the acting Commander-in-Chief of the armed forces in June 1988. On two occasions after the cease-fire agreement Ayatollah Khomeini intervened to prevent Prime Minister Moussavi's resignation, and in the end it was he who brought about the 'resignation' of Ayatollah Montazeri as his successor.

The end of the war shook the balance of the existing social, political and economic order. While the pragmatists saw in this development great opportunities to advance their own reformist agenda, plainly, so long as Ayatollah Khomeini remained on the scene they would not be in a position to isolate the Maktabis. However, all factions within the FIR had recognised that without Ayatollah Khomeini and his prevailing influence the system might not survive. As the survival of the FIR forces depended on the survival of the Islamic Republic, the two leading factions found common cause in trying to adapt the system to survive the Ayatollah's eventual departure.

As far as the republic's institutions of power were concerned they had so far been shown to be resilient enough to survive an external challenge. The key problem for the potential successors lay in the structure of power, which had been designed and moulded to suit Ayatollah Khomeini personally. It was, therefore, imperative that a process of structural reform, including constitutional reform, should begin before the Ayatollah's death, and that it should enjoy his blessing, if a smooth transfer of power was to take place in the Islamic Republic.

Ayatollah Montazeri's resignation as Faqih-designate in March 1989 ended a prolonged period of jockeying between Montazeri, Rafsanjani and Khamenei. Ayatollah Montazeri's departure from the political scene opened up new opportunities for the more junior statesmen to dominate the system. Montazeri's status as a Grand Ayatollah, however, was not affected by his political misfortunes. His return to the holy city of Qom was low-key, but as the only senior Ayatollah of any national stature in the FIR camp he could divide the leadership by serving as a focus for other FIR opposition to the Leader–President alliance.

Hojjatoleslams Rafsanjani and Khamenei (Speaker of the Majlis and state President respectively) were the two leading clerical actors who stood to gain a great deal from Ayatollah Montazeri's resignation. They had both risen through the ranks of the (theocratic) political system of the republic. Both were central committee members of the IRP. Khamenei entered the formal structures of power as the Deputy Minister of Defence, later to become the Pasdaran's representative on the Revolutionary Council. He was elected President of the republic in 1981, a post he kept until his election by the Assembly of Experts as the Faqih in June 1989. Rafsanjani's ascent of the ladder of power in the republic was particularly rapid, as more senior religious-revolutionary Islamic figures lost their lives to opposition-instigated political violence. He was elected to the first Majlis of the IRI as an MP from Tehran. Before becoming Speaker of the Majlis in July 1980, he had held the post of supervisor of the Ministry of the Interior. He was selected as Ayatollah Khomeini's representative on the Supreme Defence Council (the highest decision-making body on matters relating to the war) in 1981, and acted as its spokesman soon after. He was elected to the Assembly of Experts in 1983, and in 1984 he was also appointed a member of the Supreme Council for Cultural Revolution by Ayatollah Khomeini. He was appointed acting C-in-C shortly before Iran's unconditional acceptance of SCR 598 (*Diplomat* 25 February 1991; Jahanpour 1992).

Both Khamenei and Rafsanjani, as well as Montazeri, had held influential political positions on the 16–member Council of the Revolution (Shoray-e Enqelab), which was formed in December 1978, and which has provided much of the leadership of the republic. Both Premier Bazargan and President Bani-Sadr were members, as were Foreign Minister Qotbzadeh, Hassan

Habibi (President Rafsanjani's First Vice-President), and clerics such as Beheshti, Bahonar and Moussavi Ardebili.

The Council of the Revolution played a prominent role in shaping the politics and policies of the republic in its formative years. Indeed, it was this institution which provided the individuals who went on to lead the republic in later years. In the end it was not any of the political groupings within the FIR camp which emerged to provide answers to the question of political and spiritual succession in the republic, but rather certain clusters of individuals from the original Council of the Revolution.

The ultimate ascendency of Khamenei and Rafsanjani such that they were able to form the Leader–President alliance was a recognition of this need for the dominant personalities of the regime to surmount ideological and factional differences in the interests of providing continuity, as well as being symptomatic of Ayatollah Khomeini's aknowledgement of the need to leave structures for succession in place before his death. To formalise its ruling position, however, the constitution had to be reformed to reflect both the changes in the institutional distribution of power and the subtle new realities in the rubric of power.

Many of the FIR groups and organisations remained active, albeit at a much lower tempo. Two such key organisations were the Association of Combative Clergy (pro-Rafsanjani) and the Association of Combatant Clergy (the organisation of the radicals), which continue to maintain a high profile in channelling the energies of the competing FIR factions. However, what is evident is that throughout the war, and in the period immediately following, there were two processes taking place simultaneously. First, there was a struggle between factional competitors for power within the regime who sought to direct policy and establish ideological supremacy. Second, the institutions of the regime were themselves serving as stepping stones for the ascendancy of individuals who were able, by virtue of their realism, to overcome ideological issues in order to act as a nascent structure of power in themselves. The factionalism served to weaken the regime in such a way as to allow individuals to come to prominence and ultimately to assert their brand of leadership in a way which could facilitate secure succession. This process provided a cornerstone for the direction in which the republic has moved ever since, not least because it has set the scene for constitutional, economic and political reform relatively unhindered by the more dogmatic obstructions of ideological rivalry.

2 The emergence of the Second Republic

> Now that the war has been halted, we are in the reconstruction phase. In this phase we should think that the revolution has just started.
>
> (Hojjatoleslam Rafsanjani, December 1988)

The previous chapter demonstrated how the regime that succeeded the revolution was, under the arbitration of Khomeini, a composite of political forces struggling to attain the 'high ground' of control – and legitimacy of that control – in the new state form. The supremacy of Khomeini as unquestionably the Supreme Leader did not allow a smooth development of independent political institutions and loci of power, since such development was ultimately and constantly subject to his own arbitrary and personal intervention. The persistence of divisions within the elite was partly caused by Ayatollah Khomeini's style of leadership and the mode of his intervention in inter-elite conflict resolution (Bakhash 1989). Secondly, as Cottam has put it, 'Khomeini has not permitted any individual or faction to gain preeminence within his government' (Cottam 1989: 172). Thus it was only with his death (including the period preceding that event when preparations had to be made for the survival of the regime after his departure) that the development of independent political institutions could really effectively take place.

THE EMERGENCE OF NEW AGENDAS

The republic's acceptance of a cease-fire with Iraq alerted many Iranians and Iran-watchers to the fact that they were witnessing important changes in the Islamic Republic. The changes were reflected in the foreign policy of Iran, as well as in the balance of forces at the leadership level in the republic. The acting C-in-C, Speaker Rafsanjani, stated on 18 July 1988 that Iran's acceptance of a cease-fire 'will open a new chapter in our history' (SWB, ME/0208, 20 July 1988). Interestingly, it was the 'Young Turks' of the regime who were setting the pace of change. For example, according to Iraqi sources, the letter carrying Iran's acceptance of SCR 598 to the UN Secretary-General was not drafted by Khomeini's office, but by Khamenei, Rafsanjani and Moussavi Ardebili in the Majlis Speaker's office, on the morning of 17 July (SWB, ME/0218, 1 August 1988).

That Ayatollah Khomeini was unhappy about the decision to end the war in this manner was illustrated by the tone and tenor of his first public statement after the announcement of Iran's decision. He said:

> the acceptance of the resolution . . . was truly a very bitter and tragic issue for everyone and particularly for me . . . [*sic*] in view of the opinion of all the high-ranking political and military experts of the country . . . I agreed with the acceptance of the resolution and the cease-fire . . . death and martyrdom would have been more bearable to me.
>
> (SWB, ME/0210, 22 July 1988)

There is no mistaking the fact that the decision to end the war had been pressed, to say the least, upon Ayatollah Khomeini – despite protestations to the contrary by President Khamenei. President Khamenei stated in December 1988 that 'neither Mr Hashemi [Rafsanjani] nor I or anyone else had any idea a week before the acceptance [of SCR 598] whether the resolution was going to be accepted. It was not us who accepted the resolution; it was the Imam [Khomeini] who accepted the resolution' (*The Echo of Iran* 15 December 1988: 4). Ayatollah Khomeini, thus, was already giving way to others.

At this stage, the clearest sign of changes in policy and outlook was to be found in the foreign policy realm. Again, Rafsanjani led the way in questioning the virtues of past policies: 'The main thing is that we can stop making enemies without reason because of this new move [Iran's acceptance of SCR 598]. This has put a new road in front us. There are many people who are currently giving facilities to Saddam [Hussein] who would not have done so if our foreign policy had been right' (SWB, ME/0218, 1 August 1988).

Clearly a turning point had been reached in Iran, whereby the revolutionary idealists' stamp on the republic's foreign policy orientation had begun giving way to that of the 'realists', to use Ramazani's characterisation of the Rafsanjani camp. It is worth reiterating the point that 'In the six-year interval between July 1982 and July 1988 when Iran accepted the UN-brokered cease-fire, the idealists' foreign policy orientation often prevailed over that of the realists' (Ramazani 1989: 210). After that date the realists came to the fore. The first signs of change that many Iran-watchers had detected manifested itself in the ending of its 'confrontational foreign policy' (ibid.).

It remained unclear at this point, however, what 'a fresh stance', as Tehran Radio termed it, meant besides the change in Iran's policy towards the war. What changes in the nature of the Islamic Republic were about to occur, and in which direction, were much harder to posit in the summer of 1988, although the future President had already alluded to the necessary domestic changes which must, in his view, follow Iran's acceptance of the cease-fire. In the course of his sermon at the Friday prayers, on 1 August 1988, Rafsanjani outlined his vision of the need for a new path for the Islamic Republic, but typically stopped short of advocating a change of policy openly, disguising his views within a critique of the Maktabi positions:

> There may be some who might think that we are not prepared to compromise. They may say what is the meaning of wealth, comfort, what does solving international problems mean . . . ? There is no just government in the world and therefore we should always be as we are now. There is no need for us to change our present situation. Let prices rise as they will; let the people's problems mount up, irrespective of the burden, we are ready for martyrdom! This is not a correct view. It is not possible to organise the long life of a generation in this way.

> (SWB, ME/0218, 1 August 1988)

The message emanating from these speeches and statements was a clear one: Iran had reached a turning point in its history, and it was up to the political leadership of the country to chart a new path for it. It was as yet unclear whether the changes in policy envisaged for the republic were to be comprehensive enough to encompass the existing power structures of the country. Discussions about the future of the republic after Khomeini and about the content, nature and form of the post-Khomeini leadership were, however, put high on the agenda of the regime, mainly, but not exclusively, at the behest of Rafsanjani and his clerical allies.

THE EROSION OF THE OLD ORDER

The backdrop of the change in thinking and attitude came from an unexpected quarter, Prime Minister Moussavi, the republic's longest serving Prime Minister and an individual known for his strict adherence to the Imam's Line. In a speech made shortly before the IRI's acceptance of SCR 598, he stated: 'It is a fact that . . . we have problems and that criticisms are justified. We realise that we have not attained all the aspirations of the Islamic revolution' (SWB, ME/0167, 2 June 1988). These words provided the opening shots of a campaign of open self-criticism and public reflections at the executive leadership level, which in turn systematically and inextricably gave form to the new agendas of competing factions within the FIR, and pushed these discussions forward towards the crystallisation of positions on the future of Iran and the destiny of the Islamic Republic. Ayatollah Montazeri, the Faqih-designate, led the criticisms of the Moussavi government, and provided a forceful critique of the First Republic, advocating instead improvements in the IRI's relations with other states, more political freedom and a freer economic system (and fewer state controls) now that the war had come to an end.

Although it is practically impossible to put a firm date on the birth of the Second Republic, it is much more feasible to find the seeds of the transformation of the old order in a period of rapid change and flux (from July 1988 to June 1989). The Thermidor of the Iranian revolution, marking 'the end of the revolutionary process and the beginning of the definitive establishment of the new regime' (Mozaffari 1993: 611), forms the very basis of policy changes in Iran. The end of the war was one major feature of this period, but so also were the death of Ayatollah Khomeini and the constitutional reform process which he put in motion before his death. It is a combination of these factors, coupled with the role and influence of the faces and individuals which came to occupy the highest echelons of power after Ayatollah Khomeini's death, that help to identify the basis of post-Khomeini leadership in Iran. At the output level, also, one can see a Second Republic emerging to replace the First.

From this vantage point one can scrutinise the new leadership's approach to domestic, regional and international issues, as well as observe the type and nature of policies which were adopted. It can be shown that the policy changes have been so fundamental, their impact on the country so far-reaching, and their consequences so revolutionary that it makes little sense to continue to regard the post-Khomeini Islamic Republic as an exact replica (in structural, institutional and policy terms) of the old. Yet a strong element of continuity with the past does exist, particularly when one examines the political origins and backgrounds of the republic's post-Khomeini leadership. This, however, is not the only manifestation of such continuity. Many of the formal and informal structures of the 'old regime' remain, if not in substance then at least in appearance.

On the occasion of the tenth anniversary of the revolution President Khamenei and Ayatollah Montazeri stated that the revolution should be 'reviewed' and its successes and failures assessed. This might not be done satisfactorily, however, President Khamenei maintained, mainly because 'of one basic weakness and that is lack of a centralised executive administration' (SWB, ME/0381, 10 February 1989). This proved to be the opening shot in the debate surrounding reform of the constitution in which the executive branch of government could play the leading role in managing the affairs of the state. For the Faqih-designate, on the other hand, the main issue at this juncture was to review the leadership's past behaviour with a view to making suitable adjustments. 'We must repent of our past mistakes', he said (SWB, ME/0384, 14 February 1989). He put the emphasis on reforms which might help in the absorption of the 'specialist forces both at home and abroad', the extension of freedom of speech and political activity, and an end of censorship in the press and the electronic media.

The above, rather complementary, positions joined to add to the impetus for reform of the executive structures and 'the ways of the state' already openly discussed. These developments in themselves were perhaps not sufficient evidence of the demise of the old order, however. But two significant developments before the death of Ayatollah Khomeini were to provide tangible dimensions for it. These were the process of constitutional reform sanctioned by Ayatollah Khomeini and the resignation of Ayatollah Montazeri as the Faqih-designate in March 1989.

THE RESIGNATION OF AYATOLLAH MONTAZERI

The resignation of Ayatollah Montazeri on 28 March 1989 as the Faqih-designate some four years after his official endorsement as the successor to Ayatollah Khomeini was a significant development as far as the future of the Islamic Republic was concerned. At one level, the resignation helped to highlight the lack of stability prevalent in the system some ten years after the founding of the Islamic Republic. But, apart from underlining the deep factionalism at the heart of the system, Montazeri's resignation offered an unexpected ray of hope to those individuals who harboured ambitions in the direction of the spiritual leadership of the republic after Ayatollah Khomeini. Although Ayatollah Montazeri was not defrocked by Khomeini, unlike Grand Ayatollah Shariatmadari, who was defrocked in 1986 for challenging the Faqih's monopoly of spiritual and political power, little doubt remained that Montazeri's resignation resulted from differences between him and Khomeini. Coming in the midst of the constitutional reform debate, the resignation of Montazeri heightened the concern of the leading clerics in the republic involved with the Constitutional Review Panel to accelerate their proceedings, and, perhaps more important, to avoid being caught between the two leading Ayatollahs of the land.

The political demise of Montazeri in March raised serious questions about the issue of succession in Iran. Coming so soon after Ayatollah Khomeini's *fatwa* against Salman Rushdie in February 1989, the impression that the Islamic Republic was returning to its old pattern of confrontation in the international arena, and that domestically it was heading towards civil strife, could not have been dismissed out of hand at this point. The impression of rivalry and divisions was reinforced as the depth of the differences between Montazeri and Khomeini became public knowledge. In May 1989 the Deputy Speaker of the Majlis, Hojjatoleslam Mehdi Karrubi, announced that Ahmad Khomeini, the Ayatollah's son, was preparing a document for publication aimed at clarifying the basis and nature of Ayatollah Khomeini's opposition to Montazeri's position as the Faqih-designate (*Kayhan Havai* 17 May 1989). Karrubi, whose brother Ayatollah Hassan Karrubi was said to have represented the Islamic Republic in secret negotiations with Israeli military and defence officials in July 1985 (Menashri 1990: 377), then proceeded to declare that for two and a half years Ayatollah Khomeini had been unhappy about Ayatollah Montazeri's conduct and the activities of his office. He pointedly identified the links between Montazeri and Mehdi Hashemi, the brother of his son-in-law and the man in charge of the Islamic Republic's support for liberation and revolutionary movements (itself run from Montazeri's office), who had publicised the extensive contacts between Tehran and Washington in the autumn of 1986, as a factor in the Faqih-designate's demise. Hashemi and 40 others were arrested and confessed to committing a number of crimes against the Islamic Republic, including corruption, and subversive and 'counter-revolutionary' activities. Hashemi was executed in September 1987.

The 'Irangate' episode had caused deep animosity between Montazeri and his entourage and the government team (including Rafsanjani, Khamenei, Velayati and Karrubi, amongst others) which had led to the secret contacts with the United States and Israel. That Montazeri had been regarded by the Rafsanjani–Khamenei axis as an obstacle in their way cannot, therefore, be overemphasised in the context of the succession struggle. In addition, Ayatollah Khomeini's tacit endorsement of the government line during the Irangate affair effectively meant the isolation of Montazeri in executive circles, and particularly in policy matters affecting the state, hardly a solid foundation for the Faqih-designate to consolidate on. That the Irangate revelations soon formed part of a power struggle must also be emphasised. According to one observer, the Irangate revelations emanating from the *El–Shira'a* newspaper in Lebanon were 'part of Montazeri's and Rafsanjani's battle for power in Iran' (Segev 1988: 283). Montazeri's position, thus, can be said to have been compromised from this point onwards, barely a year after his election by the Assembly of Experts as Khomeini's successor. That he should effectively be forced out in 1989, therefore, does not mean that the roots of rivalry were recent. The struggle for power characterised in chapter 1 had continued to determine the fate of the Islamic Republic till Ayatollah Khomeini's dying days.

The end of Montazeri's political career, however, did not come until Ayatollah Khomeini's message of 22 February 1989 to the clergy. In an indirect criticism of Montazeri in this message Ayatollah Khomeini offered his 'apologies' 'to the mothers, fathers, sisters, brothers, the spouses and the children of the martyrs and the self-sacrificing devotees because of some of the wrong analyses of these days' (*The Echo of Iran* 16 March 1989: 21). In another indirect attack on Montazeri, Ayatollah Khomeini stated, on 22

March, that 'I don't have a brotherhood with anybody, regardless of his rank. My friendship with them depends on the correctness of the path they pursue' (*Iran Focus* April 1989: 4). Up to this point Montazeri (along with a number of other high-ranking clerical figures) had repeatedly called for open and unprejudiced admission of the mistakes of the past ten years. He had criticised the excesses of the past, including lack of democracy.

To the annoyance of Ayatollah Khomeini, Montazeri's letters to Ayatollah Khomeini and other figures in Iran complaining about the lack of political reform at home and about the continuation of executions of members and supporters of organisations opposed to the regime, said to number over 1,000 in the year following Iran's acceptance of SCR 598 (Bakhash 1993), were being distributed abroad by his supporters. An unexpected meeting of the steering committee of the Assembly of Experts with Ayatollah Khomeini on 27 March convinced Montazeri that the differences between him and the Faqih had become unbridgeable. His resignation the next day opened the way for others interested in the position of the Faqih to 'make themselves available'. Ayatollah Khomeini's deteriorating health, however, meant that the issue of the succession would have to be faced sooner rather than later.

Ayatollah Khomeini's death on 3 June opened the way for the election of a new Faqih by the Assembly of Experts. Even though the new constitution had not yet been put to the vote of the people, the election of the new Faqih followed its recommendations (see below for details of the 1989 constitution on the choice of Faqih). On 5 June the Assembly named Khamenei as the new Faqih, by-passing the country's senior Ayatollahs. Hasty elevation to the rank of Ayatollah accompanied his new appointment (Milani 1992). It was reported that President Khamenei had been elected against the wishes of one-third of the Khobregan Assembly, who apparently had an overall preference for Ayatollah Khomeini's son, Hojjatoleslam Ahmad Khomeini (Haeri 1989), although the national press gave a figure of 60 voting in favour of Khamenei, out of the 74 individuals present (*Kayhan* 4 and 5 June 1989). Ayatollah Montazeri telegraphed his support for Ayatollah Khamenei from his base in Qom on 16 June.

Khamenei's appointment put a swift end to the speculation about the succession debate; it also galvanised Hojjatoleslam Rafsanjani into action. He could now pursue his political career unhindered, and with the support of Khamenei. The proposed changes to the constitution would open new opportunities for Rafsanjani to climb the political power ladder further and take his chances at becoming the Islamic Republic's first executive President.

As the Assembly of Experts was constitutionally charged to elect the new Faqih, the outcome of the deliberations depended a great deal on the balance of forces in this body. Naturally, in the absence of the recognised Faqih-designate, Ayatollah Montazeri, and the non-option of a Leadership Council, the

Khobregan moved towards a compromise solution and chose Khamenei to be the new Faqih. He was elected on the basis of Article 109 of the 1989 constitution (qualities and attributes of the Leader). The procedure leading up to and the nature of this particular appointment, notes Ahrahamian, 'unwittingly undermined the theological foundations of Khomeini's Velayat-e Faqih' (Abrahamian 1991: 116). This is so largely because Khamenei's appointment was neither based on his seniority in rank, nor prevented by his not being a Marja'a-e Taqlid, both points being emphasised in the 1979 constitution and in Ayatollah Khomeini's own writings and pronouncements.

It was announced on 19 June that the date of Presidential elections would be brought forward by three weeks (from 18 August), to take place at the end of July. The Interior Minister, Hojjatoleslam Ali Akbar Mohtashemi, gave two main reasons for this decision (*Kayhan Havai* 28 June 1989). One, that in the absence of Ayatollah Khomeini it was imperative for the system to be stabilised as soon as possible and 'Ayatollah Khomeini's wishes realised'. Secondly, that since his appointment as Faqih it was not possible for Ayatollah Khamenei to be the President as well. With the Guardian Council's approval, thus, the new date for the Presidential elections and the referendum on the constitutional changes had been arrived at. It was stated that as Ayatollah Khomeini himself had recommended a two-month period for the review of the constitution and as the Review Panel had completed its deliberations there was no reason why the two events could not be combined.

It can be argued, therefore, that by September 1989 Hojjatoleslam Rafsanjani and Ayatollah Khamenei had acquired enough authority to become the two main pillars of the new regime, each instrumental in his own way in consolidating the emerging Second Republic. The former was proclaimed Iran's new President on 30 July, with 15,537,394 votes in favour, defeating his only rival (Dr Abbas Shaibani, who won 650,000 votes) by an overwhelming majority. As far as Hojjatoleslam Rafsanjani was concerned, this result compared very favourably with the previous three-candidate Presidential election in August 1985, which had returned President Khamenei with a total of some 12 million votes (Povey 1986). The referendum also approved the constitutional amendments, with 16,025,459 votes in favour (*Ettela'at*, 30 July 1989 and 1 August 1989). President Rafsanjani's Cabinet was introduced to the Majlis (for approval) on 19 August, two days after his taking the ceremonial Presidential oath.

THE CONSTITUTIONAL AMENDMENTS: PROCESS, IMPACT AND OUTCOME

The weaknesses of the 1979 constitution of the Islamic Republic in terms of vaguely defining the roles and responsibilities of the various centres of power in the republic had been evident at least since the political struggle in 1980–1 between President Bani-Sadr and Prime Minister Rajaii and his IRP-based clerical supporters. The form that that struggle took and the eventual dismissal of Bani-Sadr, at the behest of Ayatollah Khomeini and orchestrated by the Majlis (through exercising its constitutional right of the issuing of a vote of no confidence against the President), underlined the ambiguities in the constitution. At the same time, the leadership was acutely aware of the destabilising impact of such ambiguities on the entire system, particularly in the absence of Ayatollah Khomeini as the mediator and the ultimate arbiter.

The confusions associated with the lack of clarity in delineating responsibilities and in the assignment of duties in the state machinery had a direct impact on the functioning of the state, particularly in the sectors which had sprung from the revolution and the birth of the Islamic Republic. The differences between the Council of Guardians and the Majlis over legislation, for example, were one such area needing urgent attention. The Guardian Council's rejection of a high proportion of Majlis legislation as 'un-Islamic' (as much as 48 per cent according to the *Iran Times* 27 June 1989), led to the creation in February 1988 of a new mediatory body, the 13–member Council for the Determination of Expediency (literally the Council on the Discernment of What to do for the Best), which was to mediate between these two constitutional bodies. Interestingly, the creation of this body merely reinforced the existing divisions. The council from the outset was beset by difficulties, over its mandate, jurisdiction and functions. Some 97 MPs (according to IRNA 7 October 1989, 104 deputies), for instance, sent a letter to Ayatollah Khomeini in November 1988 complaining that the Expediency Council had exceeded its powers and had ratified government Bills without consulting the Majlis or the Guardian Council (*Kayhan* 7 December 1988). Ayatollah Khomeini duly responded in December by advocating limitation of the powers of the Expediency Council (maintaining that the extraordinary powers given it were mainly because of the war): 'only it should act in cases when there is difference between the Majlis and the Council of Guardians' (IRNA 31 December 1988). Ayatollah Montazeri went further, stating shortly before his resignation that the Expediency Council 'is an institute contrary to the constitution which was set up owing to the existing necessities and the war . . . in the future all affairs will be managed in accordance with the constitution' (*The Echo of Iran* 2 March 1989: 18).

President Khamenei confirmed in December 1988 that reform of the original constitution was being actively pursued by the clerical leadership of Iran. This followed the publication of a letter sent to Ayatollah Khomeini by a number of Majlis deputies complaining about the shortcomings of the original constitution. During the Friday sermon of 3 December 1988 President Khamenei stated:

> I do not claim that our constitution is free of all defects . . . In part regarding the administration of the country, whether relating to the executive or the judiciary, there are, of course, certain difficulties, certain vague points [*sic*]. In those cases when society is faced with a certain difficulty which has not been foreseen by the constitution, it is up to the leadership of the country and the leader of society to find and propose a solution.
>
> (*Kayhan* 7 December 1988)

Further support for constitutional reform came in January and February 1989 from other leading clerics, including the speaker of the Assembly of Experts, Ayatollah Meshkini (who later chaired the Constitutional Review Panel), and Ayatollah Ardebili, the Chief Justice (*Iran Focus* March 1989).

It was not until 25 April 1989, however, that Ayatollah Khomeini (himself the highest authority in the country) formally ordered President Khamenei to set up a 25-member Constitution Review Panel (20 members of which were appointed by Ayatollah Khomeini and five elected by the Majlis) to discuss the reform of the constitution. In an interview with a number of Qom theologians in March 1989, President Khamenei stated that 'our constitutional law has not foreseen a need for management in some governmental departments in such a way as to satisfy the needs of society' (*Jomhouri Islami* 4 March 1989). The Majlis, thus, was more or less bypassed in this process. Both Hojjatoleslams Khamenei and Rafsanjani served as members of the Review Panel. Ayatollah Khomeini's preferences for the main areas needing further clarification were: the Faqih issue; centralisation of the executive power; centralisation of judicial power; refinement of Article 64 of the 1979 constitution about the membership rights and number of deputies elected to the Majlis from the recognised minorities in Iran; centralisation of management of the radio and television services; and clarification and formalisation of the duties and rights of the Expediency Council (Behrouz 1989).

The main debate in this panel crystallised around two schools of thought: those who advocated a strengthening of the Prime Minister's post (and reduction of the Presidential office to a ceremonial appointment) on the one hand, and those who advocated the abolition of the premiership in favour of the presidency (making the presidency an executive office) on the other.

Meanwhile, the tensions between the offices of the Prime Minister and the President remained unresolved. Although President Khamenei remained largely uncritical of the Moussavi government, it was the Majlis and the Faqih-designate which maintained the pressure on his government. But in terms of the distribution of executive power in the republic the failures of the successive Moussavi governments to solve Iran's economic difficulties (thanks partly to the Guardian Council's opposition to the radical legislation proposed by Moussavi and supported by the Majlis) provided further ammunition for those who advocated the abolition of the premiership. It emerged in due course, moreover, that Moussavi himself had been in favour of constitutional reform in the directions foreseen by President Khamenei and Speaker Rafsanjani. He is reported to have complained openly that the root of the Islamic Republic's problems lay in the lack of concentration of power in the executive branch (*Iran Focus* April 1989).

Between 26 April and 15 June the Review Panel met 21 times. According to the regulations governing the operations of the Review Panel, three subcommittees were established to examine and propose the necessary revisions. By 11 July the final amendments to the constitution had been made. The amendments were put to a referendum on 28 July, coinciding with the Presidential elections. The proposed changes, published after Ayatollah Khomeini's death, finally removed the position of Faqih as the most powerful single authority in the land, and institutionalised the mechanisms of power and its formal distribution in the Second Republic. According to one observer, 'Without an Imam with . . . *baraka* [i.e. one like Ayatollah Khomeini], the Vilayet [Faqih] becomes simply another type of political secular state structure' (Jansen 1989: 14). It is the process of change undertaken through the consitutional reform and the developments embodied in the amendments put forward which allow one to regard the context and content of the constitutional reform as an important indication of the rise of the Second Republic.

The outcome of the review process further reinforced the position of those forces in the FIR camp who had gathered around the 'pragmatic' agenda and faction(s). The main function of the amendments was to formalise the division of power in the Islamic Republic. As will be discussed in chapter 3, the amendments to the constitution directly affected the balance of power in the Islamic Republic as well. The most significant constitutional development was the abolition of the office of the Prime Minister. Article 60 of the new constitution stated that 'The executive power shall be exercised by the President of the Republic and the Ministers, except in cases for which the Leader has been made directly responsible by this law'. Article 60 of the 1979 constitution had proclaimed: 'The executive power shall be exercised by the President of the Republic, the Prime Minister and the Ministers' (all the references to the constitutional amendments are from *The Echo of Iran* 25 August 1989 and September 1989).

According to Article 113 of the 1989 amendments,

Next to the Leader, the President of the Republic is the highest official authority of the country who is responsible for the enforcement of the

Constitution and presides over the executive power with the exception of those matters which directly relate to the Leader.

In addition, Article 87 of the 1989 constitution states: 'The President shall be obliged to obtain a vote of confidence from the Assembly [Majlis] immediately upon its formation'. Article 87 of the 1979 constitution read as follows: 'The Council of Ministers must obtain a vote of confidence'. Instead of 'government Bills and regulations' being 'notified to the President' (Article 126 of the 1979 constitution), under Article 126 of the amended constitution the President is put 'directly in charge of budgeting and planning as well as the administrative and employment affairs of the country'. Articles 133, 134 and 136 give the power to appoint Cabinet Ministers to the President and to dismiss them, and appoints him as the head of the Cabinet.

In total, the 50 or so amendments or revisions to the 1979 constitution affected the following articles: 5, 57, 60, 64, 69–70, 85, 87–91, 99, 107–13, 121–2, 124, 126–8, 130–42, 157–8, 160–2, 164, 173–6. Only three new articles were added to the 1979 constitution, Articles 109, 112 and 176. While Article 176 gave authorisation for the establishment of a Supreme Council of National Security, itself constituted under the authority of the President, Article 109 is devoted to defining the qualifications and attributes of the Faqih. The latter is particularly important, as all post-Khomeini leaders are assumed not to have the moral and 'natural' authority of the 'Founder and Leader of the Islamic Republic' and as such the qualities of future leaders have to be enshrined in the constitution. Furthermore, in the absence of the overall authority of a figure such as Ayatollah Khomeini, the new clause is designed to avoid conflict among the leading contenders for the position of the Faqih. The new article thus formalised the office of Faqih, which emerged out of the political treatise of Ayatollah Khomeini himself as the main feature of the Islamic Republic. Article 112 of the amended constitution established the Expediency Council as a legal-functional entity of the Second Republic.

At the output level also the 1989 amendments proposed changes, particularly to the sections relating to the selection and administrative responsibilities of the Faqih. These sets of changes consolidated the post-Khomeini religio-political structure of power in the Islamic Republic. Some five alterations to the 1979 constitution addressed the status of the Faqih and his role and duties. Specifically, Articles 5, 107, and 109–11 deal with these matters. Article 5 of the 1989 amended constitution is particularly important, as it erases an important qualification clause present in the 1979 version, which stated: 'If no clergy having such majority [of the people] is found, the leadership will rest with the Leadership Council composed of the clergies having the qualifications aforementioned'. Instead, the amended constitution

(Article 107) refers to the appointment of the Leader being the task of the '[religious] experts elected by the people', who

> Should they find one of the candidates more conversant with the regulations and subjects involving jurisprudence or social and political issues, or in case a candidate shall enjoy public support or shall be especially conspicuous regarding any one of the merits described in Article 109, they shall appoint him as the Leader, or else they shall introduce and elect one of the candidates as the Leader.

This is in contrast to Article 107 of the 1979 constitution, which stated that in the absence of a single Faqih figure emerging: '[the experts or Khobregan] shall decide on three or five religious leaders qualified for leadership as members of the Council of Leadership'. Under Article 109 of the amended constitution it is declared that 'Should there exist a number of qualified applicants, the individual who shall have stronger insight in matters involving jurisprudence and politics shall have preference'.

The 'single Faqih' doctrine enshrined in the new constitution was apparently formulated in order to minimise instability at the highest level in the post-Khomeini era. The Leadership Council option, regarded as an attractive formula in situations where a clear Faqih figure may not have emerged, came to be viewed as an obstacle to the survival of the post-Khomeini system by the leading clerical FIR figures. The collective leadership system also came to be regarded an inefficient model, where, by definition, differences amongst the Leadership Council members on policy and matters of judgement might lead to indecision. Secondly, many of the pragmatic forces were fully aware that the Leadership Council formula could serve to fuel rivalries and, furthermore, might in fact end up limiting the influence of individuals below the religious rank of Ayatollah. With the exception of Khamenei, who was elevated to the rank of Ayatollah when he was elected as the Faqih, Rafsanjani and the majority of his clerical allies were still Hojjatoleslams.

While many of the functions of the Faqih under the new amended constitution remained the same as under the old, there were certain instances where his powers were subject to re-examination. One such instance occurs in Article 110 of the amended constitution. In spelling out the functions and duties of the Faqih, clause 1 of Article 110 reads as follows: 'To designate the general policies of the system of the Islamic Republic of Iran after consultation with the Congregation for Determining the Expediencies [the Expediencey Council]'. No such provision existed during Ayatollah Khomeini's 'Faqihship'. At the same time, however, the influence of the Faqih has been deepened in the amended constitution. Article 110 of the 1989 constitution, for example, also lists 11 'functions and authorities' for the Leader, ranging from making appointments to the religio-political and military establishments to 'declare war or peace and mobilise the [armed] forces' (clause 5). By contrast, the 1979 constitution listed six 'functions and authorities of the Leader', including the above clause. The 1989 amendments removed the Faqih's power to dismiss the President. This can happen only at the suggestion of the Majlis when endorsed by the judiciary. Finally, the final draft of the amendments also dropped a reference to the Faqih's constitutional right to dissolve the Majlis under certain circumstances. Encountering strong opposition from the Majlis deputies to this suggestion, the new Faqih instructed the Constitution Review Panel to erase this clause altogether.

As far as the duties and responsibilities of the Faqih were concerned, the amended constitution had to adapt to new realities and the changing political environment. Ultimately, the process of adaptation had a direct impact on the defined role of the Faqih. The end of the war caused the abolition of the National Defence High Council (a relic of the war years which was disbanded after the cease-fire agreement), for instance, which in turn removed a source of constitutional leverage in the hands of the Faqih, thus affecting the mode of his interaction with the governing system. The old constitution had required the Leader 'to establish the National Defence High Council' (clause 3, subclause C, Article 110), whereas the new one requires him 'to settle the problems of the system which cannot be solved through normal channels, through the Congregation for Determining the Expediencies' (Clause 8, Article 110).

In order to ensure continuity in the system, the amended constitution made specific provisions in the event of the death, resignation or removal of the Faqih. Article 111 states that 'Until such time as the new Leader will be introduced, a council comprising the President, the Head of the Judiciary, and one of the jurists of the Guardians' Council appointed by the Congregation for Determining the Expediencies shall provisionally assume all duties of the Leader'. The 1979 constitution only required that provision should be made for the Khobregan to be convened 'for the purpose of studying and implementing this Article [111]'.

Another significant amendment is to be found in its treatment of the judiciary. Firstly, it abolished the five-member Judicial High Council as the highest judicial authority in the republic and replaced it with a single appointment (made by the Faqih), to be known as the Head of the Judiciary (Chief Justice) (Article 157). Constitutionally, he is Chief Justice for a five-year period and responsible for all judicial administrative and executive matters. Secondly, the Minister of Justice is responsible to the Chief Justice. Indeed, the Minister is to be chosen by the President from 'among those proposed to the President by the Head of the Judiciary' (Article 160). Thirdly, instead of the Faqih appointing the religious-based positions of the President (or Head) of the Supreme Court and the Public Prosecutor-General (as was the case under Article 162 of the 1979 constitution), the appointments are to be made by the Head of the Judiciary. Fourthly, the Head of the Judiciary is empowered to change or remove a judge (under strict and very special circumstances and not against the will of the judge(s) concerned) after consultation with the Head of the Supreme Court (Article 164). It is clear, therefore, that, consistent with the procedures regarding the presidency of the republic and that of the choice of the Faqih, in this respect also the 1989 amendments moved towards the centralisation and 'personalisation' of the structures of power.

These changes reflect the constitutional/legalistic aspects of the Second Republic. One final feature of the 1989 amendments needing further attention is the formalisation of the Expediency Council as a constitutional entity in post-Khomeini Iran. Under Article 112 of the amended constitution the Expediency Council is recognised as a body

> formed for the purposes of determining the proper acts and things deemed expedient in cases where a ratification of the [Majlis] shall be rejected by the Guardians Council on grounds of inconsistency with the principles of the Holy Sharia or the Constitution [*sic*]. The Congregation shall be formed upon the instructions of the Leader.

The deadlocks of the earlier era, therefore, had given birth to a new (largely) clerical body which was then enshrined as a permanent structure of the Second Republic. Its membership expanded to 20 under Ayatollah Khamenei, the Expediency Council was reconstituted in October 1989 according to the amended constitution. Now under his firm control, the Faqih proceeded to select the membership of the Expediency Council, ensuring that the main streams of political opinion in the republic were represented in this body. 'The presence of well-known political figures of the country, even though from the two main political streams of the country, is . . . [an] important characteristic of the newly formed council', according to an editorial in the *Tehran Times*, an English-language newspaper known to be close to the government (*Tehran Times* 8 October 1989). President Rafsanjani was elected Chairman of the Expediency Council by the membership on 10 October1989.

Certain aspects of the 1979 constitution, however, were regarded as unalterable. These included the Islamic nature of the system; the Islamic basis of all the laws and regulations; the spiritual bases and Islamic objectives of the republic; the republican nature of the system; the legal guardianship (Faqih) introduced by Ayatollah Khomeini; the official religion of Iran as 'Asna Ashari' based on the 'Twelfth Imamism'; the conduct of the country's affairs by reference to public vote.

POLICY CHANGES IN POST-KHOMEINI IRAN

Basically, three areas of policy change can be identified in the Second Republic, these being the main functional features of the post-Khomeini state: first, domestic politics; second, economic and social policy; third, foreign policy. Not all of these have been pursued with the same vigour by the new administration. Of the three areas, the main focus has been on economic and foreign policy.

The changes in the foreign policy realm have been dominated by the need to improve Iran's regional and international standing through co-operation and dialogue with the West, the (former) USSR, the Gulf Arab states and other Arab and regional actors. This stemmed partly from Iran's economic needs in the era of reconstruction, and partly from recognition of the fact that the republic's diplomatic isolation had had severe repercussions for Tehran's regional status.

The need for economic reform and policy change was the dominant theme of the Rafsanjani presidency. In a series of speeches, President Rafsanjani outlined the policies of his first term in office and reiterated them in two major policy-oriented speeches (at the swearing-in ceremony of 17 August 1989 and the Friday prayer sermon of 1 September 1989) soon after his election. Against the background of a deteriorating domestic economy, the new government's strategy was based on raising industrial production and accelerating economic growth. The control of inflation and a reduction in the government's budget deficit were regarded as major priorities of the Rafsanjani administration, but so too were the raising of foreign finance for reconstruction and economic development, the raising of tax receipts by the government, deregulation, liberalisation, and privatisation of the economy. The heart of the new economic policies was to be found in the Five Year Development Plan, formulated in 1989 and scheduled to start in 1990.

Throughout, the emphasis was on economic co-operation with the West and others, which in turn depended on correct, if not warm, diplomatic ties. As Hojjatoleslam Rafsanjani stated in the course of his Friday prayer sermon of 1 September, 'I will not now engage in fantasies of an independent and self-sufficient society', plainly endorsing further integration into the international system (SWB, ME/0552, 4 September 1989).

On political reform the Second Republic has been much more cautious about advocating change and even slower to implement it. Recalling the discussion in chapter 1 on factionalism and the tendency towards monopolisation of power by the FIRs, it is hardly surprising that political reform has not been taken seriously. As Nader Entessar notes, 'the Islamic Republic has yet to devise a formal and institutionalised system of political participation' (Entessar 1992: 225).

Historically speaking, it can be seen that in fact a certain element of continuity exists with Iran's pre-revolution experience, as for much of the Shah's rule only three political parties were allowed to operate in Iran, none of them freely. The political parties concerned were the Iran Novin (the governing party), Mardom and Pan-Iranist. In 1976 the Shah decreed the end of the old party system, creating in its place a single-party political system (the new party was called Rastakhiz) and disgarding the 'loyal opposition'. In the Islamic Republic the 'ruling party', the IRP, was disbanded even before the emergence of the Second Republic, and no new political party had appeared to represent the post-Khomeini leadership of Iran, or indeed to represent the FIR opposition forces.

Although the regime initiated some political changes as early as December 1988, mainly by considering the implementation of the Political Parties' and Groups' Activities Act of 1981 (suspended for the previous seven years), little tangible progress has been made in the direction of political freedoms. Hojjatoleslam Rafsanjani even talked of communists being allowed to operate freely in the future (IRNA 7 December 1989). It is worth recalling that the war was given as the official reason for the suspension of the Parties Act (see the Interior Minister's interview in *Kayhan*, 14 December 1988). The change in the political atmosphere enabled some 24 groups and personalities to apply to the Interior Ministry for formal recognition (*Kayhan* 18 January 1989). By mid-February over 30 parties had submitted applications (SWB, ME/0384, 14 February 1989), none of which received a licence to operate. No changes to the constitution were envisaged in regard to political organisational rights and freedoms in Iran, despite the establishment in 1993 of a human rights committee attached to the Majlis.

Article 26 of the constitution stated that:

> Political parties, and professional associations and societies as well as societies subscribing to Islam or other recognised minority religions, are free to operate, provided that they do not violate the principles of independence, freedom, national unity, Islamic criteria or the foundations of the Islamic Republic.

Freedom to hold marches and public gatherings is provided for in Article 27 of the constitution. That said, since 1981 all opposition political parties have been banned; even the ruling party itself, so to speak, the Islamic Republican Party, was disbanded at the behest of its leaders in June 1987. It is ironic that the only group out of the 80 which emerged soon after the revolution which has survived in the Islamic Republic, Bazargan's Nehzat-e Azadi movement, is normally regarded as a voice of the opposition. It has not, however, been allowed to function as a political party.

Regardless of the rights to political organisation granted in the constitution, political groups and organisations have to comply with the principles laid down in the 1981 Parties Act. The Act does not of course allow the emergence of 'irresponsible' political organisations. The Act's 19 articles strive to obtain conformity rather than diversity. Article 1 categorically declares that political organisations must 'conform to the overall principles of the Islamic Republican system'. Article 14 of the Act states: 'Groups applying for permits must clearly state their allegiance to the Constitution of the Islamic Republic of Iran in their articles of association and manifestoes', and Article 15 warns, 'Any changes in the leadership, manifesto or articles of association of the groups must be announced to and reviewed by the committee stated in Article Ten'. The Act also reserves the right of the 'Article 10 committee' to dissolve organisations found to be functioning beyond the boundaries set by the state.

Freedom of association and political organisation outside the parameters already laid down in the Islamic Republic, it seems, would cause serious problems for the 'agenda' in Iran, and would ultimately result in challenges to the very legitimacy of the entire system. This is clearly not desirable in a republic which has to maintain a form of rule inherited from a revolutionary process, itself the 'child of more than one father' and lacking the guiding hand of Khomeini. Lack of 'diversity' in politics, furthermore, is utilised in the Islamic Republic to reinforce the uniformity of the system – despite the openly recognised and all-pervasive differences within its edifice.

As already stated, many of the above features of the Second Republic amount to a sharp departure for the Islamic Republic from its past (the first decade of its existence). But far from moving towards new horizons, much of the data indicates that the new regime is in fact moving back in time – albeit under a vastly different leadership and political system – to try and fulfil the policies and priorities pursued by Imperial Iran. Ultimately, without the war, a combination of geopolitical exigencies and Iran's position in the international division of labour have re-emerged to influence greatly the direction and tempo of future development of the Islamic Republic. As Abrahamian has observed, Ayatollah Khomeini's heirs 'no longer talk of land reform, income redistribution and nationalization of foreign trade . . . They talk less about social justice and the rights of the shantytown poor, and more about productivity, privatization, business incentives, managerial skills and free-market mechanisms' (Abrahamian 1991: 119).

3 The politics of power in post-Khomeini Iran

Machiavelli had a concept called the concept of *virtu*. The substance of this concept is that man can change his environment qualitatively, but depends upon two essential things and their meeting together. First, favourable circumstances, and then the leadership which is able to understand these circumstances, react instinctively with them, seize the favourable moments, and then act with determination to fulfil them. When these two characteristics meet, a qualitative change in the situation becomes possible.

> (Hanna Batatu, in *Perspectives on the Middle East 1983*,
> Washington, DC: Middle East Institute, 1983)

As already discussed in chapter 2, the dismissal of Ayatollah Montazeri as the prospective leader of the Islamic Republic, and the crisis following the Salman Rushdie affair in the spring of 1989, helped to disguise a real trend towards the Second Republic, then in its embryonic state following the appointment of Hojjatoleslam Hashemi Rafsanjani as the Commander-in-Chief of the armed forces in June 1988 – only weeks before Iran's unconditional acceptance of SCR 598.

The loss of the 'moderate' Montazeri was interpreted by analysts as a blow to the pragmatic/realist line prevalent in Iran at that time, and the Rushdie affair was seen as a sign which marked the ascendency of the radical elements within the Islamic Republic – in time to consolidate power before the Ayatollah's impending demise. Given the new agenda of the republic since Ayatollah Khomeini's death, an alternative presentation of these two events can be made, and one which can be regarded as advancing the cause of the pragmatists (or realists in relation to economic and foreign policy).

Far from weakening the hand of the realists, Ayatollah Montazeri's dismissal helped this loose grouping in two important ways. Firstly, it removed a potential source of political power against the Khamenei–Rafsanjani coalition *before* Khomeini's death, thus strengthening the general realist platform in the medium term (i.e. after Khomeini's death), despite the short-term negative impact of losing a leading 'moderate' figure. Secondly, as the evidence in chapter 2 suggests, more ambitious realists may actually have been involved in the anti-Montazeri campaign, setting him up as the figure to draw the fire and venom of the hard-liners and other radicalist forces. Paradoxically, in this sense his political future was the sacrificial lamb that served to unite the leadership of the republic. In Ayatollah Montazeri's fall from grace all factions received a positive fillip to their own fortunes.

The pragmatists saw in his downfall their own rise to power in the medium term, and the 'radicals' interpreted the absence of Ayatollah Montazeri as a mortal blow to 'moderation' and an immediate gain for their own line. The Rushdie affair, on the other hand, can be regarded as an aftertaste – a shock reaction – to the pace of change in the Islamic Republic's foreign relations and its fast-changing domestic indicators of accepted political behaviour. Its medium-term impact, it must be noted, has been minimal, adversely affecting directly (for a short period) Tehran's relations with only one (non-Islamic) country, the United Kingdom. Domestically, the Rushdie affair did not affect the balance of forces, never instigating an inward rupture or indeed any contradictory outpouring of sentiments among the political elite.

THE REINS OF POWER IN POST-KHOMEINI IRAN

The almost totally smooth and steady transfer of all the important and decisive reins of power to the pragmatists after Ayatollah Khomeini's death has had profound implications for the regime. Hojjatoleslam Khamenei's designation as the Faqih, over the heads of many other very able and senior Ayatollahs on the one hand, and the election of Hojjatoleslam Hashemi Rafsanjani (the Speaker of the Majlis for the previous nine years) in August 1989 to the office of President on the other (a position held by Khamenei himself for the previous eight years), consolidated greatly the role of these two individuals in the post-Khomeini structure of power. The proposed constitutional amendments carried easily by the Majlis and the electorate (at the same time as the Presidential elections) put the necessary flesh on the skeleton of the 'new' republic.

As already stated, the loss to the presidency of the Prime Minister's portfolio can be seen as the most important structural change in the republican system of government in Iran. Other important amendments to the constitution, the creation of new centralised bodies (the Supreme Council of National Security, for instance) were to all intents and purposes new developments in post-Khomeini Iran. Ultimately, the changes in the republic's constitution typify the changes in the power structure of the regime and the distribution of institutional control, which are after all the essence of the Second Republic.

Certain qualifications, however, have to be borne in mind when speaking of the 'Second Republic', particularly in terms of the extent of continuity in the system. Many of the bureaucratic structures utilised and created by the post-Khomeini leadership are not significantly different from those of the First Republic, nor indeed very distinct from the Imperial state machinery created by decades of Pahlavi rule. The membership of the Expediency Council, for instance, was enlarged in the Second Republic from the original 13 to 20. Its new make-up is also somewhat different: according to the 1989 constitution the President chairs the council, the members of which are appointed by the Leader. In its current form, thus, the control of the council remains with the 'Leader–President' coalition. Despite the presence of Ahmad Khomeini, former Majlis Speaker Mehdi Karrubi, former PM Moussavi and former Prosecutor-General Mohammad Khoini'a as the Old Guard hard-liners and their counterweights in Rafsanjani and Ayatollah Yazdi and Mahdavi Kani in the council, it is clear that the 'institutional' appointments ensure a bias toward the realists' (or pragmatists') line. Constitutionally, besides the six Islamic jurisprudent members, the heads of the three branches of government and the Minister of the Interior, there will always be present the Cabinet Minister and the head of the Majlis committee concerned with the matter under discussion. It is notable also that Hojjatoleslam Mohtashemi (the former Interior Minister), regarded as one of the leaders of the Maktabi FIR faction, was not appointed a member of the Expediency Council when it was reconstituted by Ayatollah Khamenei.

Since the 1979 revolution the clerical establishment (estimated to number anything from 90,000 to 200,000) (Hiro 1985; Schahgaldian 1989) has formed the very heart of the regime, providing the state with one Prime Minister, three Presidents, four Majlis Speakers, two Faqihs and a host of other functionaries and officials (including the voting clerical 50 per cent membership of the Council of Guardians). The country's Ayatollahs (around 200 in number) are present in the most critical of institutions and bodies in the republic. Since 1989 the President, the Faqih, the Majlis Speaker, the Head of the Judiciary and Chairman of the Supreme Court have been clerics, some attaining office through selection (largely) by other clerics and others through popular elections. Thus individually and collectively the clerics have dominated the most crucial levers of power in the land. Despite their endemic factionalism (Behrooz 1991) they continue to form the backbone of post-Khomeini Islamic Republican Iran. One useful way of examining the balance of power in the republic between the various clerical factions and personalities is to draw a distinction between those who have power and those who enjoy authority. So, for instance, power is much more a politico-religious concept (the Faqih) in Iran, whereas authority can be seen to have purely religious roots embedded in the hierarchy of the Shii sect of Islam.

Despite the rather fragmented nature of power relations, today's Islamic order in Iran is built around two key institutions, the Leader (Rahbar) and the President. As shown in Table 1, these two pillars control much of the country's politico-religious and governmental machinery. Other state organs which are of significance in explaining the structure of power in post-Khomeini Iran are: the Council of Guardians, the Majlis, the Expediency Council, the Assembly of Experts, the head of the judiciary (the Chief Justice), the National Security Council, the Cabinet, the foundations, Friday prayer posts, membership of or access to the coercive machinery of the state, Islamic associations and 'unity' committees. (The relationship between the most important of these institutions was discussed in chapter 2.) Add to these religious rank and authority as another factor in the structure of power in modern Iran and you have a complex set of relationships which are in part based on personal contacts and authority, factional allegiances, kinship and marriage ties and a series of 'multi-directorships', and in part based on the authority derived from the office itself.

Table 1 Agencies of formal power in Iran

Agency	Year founded	Function
Faqih	1979	Spiritual leader
Executive Presidency	1989	Executive leader
Cabinet	1979	Control of Ministries
Assembly of Experts	1979	Nominate and choose the Faqih
Council of Guardians	1980	Ratify Majlis legislation and supervise elections
Majlis	1980	Approve government policy
Expediency Council	1987	Arbitrate between Majlis and CoG
Reconstruction Policy Making Council	1988	Formulate reconstruction policies
Head of Judiciary	1989	Oversees courts
Joint Chiefs of Staff	1991	Co-ordinate defence policy

Velayat-e Faqih

Though some authors view the power of the office of the Faqih as having been reduced since Ayatollah Khomeini's death – in the words of Bakhash, 'the standing of the office has already been much diminished, and this process of the declining office of the faqih could continue' (Bakhash 1993: 82) – constitutionally and practically the Leader's position remains the locus of power in the republic, around which are spun the other offices of the state. A position created and occupied by the leader of the revolution, the Faqih system remains in place after the death of the patriarch as the embodiment of his Islamic Republic. The very basis of the legitimacy of the Islamic Republic is to be found in this doctrine and the system of power in modern Iran feeds from it.

In order to institutionalise the authority of post-Khomeini Faqihs and the principle of the Velayat-e Faqih system, the 1989 revised constitution enshrines the many informal levers of power that the late Ayatollah Khomeini himself controlled (Jahanpour 1990). As mentioned in chapter 2, the 1989 revised constitution deepened the influence of the Faqih in the system, adding substantially to his formal functions. The revised constitution states, for instance, that the President is accountable to the populace as well as the Faqih (in the 1979 constitution he was accountable only to the populace), that he must submit his resignation to the Faqih and, in the event of incapacity (and the unavailability of his first Vice-President), the Faqih is to appoint a new President.

The Faqih's role and responsibilities under the 1989 revised constitution can be summarised as follows (Behrouz 1989):

1 Supreme commander of the armed forces.
2 Determining the general policies of the IRI (in consultation with the Expediency Council).
3 Supervising the general implementation of agreed policies.
4 Ordering referenda.
5 Power to declare war and peace and general troop mobilisation.
6 Appointing and dismissing:

  (a) Members of the Council of Guardians.
  (b) Head of the judiciary.
  (c) Director of radio and television networks.
  (d) Chief of staff of the armed forces.
  (e) Commander-in-Chief of the IRGC.
  (f) Commander-in-Chief of the military and security forces.

7 Resolve differences and regulate relations among the three branches of the government.
8 Resolve, through the Expediency Council, problems which cannot be resolved by ordinary means.
9 Signing the decree naming the President after popular elections.
10 Impeaching the President for reasons of national interest pursuant to a verdict by the Supreme Court confirming his violation of his legal duties or a vote of no confidence by the Majlis.

Behrouz sees the 1989 revisions as not only centralising power within the system but also restricting the free hand of the leader by tying his most important decisions to prior consultations with the Expediency Council: 'contrary to the past, he could not take a step outside the framework of the Constitution' (Behrouz 1989: 17).

The Faqih exercises power through four main avenues: (1) his private office, (2) his provincial representatives, (3) his representatives in national organisations and (4) as C-in-C of the armed forces. His private office provides him with intelligence and information about day-to-day matters, arranges his meetings, visits, etc., as well as keeping him informed of political developments at home. In 1991 he appointed Hojjatoleslam Mohammadi-Golpaygani to head his private office (one of his advisers since November 1989). The Leader's four advisers who form part of his private office include two military officers (Brigadier-General Hossein Hasani-Sa'di and Rear Admiral Mohammad H. Malekzadegan) and two clerics with the rank of Hojjatoleslam (Mohammad A. Tashkiri and the above-named).

Ayatollah Khamenei has 22 provincial representatives covering the length and breadth of Iran, thus representing the *horizontal* extent of his power. They are accountable to his office and report to him direct on developments in the provinces and the impact of government policies and major issues outside the capital. Ayatollah Khamenei kept on 16 of the late Ayatollah's appointees, some of whom had been in their post since the early days of the revolution (Jahanpour 1992). By keeping in service many of Ayatollah Khomeini's provincial representatives Ayatollah Khamenei not only managed to minimise antagonism against him in the provinces but enabled himself to plug into the late Faqih's extensive national network and thus carved a solid power base for himself on the foundations provided by the late Imam. Consistent with Ayatollah Khomeini's practice, almost all Ayatollah Khamenei's provincial representative appointments were clerics.

In addition to the 'horizontal' net of representatives, the Faqih, through his representatives in national organisations, keeps a *vertical* sphere of influence in the country as well. Ayatollah Khamenei has 23 representatives in national organisations, ranging from the various branches of the armed forces and the Pasdaran to a number of foundations, Islamic bodies (including the Hajj office) and civil organisations. The most important of his appointments in national organisations are: the Central Directorate of Mosque Affairs (Ayatollah Mohammad Reza Mahdavi Kani, the former Secretary-General of the pro-Rafsanjani Association of Combative Clergy), the media (Hojjatoleslam Mohsen Do'agu), the armed forces (including Pasdaran) (five representatives, all clerics) and the National Security Council (on which he has two representatives: Hojjatoleslams Ahmad Khomeini and Hasan F. Rouhani, also registered as President Rafsanjani's national security adviser) (Jahanpour 1992). Eighteen of the national representatives (including two in the National Security Council) were clerical appointees (two Ayatollahs and 16 Hojjatoleslams).

The Faqih also appoints the secretariat and executive committee members of the Central Council of Friday Prayer Leaders, the organisation which supervises and directs the affairs of the Friday prayer leaders nationally, and through this council monitors, directs and, if need be, alters the tone and tenor of the national debate.

The executive President

President Rafsanjani is the first executive President of the republic and as such wields a great deal of power. He used this office to consolidate his position in post-Khomeini Iran and also to co-opt and neutralise 'many of his radical rivals by dropping them from the Cabinet and other important positions, or by appointing them to largely ceremonial posts and advisory positions lacking executive authority' (Bakhash 1993: 73). However, it would be incorrect to reduce his power base to this high office. Apart from being President, which enables him to choose the country's Ministers and direct the country's economic, political, foreign and public policies, he chairs the National Security Council (which formulates foreign policy as one of its many central functions), the Expediency Council, and a series of other executive councils. He is the executive branch's representative on the council of the three branches of government (the executive, the judiciary and the legislature), the First Deputy Speaker of the Assembly of Experts and Chairman of the influential Anti-Narcotics Headquarters.

The President is one of only three positions in the country which can rely on a national network (the other two being the Leader and the Head of the Judiciary's office). Apart from his nine or so deputies, Rafsanjani has control of the Presidential Bureau through which he maintains his organisational structure, and relies on a large body of 'presidential advisers' for support and policy direction. He has 19 advisers who offer him guidance and insights on a wide range of topics, including economic, foreign and international affairs, women's and social affairs. Through the country's 23 Ministries (until 1994) President Rafsanjani exercises his influence in the implementation of his administration's policies, but through his other posts he exercises direct power in formulating the republic's domestic and foreign policies. Each Ministry offers the President a unique window on the nation and its affairs. Of particular importance to the extent of his power and influence in post-Khomeini Iran are the Ministries of Foreign Affairs, Economics and Finance, Intelligence, Petroleum, Islamic Guidance and the Interior. His considerable personal skills ensure that he uses his office effectively and decisively.

Other institutional bases of power

The 12-member Council of Guardians, the 270-member Majlis, the 20-member (excluding the temporary members) Expediency Council, the 83-member Assembly of Experts, the head of the judiciary (the Chief Justice), who takes responsibility for the Minister of Justice, the 11-member National Security Council (Hojjatoleslam Rouhani is counted twice, as the Secretary and as Khameini's representative), the 23-member Cabinet, the various foundations, Friday prayer posts, membership of or access to the coercive machinery of the state, Islamic associations and 'unity' committees are the other institutions and offices from which power and influence can be derived.

The Council of Guardians, the Majlis and the Assembly of Experts represent direct paths to the inner circle of the elite; membership of these organisations in turn opens doors to some of the other key bodies. The complex relationship between the Council of Guardians, the Majlis, the Expediency Council, the Assembly of Experts and the Interior Ministry partly determine the membership make-up of these bodies, through which much of the power struggle between individuals, factions and lines of thought are conducted. Where membership of an institution is to be determined by the populace the vetting procedure, handled by one or more of the above bodies, can sometimes make or break factions and personalities. Ironically, the built-in checks and balances between these bodies, originally designed to prevent monopolisation of power by any one institution (or head of an institution), has in practice merely deepened the competitive nature of factionalism in Iran (Schahgaldian 1989). Headship of the powerful foundations in modern Iran of course would also provide individuals and factions with independent financial resources.

While membership of the other bodies mentioned above may not offer a direct route to the highest echelons of power, belonging to an institution with muscle usually enhances the careers of those who already have strong ties with the clerical establishment, and in turn reinforces the line coming out of the capital. Outside Tehran, being a governor (or working in the governor's office), head of the security forces (or a high-ranking officer in the security forces), a regional member of the Assembly of Experts, the Faqih's representative or being a Friday prayer leader cannot only enhance one's standing in the local community but also implement the will of those trying to dominate the centre and control the periphery.

The question of Marja'aiyat is highly relevant to the struggle for power, if not the structure of power in post-Khomeini Iran, and has became more so with the death of a number of Grand Ayatollahs in recent years. While Ayatollah Khomeini was alive the Marja'a and the Faqih were embodied in one office – his. Through his doctrine the clergy became the main operators of the state. With his death, and the subsequent appointment of a relatively junior cleric as the new Faqih, a dislocation emerged between the constitutional status of the Faqih and the traditional hierarchy and grid of the Shii system of rank and seniority. The diminishment of the ranks of the Ayatollah Ozmas, with the death of Shariatmadari, Khomeini, Khoi (in Najaf), Mar'ashi Najafi, and Golpaygani, had left only Grand Ayatollah Tabataba'i Qomi as the main religious figure with an established degree of seniority from before the revolution. The demise of three Grand Ayatollahs (Mara'ashi Najafi, Khoi and Golpaygani) so soon into the new Faqih's appointment caused a serious crisis for the post-Khomeini system, for it was this system which had sought to transform Shiism from 'a polycephalic faith to a unicephalic or monolithic one' (Milani 1992: 189).

Grand Ayatollah Golpaygani's death in December 1993 precipitated the crisis, which was deepened even further by the fact that his family refused to allow Ayatollah Khamenei to lead the funeral ceremonies, thus denying him the opportunity to choose the deceased's successor (Haeri 1994). The question of Marja'aiyat affected Iran's position in three ways; firstly, it threatened to split the entire international Shia community; secondly, lack of unity in Tehran and Qom threatened to undermine the standing of the Iranian leadership within that community; and thirdly, it threatened to drive a wedge between the Iranians and their fellow Shii in the Arab world, particularly those in Iraq and Lebanon.

In Lebanon the issue divided Iran's closest ally, the Hezbollah, down the middle. Sheikh Fadlallah chose to back Ayatollah Mirza Ali Sistani of Najaf (a former student of Ayatollah Khoi) in the succession struggle, while the Lebanese movement's political leader, Hassan Nasrallah, gave his support to Ayatollah Khamenei (Haeri 1994). Fadlallah, along with Baqer Al-Hakim and Mohammad Shams Addin, signed the petition asking Khamenei to support Sistani's candidacy (*Issues* January 1994). In Iraq, too, Ayatollah Sistani was viewed as the front runner and the Iranian Shia were urged to facilitate the emergence of an Arab Marja'a in Najaf. Meanwhile, in Iran, a four-way race developed for the position of a single Marja'a-e Taqlid, between Ayatollah Araki (closest to Ayatollah Khomeini and who became the source of emulation for his followers after his death), Ayatollah Tabataba'i Qomi (Ayatollah Khamenei's former teacher), Ayatollah Montazeri (Ayatollah Khomeini's former chosen successor) and Ayatollah Mohammad Rouhani (based in Qom and a known opponent of Ayatollah Khomeini). Another player in this struggle was Ayatollah Shirazi, who tried to drum up support for his own candidacy among the Gulf Arab Shia population, but to no avail. Ayatollah Rouhani is supported by many Shia scholars in Iraq, Lebanon and Pakistan (*Nimrooz* 30 December 1993) and Ayatollah

Tabataba'i Qomi is followed by many Shia of Lebanon, Kuwait, Pakistan and the Eastern Province of Saudi Arabia (ibid.).

After failing to establish Ayatollah Khamenei as the new Marja'a, the Iranian leaders set about isolating both Ayatollahs Montazeri and Rouhani, and pressed for the recognition of Ayatollah Araki as the Marja'a, thus trying to ensure the continuity of the line within the Velayat-e Faqih system. Nevertheless, a division had become apparent between the government figures in Tehran, who demanded Ayatollah Khamenei's candidacy as the Marja'a, and the senior religious figures in Qom, who insisted that the Marja'aiyat should remain with the Qom theologians. The compromise solution was found in Khamenei's acceptance of the 107-year-old Ayatollah Araki as the source of emulation. This arrangement had two principal implications. First, it reinforced the chasm which had emerged within the Iranian theocracy since Ayatollah Khomeini's death: the existence of a Faqih (a constitutional position based on politico-religious authority) and an independent source of emulation for the Shii faithful. Second, it left the issue of the source of emulation for the non-Iranian Shii, particularly those in Iraq and Lebanon, and their demands for an Arab Marja'a conspicuously unresolved. With Khamenei in mind, religious figures (like Ayatollahs Yazdi and Meshkini) in Iran began emphasising the importance of political experience as an important quality of the Marja'a and called for a return to having the Faqih as the source of emulation for all Shii too (*Salam* 18 December 1993). The precedent for the supremacy of political over religious authority had been set by Ayatollah Khomeini himself when, shortly before his death, he drew attention to the importance of the former as the overriding quality of any future Faqih (Abrahamian 1993).

IRANIAN ELECTORAL POLITICS SINCE 1989

Majlis and the Cabinet: an analysis of the 1989 encounter

Hojjatoleslam Rafsanjani was re-elected Speaker of the Majlis for the eighth consecutive time in June 1989 with 230 votes of the 241 deputies present in favour, one against and 10 abstentions, but was not to hold this post for long; he was to be elected as the first executive President of the Islamic Republic in July 1989, winning 13,468,355 out of the 14,192,802 votes cast (IRNA). As expected, all the members of President Rafsanjani's 1989 Cabinet of 22 (a new Ministry, the Ministry of Co-operatives, was created in January 1992, headed by the former Minister of Industry in the Moussavi Cabinet, Gholam Reza Shafei) received an unprecedented vote of confidence from the 261 Majlis deputies of the third Majlis present at the Majlis session in late August 1989, an experience which was not to be repeated in the fourth Majlis's dealing with President Rafsanjani's second Cabinet of 1992. Ironically, the fourth Majlis was much more in tune with the President's agenda and had been 'purged' of many of the radical Maktabi elements by a combination of Guardian Council intervention and voter preferences.

Hojjatoleslam Sobhanian had told the *Tehran Times* only a few days before the 1989 vote that 'all agreed that the proposed Ministers should get clearance from the Majlis' (*Tehran Times* 24 August 1989), despite the many reservations expressed by a number of deputies and the new Speaker (Rafsanjani's deputy, Hojjatoleslam Mehdi Karrubi) himself. In a telling speech to the deputies the new Speaker pointed out that the Majlis still retained enough powers to monitor and scrutinise the activities of the Ministers and, if need be, dismiss them from their posts: 'our hands will not be tied if a Minister gets the vote', he said assuringly in his address (SWB, ME/0549, 31 August 1989).

Of the 22 appointments, 12 were new nominees, but had already served the Islamic Republic in other capacities. One feature of the 1989 Cabinet was its technocratic character, including many individuals with little, if any, Maktabi credentials. Indeed, a number of them had been engaged in political battles with the Maktabis for some years, most notably Mohsen Nourbakhsh (the former Governor of the Central Bank and a Tehran Majlis deputy, elected in 1988) and Iraj Fazel (the former Higher Education Minister). Both these individuals were to be absent from President Rafsanjani's 1993 Cabinet: the latter lost his job under Majlis pressure in January 1991 and the former was unable to win the Majlis's vote of confidence in 1993.

The general 'de-ideologisation' of executive power gained further momentum with such technocratic appointments, prompting many influential figures in Iran to dub President Rafsanjani's 1989 team the 'Cabinet of construction' (*Abrar* 30 August 1989; *Ettela'at* 30 August, 1 September 1989). Indeed, the strength of this trend was such that it was to distinguish the second Rafsanjani administration as an almost entirely technocratic one. The emphasis in 1993 was on the expertise, technical skills and administrative abilities of the Ministers and not on their 'Islamic virtues' and revolutionary zeal. As one scholar suggested, a consequence of the shift from Khomeini's 'Islamic totalitarianism' to Rafsanjani's 'pragmatic Islamism' would be the increasing likelihood of the 'progressive marginalization of the Islamic extremist groups' (Mozaffari 1993: 614). When introducing to the fourth Majlis his second choice to head the Economics and Finance Ministry, the qualities that the President emphasised were precisely technical competence and relevent qualifications: 'Under present circumstances he [Morteza Mohammad Khan] is the most suitable person for the post . . . He has a Master's degree in Economics, which is consistent with his duties, and his submitted

PhD is going through its final stages of approval' (*Kayhan Havai* 13 October 1993).

Table 2 The Cabinet and Majlis deputies' voting pattern, 29 August 1989

Name	Post	For	Against	Abstention	Total
I. Kalantari	Agriculture	186	53	20	259
A. Vahaji	Commerce (new)	147	93	18	258
G. Forouzesh	Construction Jihad	221	30	10	261
A. Torkan	Defence and Logistics (new)	242	10	9	261
M. Nourbakhsh	Economics and Finance (new)	195	43	19	257
M. A. Najafi	Education	160	86	12	258
B. Namdar-Zanganeh	Energy	245	5	7	257
A. A. Velayati	Foreign Affairs	213	35	10	258
I. Fazel	Health (new)	165	86	9	260
M. H. Nezhad-Hosseinian	Heavy Industries (new)	219	26	11	256
M. Mo'in	Higher Education (new)	237	14	6	257
S. Kazerouni	Housing	145	97	14	256
M. R. Nematzadeh	Industries (new)	217	28	12	257
A. Fallahiyan	Intelligence (new)	158	79	18	255
A. Nouri	Interior (new)	224	20	15	259
M. Khatami	Islamic Guidance	246	10	4	260
A. Shoushtari	Justice (new)	209	30	18	257
H. Kamali	Labour (new)	224	18	16	258
M. H. Mahloji	Mines and Metals (new)	150	85	22	257
G. Aqazadeh	Oil	231	18	10	259
M. Gharazi	Posts, Telegraphs and Telephone	230	16	11	257
M. Sa'edi-Kia	Roads and Transport	222	21	9	252

Source: Islamic Republic of Iran News Agency (IRNA) 30 August 1989.

Notes: 261 of the Majlis's 270 deputies were present on 29 August 1989. Ministers had to receive a minimum of 131 votes (half the deputies present plus one) for approval.

In so far as empirical interpretation is possible, the position of the seven most and least popular Cabinet Ministers in terms of Majlis voting patterns may throw some light on the relationship between the legislative and executive branches of government in the Second Republic. One feature of the 1989 Cabinet, highlighted in Table 2, was the balance between continuity and change sought by Rafsanjani. As the appointments themselves make clear, continuity was sought in the areas deemed important to the smooth functioning of the state and the reconstruction efforts of the government, most notably

Agriculture, Construction Jihad, Energy, Foreign Affairs, Oil, and general communications and transport Ministries. In terms of changes compared with the previous government, the replacement of statists from key Ministries such as Heavy Industries, Commerce, and Economics and Finance removed the potential barriers to the planned deregulation and liberalisation of the economy by the Rafsanjani administration.

Looking at Table 3, one is struck by the significant popularity gap that divided the Ministers most popular with the deputies from their least popular colleagues in 1989. Hojjatoleslam Mohammad Khatami's (Islamic Guidance Minister) favourable vote of 246 contrasts sharply with that of Serajaddin Kazerouni's (Housing Minister) 145 votes – a difference of 101 votes. If we add the abstentions in each case to the negative vote cast in order to arrive at the true total negative vote, then Khatami's net pro vote would stand at 242, whereas Kazerouni's would be reduced sharply to stand at only 131, just on the 'pass mark' and 111 votes behind Khatami's score. The gap does narrow, however, as we approach the edges of each category.

Table 3 Seven most popular Cabinet Ministers, 1989

Minister	For	Against	Abstention
1 Khatami	246	10	4
2 Namdar-Zanganeh	245	5	7
3 Torkan (new)	242	10	9
4 Mo'in (new)	237	14	6
5 Aqazadeh	231	18	10
6 Gharazi	230	16	11
7 Nouri (new)	224	20	15
8 Kamali (new)	224	18	16

Table 4 provides details of the status of the least popular Ministers – those with the highest negative votes. Five of the new Ministers chosen by President Rafsanjani figure among the seven least popular Ministers, marking a substantial reservation by the Majlis of the nature of Rafsanjani's Cabinet. It is also noteworthy that a new clerical Cabinet Minister, Hojjatoleslam Fallahi-yan, appeared on the list of the seven least popular Ministers – appearing as the fifth least popular Minister in Table 4. As already noted, the least popular Minister as far as the Majlis was concerned was Kazerouni, although in terms of abstentions Kazerouni scores lowest among the seven Ministers. The least 'least popular' Minister (Nourbakhsh) in this categorisation does well overall, being only 29 votes behind the seventh 'most popular' Ministers category, Hojjatoleslam Nouri and Hussein Kamali, a three-term member of the Majlis (1981–9) and Chairman of its labour and employment affairs committee.

In addition, it can be observed from Table 4 that the seven 'least popular'

Table 4 Seven least popular Cabinet Ministers, 1989

Minister	Against	For	Abstention
1 Kazerouni	97	145	14
2 Vahaji (new)	93	147	18
3 Najafi	86	160	12
3 Fazel (new)	86	165	9
4 Mahloji (new)	85	150	22
5 Fallahiyan (new)	79	158	18
6 Kalantari	53	186	20
7 Nourbakhsh (new)	43	195	19

Ministers also recorded fairly high abstention votes. The addition of the 'abstention' votes to the ones 'against', therefore, would record a greater net loss for this category than it would for the 'most popular' tier of the Cabinet. As Table 5 shows, an average of 11–13 (ranging from 14 to 22) votes can be subtracted from each Minister's score in the 'least popular' category (Table 4) in order to arrive at their 'true' popularity/unpopularity rate.

Thirdly, seven of the 12 new appointments appear on the highest absten-

Table 5 Seven Cabinet Ministers with greatest number of abstentions, 1989

Minister	Abstention	Against	For
1 Mahloji (new)	22	85	150
2 Kalantari	20	53	186
3 Nourbakhsh (new)	19	43	195
4 Vahaji (new)	18	93	147
4 Fallahiyan (new)	18	79	158
4 Shoshtari (new)	18	30	209
5 Kamali (new)	16	18	224
6 Nouri (new)	15	20	224
7 Kazerouni	14	97	145

tion rate data. This pattern of voting could be interpreted as a warning to the President. Indeed, this voting pattern served as the most effective and least destabilising way of registering dissent by the third Majlis deputies. Bearing in mind the balance of power in post-Khomeini Iran, short of an outright rejection vote against President Rafsanjani's first Cabinet, the deputies seem to have chosen to challenge his executive authority in the least damaging style by raising doubts over the 'new' portion of the Rafsanjani Cabinet.

In comparison with the harsh treatment by the Majlis of the Moussavi government's proposed Ministerial appointments (never approving his Cabinet appointments outright in the eight years of its existence), the 'radical' third Majlis gave the new President and his new powers explicit support, particularly as none of Rafsanjani's appointments received a vote of no confidence.

As the abstention voting pattern in Table 5 shows, however, the efforts of the President and his allies were unsuccessful in creating full and unconditional support for the Rafsanjani mandate. Therefore a potent source of trouble to the new leaders remained. If we were to reinterpret the figures, the total negative vote (abstentions plus negative votes) could be said to show that the Majlis's rejection of the Cabinet (realistically set at about one-sixth of the proposed Cabinet) would rise to an unacceptable proportion engulfing nearly one-third of the Rafsanjani Cabinet. In other words, some 50 MPs out of 261 present in the chamber consistently opposed the Cabinet nominations.

As the secret ballot prevents us from empirically examining the voting pattern of each deputy, the speeches and the relative consistency in the abstention figures would suggest that a hard core of the deputies objected to the 1989 Rafsanjani Cabinet. Yet as a whole the majority of the deputies supported the Rafsanjani Cabinet. One interpretation of the Majlis's approval of the Cabinet was the implicit recognition that without Rafsanjani's guidance the serious divisions among the ranks of the clergy (over the social, ideological, cultural, political and economic life of the country) could lead to irreparable splits in the unique mosque–state structures of the Islamic Republic.

As a final point on the popularity ratings, it is perhaps a sign of the times that while the most popular Cabinet Minister was a cleric, he still received more total negative votes (14) than his nearest rival, a non-cleric *kolahi* individual, with only 12 negative votes. In the 'least popular' category also a cleric is found whose total negative vote stands at 87 – about one-third of the Majlis voters. In essence, therefore, exactly one-third of the third Majlis did not approve of the appointment of a new cleric, Hojjatoleslam Fallahiyan, to the Cabinet. By contrast, though never ranking as one of the 'most popular' Cabinet nominations (not being among the top eight) in 1993, nonetheless Fallahiyan is not by any means one of the least popular Ministers, receiving only 51 total negative votes from the fourth Majlis.

The key appointment

In an analysis of the emerging power structures of the Second Republic a study of the make-up of the executive President's Cabinet is particularly important. A key appointment in the 1989 administration was that of the Interior Minister, not only because of the individual appointed but also because of the personality who was replaced, the leading radical opponent of the President's policies, Hojjatoleslam Mohtashemi. This notable absence from the 1989 Cabinet, despite the letter of some 130 Majlis deputies to the President calling for the reinstatement of Mohtashemi only weeks before the Majlis vote, is significant in so far as it is an indication of the changing balance of power amongst the influential clerics in post-Khomeini Iran. The tussle between the President and the Majlis over the position of Mohtashemi was eventually settled in Rafsanjani's favour, as the Majlis's voting pattern in August 1989 in favour of Hojjatoleslam Abdullah Nouri illustrates. In the end, the third Majlis did give its support to President Rafsanjani's chosen Interior Minister: 224 of the deputies supported Nouri's appointment as the new Interior Minister in the Cabinet. He received 20 votes against and 15 abstentions, a total negative vote of only 35. By contrast, Hussein Kamali, who was also seventh on the 'most popular' list, accumulated a total of 34 negative votes.

Although in relative terms he remained the most unpopular Minister of the top seven in 1989, compared with Mohtashemi's performance in the 1985 Majlis vote of confidence, Nouri's score was much better; out of 258 votes cast in the October 1985, Mohtashemi received 163 votes in favour and 32 against, with 63 abstentions, a total negative vote of 95 – nearly three times Nouri's in 1989.

Nouri's key role in the Second Republic did provide the perspective for appreciating the need for replacing Mohtashemi as the Interior Minister in the new Rafsanjani line-up. Although something of a hard-liner by the standards of the rest of the 1989 Cabinet, Nouri had been moving up fast to become a senior member of the Cabinet. On the one hand the Ministry he headed provided the 'Leader–President' faction with two important advantages. Firstly, direct access to the provinces outside the mosque network; and, secondly, the most efficient instrument for implementing policy and gauging national public opinion on both policy and security matters.

On the other hand, Nouri's appointment as the chairman of the newly created National Security Council, which, according to the 1989 constitutional changes, not only formulates and co-ordinates national security and defence policies but also directs the republic's political programme, brought the commanding heights of the state's political and politico-military structures under the direct control of the Cabinet. Furthermore, Nouri's role as Ayatollah Khomeini's representative to the Guards from early 1989 had helped his career. Through Nouri's appointment as the Interior Minister, Rafsanjani attempted to maintain a support base – albeit indirectly – in the Pasdaran, at the same time as appeasing the militant and armed hard-liners of the regime (with whom Nouri was said to maintain contacts). The latent support from the IRGC could have become crucial for the President, particularly since formal control of the armed forces, the post of C-in-C, was returned to the Supreme Leader soon after the transfer of the constitutional duties of the Faqih to Ayatollah Khamenei.

The elections to the fourth Majlis

The Council of Guardians announced on 1 April 1992 that just over 1,000 of the 3,150 hopeful MPs had been barred from standing for parliament, including 30 of the incumbents. Thus some 2,050 individuals who had received a 'clean bill of health' from the screening committee of the Council of Guardians entered the competition for the Majlis's 270 seats. Through a thinly disguised attack on the radicals in his Friday prayer speech Ayatollah Khamenei opened the electoral campaign against the radical factions in March 1992. He made four key points: firstly, that he fully supported the Council of Guardians in the application of its selection procedure for candidates; secondly, that his support for the President and his government was explicit and total; thirdly, he undermined the status of the radical factions by his indirect reference to them as *fetnehgar* (seditious); and, finally, he asked the people to vote for those candidates who would use their new appointments constructively and in the interest of assisting the government to complete its reforms (*Ettela'at* 28 March 1992). Ayatollah Imami Kashani, a leading member of the Council of Guardians, also supported the pragmatists and attacked the radicals during Tehran's Friday prayer on the eve of the elections.

Strong protestations were made to the President and the Faqih about what the radicals called the Council of Guardians' 'jeopardisation' of the election procedure (*MEED* 10 April 1992). In a direct criticism of the pragmatists and conservatives Karrubi said on election day (10 April): 'if [those] devoted forces [who are] committed to the revolution had not been removed from the election scene it would have been better' (*Abrar* 11 April 1992). On the same day Rafsanjani declared that 'the people know the criteria very well . . . and I am convinced that our society has chosen the Five Year Plan and in these elections too will endorse it [i.e. chose those candidates who support the administration's policies]' (*Abrar* 11 April 1992).

The fourth Majlis started work on 28 May, and elected Hojjatoleslam Nateq Nouri, a leading member of the Association of Combative Clergy of Tehran (Jameh-e Ruhaniyat-e Mobarez-e Tehran) and former Interior Minister in the 1980s, as its third Speaker, in place of Hojjatoleslam Karrubi (a high-profile figure in the rival organisation the Association of Combatant Clergy of Tehran, Jameh-e Ruhaniyun-e Mobarez-e Tehran), who failed to keep his seat in the fourth Majlis. The latter association failed to return any deputies from the largest and most important constituency of all, Tehran

Table 6 Number of clerics in the Majlis since 1980

	1980–4	1984–8	1988–92	1992–6
Clerics	98	122	71	49
Non-clerics	118	147	189	219

Source: Haghayeghi (1993).

Note: The total number of clerics in the Majlis varies according to catagorisation. The above figures refer only to 'people of the cloth'.

(Sarabi 1994). A total of 18.8 million votes were cast in the first round (10 April) and 7.5 million in the second round (8 May) of the elections (*MEED* 12 June 1992). Numerically this was higher than all previous Majlis elections (first Majlis: 10,833,843; second Majlis: 15,815,986; third Majlis: 16,988,799), but the growth in the number of participants in general elections must be seen in the context of an average annual population growth rate of around 3.8 per cent since the revolution (Vakili-Zad 1992). As many as 30 women candidates were nominated for election in Tehran, a record number in the republic. Just 82 deputies from the third Majlis were re-elected, with 181 deputies entering the Majlis for the first time. Only 38 deputies from the first Majlis had retained their seats in the second and third and only 12 MPs from the first Majlis survived the latest round (Jahanpour 1992). The rest were new deputies competing for a place for the first time. The fourth Majlis also sees the highest number of women deputies: nine compared with four in the third Majlis.

The fourth Majlis is said to represent about 70 per cent support for the President; by contrast the third Majlis had a hard-core of about 40 radicals opposing the administration's domestic economic and foreign policies (Vakili-Zad 1993; Siavoshi 1992). That said, it was the so-called radical third Majlis, a legacy of the First Republic, which approved much of the Rafsanjani administration's economic reform programme, including foreign borrowing and the creation of FTZs, and helped in laying the basis of the policy changes on the republic's home and international fronts. Ironically, having seen the back of the radicals, it is the social conservatives in the fourth Majlis who have been warning the President of rising discontent among the people and the need for 'social justice' in his second administration's policies (ibid.). It should also be remembered that it was the third Majlis which gave the President's proposed Cabinet a 100 per cent vote of confidence in 1989 and not the fourth, considerably friendlier, Majlis in 1993.

Hojjatoleslams Mehdi Karrubi, Ali Akbar Mohtashemi and Mohammad Khoini'a, among the leading Maktabis in the third Majlis, failed to get re-elected. The controversial vetting procedure referred to above blocked the nomination of a number of leading radicals: Assadollah Bayat, Ayatollah Sadeq Khalkhali, Hojjatoleslams Hadi Ghafari and Mousasvi Tabrizi, Ibrahim Asgharzadeh, Behzad Nabavi and Mrs Atefeh Rajaii (*MEED* 17 April 1992). Hojjatoleslam Hadi Khamenei (the Faqih's brother, who has strong ties to the radicals) also failed the vetting procedure but was allowed to stand. He too was unable to keep his seat in the fourth Majlis, having been a deputy since 1980.

The composition of the fourth Majlis illustrates graphically the passing of the old and the rise of a new generation of parliamentarians with much looser ties with the First Republic and Ayatollah Khomeini decade.

Majlis and the Cabinet: an analysis of the 1993 encounter

Compared with 1989, the President's 1993 list of 23 Cabinet Ministers contained fewer changes. Only seven changes in total were introduced, in the following Ministries; Roads and Transport, Defence and Armed Forces Logistics (existing Minister shifted to another Ministry), Interior, Housing, Higher Education, Commerce and Health. Despite intense lobbying by non-governmental organisations and Majlis factions, and speculation in the media, the Ministers of Agriculture, Construction Jihad, Energy, Foreign Affairs, Oil and Posts, Telegraphs and Telephones held on to their portfolios. All these key Ministers had not only served in President Rafsanjani's first administration but had held the same Ministerial posts in the last Moussavi government. This would seem to make clear the President's instinct for continuity and recognition of the need to maintain a balance in the Cabinet. Naturally a degree of inter-factional fighting had played its part in guiding his choice of Ministers in 1993. His overriding concern, however, was continuity with the domestic and foreign policy agendas he had set himself and the nation. This view is supported by the fact that 16 of the proposed list of 23 Ministers were scheduled to keep their existing posts, of whom only one (Nourbakhsh) did not manage to clear the Majlis's vote of confidence hurdle. Apart from this snub, the data would support the contention that overall the largely non-Maktabi fourth Majlis was as kind to the President as its predecessor.

Finally, though he was said to be suffering from ill health, in view of the significance of the Interior Ministry job, Hojjatoleslam Abdullah Nouri's absence from the 1993 Cabinet may have been the price he had to pay for failing to give advance warning of and contain the widespread 1992 riots in Iranian towns and cities (*Financial Times* 17 August 1993).

The Majlis's confrontation with the 1993 Cabinet came down to its rejection of the President's Economics Minister, the architect and executor

Table 7 The Cabinet and Majlis deputies' voting pattern, 16 August 1993

Name	Post	For	Against	Abstention	Total
I. Kalantari	Agriculture	215	23	23	261
Y. Al-e Eshaq	Commerce (new)	222	12	26	260
G. Forouzesh	Construction Jihad	152	70	27	249
G. Shafei	Co-operatives	229	9	18	256
M. Forouzandeh	Defence and Logistics (new)	233	5	20	258
M. Nourbakhsh	Economics and Finance	127	75	49	251
M. A. Najafi	Education	147	73	36	256
B. Namdar-Zanganeh	Energy	202	37	18	257
A. A. Velayati	Foreign Affairs	207	17	33	257
A. R. Marandi	Health (new)	246	4	11	261
M. H. Nezhad-Hosseinian	Heavy Industries	231	12	16	259
M. R. Hashemi-Golpaygani	Higher Education (new)	220	12	29	261
A. A. Akhundi	Housing (new)	193	37	22	252
M. R. Nematzadeh	Industries	194	29	29	252
A. Fallahiyan	Intelligence	204	24	27	255
A. M. Besharati	Interior (new)	225	14	21	260
A. Larijani	Islamic Guidance	219	12	29	260
A. Shoushtari	Justice	233	7	18	258
H. Kamali	Labour	223	18	17	258
M. H. Mahloji	Mines and Metals	166	54	38	258
G. Aqazadeh	Oil	134	88	25	247
M. Gharazi	Posts, Telegraphs and Telephone	192	38	21	251
A. Torkan	Roads and Transport (new)	176	34	48	258

Source: Abrar 18 August 1993.

Notes: 261 of the Majlis's 270 deputies were present for the vote. Ministers had to receive a minimum of 131 votes (half the deputies present plus one) for approval. The Defence Minister, Akbar Torkan, was proposed as the new Roads and Transport Minister in place of Mohammad Sa'edi-Kia. The Health Minister, Iraj Fazel, was dismissed by the Majlis on 13 January 1991. Hojjatoleslam Khatami resigned as the Islamic Guidance Minister on 17 July 1992 and was replaced by Ali Larijani. In early 1994 Larijani in turn was removed from this post through a decree issued by the Faqih and appointed as the new head of the state-controlled television and radio organisation. Engineer Moustapha Mirsalim, a well known moderate, was chosen by the President to head the Islamic Guidance Ministry. Out of 224 MPs present, 178 voted in his favour, 27 against and 19 abstained. The President's brother, Mohammad Hashemi, who had headed the television and radio organisation for 13 years, was removed from this post in February 1994. On 14 February, the President appointed him as Senior Deputy Foreign Affairs Minister.

of the post-1989 economic reform strategy. The rejection of his nomination by the Majlis not only threatened to undermine the entire basis of the reform programme, but managed to raise a question mark over the direction of policy changes in the country and the administration's ability to contain the economic crisis on the one hand, and reverse it on the other. Thus, when the Majlis refused to endorse the reappointment of Nourbakhsh, the President appointed him as his Vice-President in charge of Economic Affairs. In his decree appointing Nourbakhsh to this new post, the President pointedly underlined Nourbakhsh's experience as the architect of the economic reforms:

> In view of the . . . valuable experience you gained during the period of reconstruction and reform of the economic system, and in order that the principled policies of economic adjustment and the comprehensive second five-year plan may continue, I appoint you to the post of Vice-president in charge of economic affairs.

> (SWB, ME/1770, 18 August 1993)

Nourbakhsh remained in the President's team but out of the reach of the Majlis. Indeed, his position was restrengthened in September 1994, and his role made more central again, when he replaced Adeli as the Governor of the Central Bank – a post that Nourbakhsh had held from 1982 to 1988.

The President's second decree reiterated his administration's commitment to the reform process by appointing Nourbakhsh's ally and First Deputy Minister, Mohammad Javad Vahaji, as supervisor of the Economics and Finance Ministry. His final choice of Economics Minister was introduced to the Majlis in October 1993. He too was known for his pragmatism and support for the administration's economic policies. He was criticised by one deputy for not paying enough attention to the issue of social justice in his proposed economic programme (*Kayhan Havai* 13 October 1993). As one of Nourbakhsh's Deputy Ministers and head of the country's Customs Administrative Organisation from September 1989, he was often at the sharp end of the trade liberalisation and deregulation strategy of the administration, and his nomination as the new Minister of Economics and Finance signalled the President's determination to stay the course and confront the Majlis head-on. This gamble will pay off only if the economy improves markedly before the end of Rafsanjani's second term of office.

Despite the misgivings of some of the deputies, on 16 October 1993 the Majlis gave Mohammad Khan the vote of confidence that the administration was seeking; of the 223 MPs present, 151 voted in favour, 46 voted against and 26 individuals abstained – a relatively high negative vote compared with the August 1993 vote for the rest of the Cabinet. The most popular Minister in the 1993 Cabinet line-up was the former Minister of Health in the last Moussavi government, Dr Marandi. In terms of number of votes cast also, Marandi (along with the new Minister of Higher Education) topped the list (261). The second most popular Minister of the 1993 nominations was

Table 8 Eight most popular Cabinet Ministers, 1993

Minister	For	Against	Abstention
1 Marandi (new)	246	4	11
2 Shoushtari	233	7	18
3 Forouzadeh (new)	233	5	20
4 Nezhad-Hosseinian	231	12	16
5 Shafei	229	9	18
6 Besharati (new)	225	14	21
7 Kamali	223	18	17
8 Al-e Eshaq (new)	222	12	26

Table 9 Eight least popular Cabinet Ministers, 1993

Minister	Against	For	Abstention
1 Aqazadeh	88	134	25
2 Nourbakhsh	75	127	49
3 Najafi	73	147	36
4 Forouzesh	70	152	27
5 Mahloji	54	166	38
6 Torkan*	34	176	48
7 Gharazi	38	192	21
8 Akhundi (new)	37	193	22

* New in this post.

Hojjatoleslam Shoushtari, whose 1989 favourable vote of 209 was only just about average for the last Cabinet. Rather similar to the 1989 experience, four of the new faces appear on the 'most popular' list, but unlike in 1989 only one individual receives more than 15 negative votes. The popularity of the new nominations with the fourth Majlis is further underlined by the data; as Table 9 shows, only one of the new nominations appears on the 'least popular' list of eight. In 1989 five of the new nominations appeared on the 'least popular' list of seven. Again not dissimilar to the 1989 Majlis vote, a significant popularity gap separated the most popular Minister from the most unpopular – some 119 votes separated the most popular person from his least popular counterpart. Adding the abstentions to the negative vote in each case to arrive at the total negative vote shows that Marandi's total negative vote was only 15 while Nourbakhsh's was 124.

Although Nourbakhsh was unable to obtain the vote of confidence needed to stay in the Cabinet, it emerges from Table 9 that in fact he did not receive the highest number of negative votes in 1993; it was Aqazadeh who scored the highest number of votes against his nomination. The key to understanding Nourbakhsh's inability to clear the hurdle, therefore, despite the 10 spoilt papers in his case, can be found in the rather high abstention rate against him. Compared with the next least popular on the list of Ministers, Aqazadeh (who incidentally saw 14 spoilt ballot papers), Nourbakhsh suffered 24 additional abstentions. Looking at Aqazadeh's vote more closely, it is clear from the data that the incumbent Oil Minister's standing with the fourth Majlis is quite different from that of the third. With declining oil revenues and economic hardships stemming from Iran's financial crisis as the backdrop, the Minister who received only 18 negative votes from the third Majlis and a total negative vote (negative votes plus abstentions) of 28 in 1989 suffered a total negative vote of 113 in 1993 – the second highest. Indeed, his case is the most interesting of all the 1993 nominations; being one of the most popular Ministers in the 1989 Cabinet, he was just three votes clear of rejection by the fourth Majlis.

Table 10 Eight Cabinet Ministers with greatest number of abstentions, 1993

Minister	Abstention	Against	For
1 Nourbakhsh	49	75	127
2 Torkan	48	34	176
3 Mahloji	38	54	166
4 Najafi	36	73	147
5 Velayati	33	17	207
6 Hashemi-Golpaygani (new)	29	12	220
7 Larijani*	29	12	219
8 Nematzadeh	29	20	194

* New to this job since 1989.

Table 10 reveals that in 1993 only one of the new Ministers appears on the highest abstention rate data; four others (Nourbakhsh, Torkan, Mahloji and Najafi) with high negative votes feature on this list, thus marking about one-fifth of the 1993 Cabinet nominees the most unpopular Ministers with the fourth Majlis. Figures also show that in comparison with deputies of the third Majlis, the fourth Majlis's parliamentarians used their abstention vote much more liberally. In 1989, for instance, only two nominees received more than 20 abstention votes (Mahloji and Kalantari); in 1993 all the eight Cabinet nominees appearing on the 'highest abstention' list in Table 10 had well over 20 MPs abstaining from the vote. In 1993 17 Cabinet nominees witnessed abstention rates of 20 and over (i.e. over 20 MPs abstaining from the vote);

in 1989 only twice did more than 20 MPs abstain from voting. This pattern of voting may indicate the fourth Majlis's deep-felt reservations about the proposed Cabinet, but it also reveals their unwillingness to undermine the President's second administration by voting against his Ministerial nominees – it should be noted that the total negative vote of half the nominees listed in Table 10 did not exceed 50.

The Presidential elections of June 1993

The sixth Presidential elections took place on 13 June 1993, with four candidates out of the 124 hopefuls standing, and the incumbent winning 63 per cent of the total votes cast. His nearest rival, Ahmad Tavakoli (former Labour Minister and Economics Editor of the pro-market daily, *Resalat*), received 24 per cent of the vote and majority support in Kurdistan province; Abdullah Jasbi and Rajabali Taheri obtained 9.1 per cent and 2.4 per cent of the popular vote respectively. Thus almost exactly 35 per cent of the voters voted against the President. Little separated the candidates' policies from each other (see *Kayhan Havai* 3 June 1993), which may explain the relatively low turn-out of 56 per cent of the 29 million-strong electorate, fewer than the elections for the fourth Majlis. Unhappiness about the economic situation and general apathy amongst the voters were cited by local papers as the main reasons for the low turn-out (*Salam* 14 June 1993; *Kayhan* 14 June 1993). The absence of a real choice and of real alternatives (in terms of programmes and personalities) to the incumbent seems to have militated against large-scale participation in the Presidential elections. In the 1989 Presidential elections 70 per cent of the electorate voted, 94 per cent of them voting for Hojjatoleslam Rafsanjani.

Rafsanjani saw in his victory emphatic popular support for his policies: 'While passing through the difficult period of economic adjustment and reconstruction', he said, 'the people, two-thirds of them, have approved the difficult path of adjustment and given their approval to this programme' (SWB, ME/1714, 14 June 1993). But others, including the radicals and Bazargan's Freedom Movement (*Nimrooz* 30 July 1993) saw serious signs of discontent in the voters' behaviour. Firstly, the low turn-out indicated dissatisfaction with the 'system', particularly as all the leadership was encouraging massive participation; secondly, the vote showed slackening of support for the President (and his economic reform programme); and thirdly, the popular perception that real choice was not allowed by the leadership was reinforced by the statements of the radicals before and after the election, and actually harmed the credibility of the entire system (Economist Intelligence Unit, third quarter 1993).

Although the election results did dent the President's prestige, in terms of

Table 11 Presidential election results, June 1993

Candidate	Number of votes	% of total
Rafsanjani	10,553,644	63.2
Tavakoli	3,976,165	23.8
Jasbi	1,515,632	9.1
Taheri	401,579	2.4
Spoilt papers	253,230	1.5
Total	16,700,250	100.0
Vote cast as % of electorate		57.6

Source: IRNA 14 June 1993.

posing a challenge to his authority, he moved quickly to turn them into a victory for himself and his line against the radical factions. After receiving a letter of support and congratulations from 175 deputies of the 270 seat Majlis on his election victory (SWB, ME/1714, 14 June 1993), he also moved to reinforce his cordial relations with the fourth Majlis. It should be recalled that the shock of the confidence vote for his proposed Cabinet did not occur until August. Whether his relatively poor showing in the polls had undermined his administration's standing with the Majlis is hard to determine with any certainty, owing to the fact that although Nourbakhsh did not receive endorsement from the fourth Majlis, as we have seen, the rest of the President's nominations were by and large reasonably well received.

The Rafsanjani Cabinets in modern historical perspective

As Table 12 highlights, although clerics were well represented in President Rafsanjani's 1989 Cabinet (four Ministers), by 1993 only two remained in the Cabinet. Of the four Hojjatoleslams in the 1989 Cabinet only one (Khatami) had served in the previous council of Ministers; the two clerics in the 1993 Cabinet had served in President Rafsanjani's first administration. The appointment of the four clerics to the posts of Islamic Guidance, Justice, the Interior and Intelligence had left the 'political' posts in the 1989 Cabinet in the hands of the Shii clergy while the technocrats were left in charge of the 'functional' Ministries. Hence the 'Islamic' nature of the republic had remained intact and the clerics continued to rule Iran as this Islamic country's 'natural' rulers.

By 1993 the clerics had control of the Justice and Intelligence Ministries, and the broad division of labour mentioned above had evaporated, with the most religious-oriented of all Cabinet posts, that of Islamic Guidance, being occupied by a non-cleric, Ali Larijani (who nonetheless had very strong

Islamic credentials), who took up his new post on 17 July 1992. The appointment of Mohammad Besharati as the Interior Minister in 1993 is equally significant in this light, as this was the first time (since a brief period in 1981) that a cleric was not in charge of this Ministry. Two peculiarities in the clerical appointments need to be mentioned here, both arising from political imperatives of the Islamic Republic itself. Firstly, the religious ranking of none of the four clerical Ministerial appointments in 1989 and of two in 1993 exceeded the Hojjatoleslam level, thus remaining on a par with the President's own religious rank. This was partly intended as a way of preventing the undermining of the moral and religious authority of the highest executive power in the land from within the governmental establishment. Secondly, the equality of rank among the clerical Ministers themselves helped to remove the factor of religious differentiation among these Ministers. In this fashion, the undermining of governmental by religious authority was prevented, since religious rank had in effect been eliminated as a distinct basis of authority within the executive machinery of the government.

The country's shift towards technocracy – arguably best exemplified in the most authoritative and professional Cabinet of the Shah's long reign, the 1967 Cabinet of Prime Minister Amir Abbas Hoveyda – was likewise reflected in Rafsanjani's second term of office. Compared with Bazargan's 1979 government, Rafsanjani's Cabinets have been distinctly more technocratic. Whether this again illustrates control of the state by an influential executive body, as was true under the Shah's longest-serving Prime Minister, remains to be seen.

Table 12 Qualifications of Iranian Cabinet members, selected Cabinets

Qualification	1967	1979	1989	1993
No. of Ministers	24	23	22	23
MD/PhD	15	9	7	8
Engineer	5	4	9	9
Untitled	3	9	2	4
Lt-General	1	1	0	0
Hojjatoleslam	0	0	4	2

Sources: Ettela'at 19 October 1967; IRNA; *Abrar* 18 August 1993.

Notes: The 1967 Cabinet had one woman Minister. None of the Cabinets since the revolution has had a woman Minister. The number of Ministers in the Rafsanjani Cabinet was increased by one in January 1992. The merger of a number of Ministries initiated in 1994, will again reduce the number of Ministers in the Cabinet.

Table 12 illustrates the changes in the qualification patterns in the different Cabinets. On paper the qualification standards of the Rafsanjani Cabinets compare favourably with those of both the Bazargan (1979) and the Hoveyda (1967) Cabinets. Rafsanjani's Cabinets, however, contained the highest proportion of 'engineers'. This designation is misleading because, although it can demonstrate technical expertise and 'modernity', it also represents a title embedded in Iran's socio-economic hierarchy, usually given to all those with a technical Bachelor's or Master's degree. Nevertheless, in social class terms *mohandes* (engineer) is a revered title denoting high social standing, professional competence and proven ability. In this context, President Rafsanjani's choice in 1989 of 'engineers' from the pool of eligible candidates available to him could be said to symbolise progress and modernity, and furthermore a commitment to the rejuvenation and reconstruction of the country.

It is important to note that President Rafsanjani's two Cabinets mark the first instances in the contemporary history of Iran when no military personnel have been present in the Cabinet. This could be interpreted as a good omen in the context of Iran's recent turbulent relations with its neighbours. But it could also be sounding the death knell of the Iranian military machine muscling in with the other social and political groups in the country for power. For whatever reason, by turning away from its historic opportunity to gain power in the 1977–9 period, the Iranian military may well have lived through long years of war in the 1980s only to witness its own political demise in the 1990s. The fate of the military, thus, seems to depend both on the political stability of the Second Republic and tranquillity in the region and on the success of the rearmament efforts under way since 1989. The latter requirement is likely to proceed unhindered, however, with the appointment in 1993 of Mohammad Forouzandeh (former Deputy Chief of the General Command of the Armed Forces) as Defence Minister in place of Torkan. Forouzandeh is an experienced individual who enjoys close relations with the Pasdaran and is intimately acquainted with Iran's military and logistical needs.

PLURALISM AND THE SECOND REPUBLIC

It should be clear that on balance the advent of the Second Republic has been interpreted as a positive development in this study, and as such I have concentrated my efforts on understanding the 'new' regime without commenting too extensively on its repressive nature. Certainly in the economic sphere the post-Khomeini leadership has attempted to move towards liberalisation and openness. Its policies are a break from the generally statist traditions of the last decade (Mozaffari 1993). This trend can be demonstrated by closer consideration of a key appointment in the post-1989 regime. The elevation of Ayatollah Yazdi, the former Deputy Speaker of the Islamic parliament, who failed to win re-election to the Majlis in the 1987 parliamentary elections, to Head of Judiciary instead of the former Prosecutor-General Hojjatoleslam Khoini'a is the case in point. His appointment signalled the clarity of purpose of the pragmatist coalition in that Ayatollah Yazdi is a well known 'moderate' and strongly in favour of denationalisation and the deregulation of the economy.

A recent survey of 'fundamentalist tendencies in North Africa' in 1993 concluded that no Muslim country in the Middle East except Turkey can be regarded as democratic because the rest do not display all the main features of democratic government: a government responsible to an elected parliament, the division of powers between the executive, the judiciary and the legislature, political pluralism and the rule of law (Borderas 1993). The author of the report may well be pleasantly surprised to discover that in fact by his yardstick the Islamic Republic is at the very least a fledgling democracy – even the President admits that many of the features of the Iranian political system can be seen to resemble a democratic Western model! In his words:

> During the past 14 years . . . the Islamic Republic of Iran has relied on referenda and the establishment of popular institutions as its main tools. In more than 12 elections with the participation of the people (men and women), the Iranians have elected their governmental system, President and Majlis deputies and have ratified their constitution. They have elected in two turns the members of the Assembly of Experts whose duty it is to choose the Leader. The presence of representatives from religious minorities in the Majlis with equal rights [is established] . . . and the guarantee of this right to the constitution signifies the depth and genuineness of our commitment to democracy.
>
> (*Ettela'at* 21 February 1993)

The Iranian system passes the first two tests of democracy (Borderas 1993) with ease and its leaders can claim to be governing the people by the rule of law. Thus it can satisfy three of the four features, but the sticking point would be the issue of political pluralism. Therefore the Iranian model's most distinguishing feature would not be its arbitrary form of government, or naked dictatorship imposed by an unelected political class – because these are not the traits of this system – but rather in the way in which political action and the given boundaries of political norms and behaviour are controlled institutionally.

It is hard to deny that in the political sphere the existence of a collective consensus in the 'Leader–President' coalition and the coalition's opponents in a 'loyal opposition' of sorts resembles a form of pluralism, albeit of the few for the benefit of the few. But it is the absence of political pluralism in its wider sense that worries observers of the Iranian political scene. The regime's violations of basic human rights have been a subject of study and an object of criticism by many international and Western-based agencies, including the United Nations Human Rights Commission, Amnesty International, Middle East Watch and European human rights bodies. Some observers, however, go so far as to argue that an Islamic political system 'is distinguished from all others in that it is *inherently* anti-democratic' (Ja'far and Tabari 1984: 345). Factionalism and open political struggle in the Iranian case should not be mistaken for untrammelled political freedom; while voting is a major feature of the Iranian system, mass political participation in the country's affairs has remained restricted (Bakhash 1993). As we have seen already, despite the recent important constitutional changes, the exceedingly important clauses of the constitution regarding liberty and freedom still remain unimplemented. Political persecution and execution of opponents has continued, both at home and abroad. The prospects for a general national consensus remain bleak and Iranian political activity, both at home and abroad, continues to be divisive. It would be idealistic, therefore, to expect a quick and total transformation of the regime in such a short period and in such uncertain times.

In terms of control the steps taken in the early days of the republic to control the opposition's means of communications and propaganda remain in force. Organised political action, even by those non-clerics still loyal to the principle of an Islamic Republic, was not permitted even half a decade or more after the advent of the new government. The SR and LIF forces remain excluded from mainstream political activity. Many of the former Prime Minister Bazargan's supporters, for instance, were rounded up in the summer of 1990 and the activities of his organisation effectively curtailed.

Finally, it should be made clear that not only was the break with Khomeini's Iran not absolute and complete, but, despite the significant institutional changes, strong personal links with the Khomeini era remain. This should not be surprising in view of the discussion in chapter 1 as, even while aiming to transform the Islamic Republic, the leaders of the 'Leader–President' alliance themselves could still find legitimacy only in their own past and under the system of rule which themselves had helped Ayatollah Khomeini to create.

INSTITUTIONAL COMPETITION AND STRUCTURAL CHANGE

Despite the reforms so far implemented, therefore, the current leaders have not entirely broken with the past. The constitution of the Second Republic has come to resemble the constitution of the French Fifth Republic, with the powers of the presidency fully reinstated. As in the French system, in Iran's near-Presidential system the voters elect both the President and the parliament, but, unlike the former, the Iranian President can appoint his Cabinet only with the approval of the parliament. In terms of his executive position, however, the role of the Iranian President is closer to that of his American counterpart, for although the Iranian Cabinet needs the support of the parliament, unlike in France he does not choose a Prime Minister to head the Cabinet – he controls the direction of the executive and central government agencies by chairing the Council of Ministers. Such comparisons with other Presidential systems, however, should not disguise the unique features of the Islamic Republic. Apart from the intricate relationship with the parliament, Iran's is the only presidential system in which the popularly elected head of the executive branch must seek the approval of an unelected figure (the Faqih) before he can take up office, and in which the President and his executive team are 'subordinated to a religious authority' (Milani 1993).

In the absence of Ayatollah Khomeini the constitutional changes have resulted in a balance of power emerging between the President and the Faqih. Although the roots of competition between these two institutions and their respective representatives in the Second Republic may not have been eliminated, expediency dictates that the two should more than tolerate each other and help implement policies which serve the interests of the new regime, and administer those which are designed to undermine the position of 'radicals' within the ranks of the ruling elite. As was demonstrated in the run-up to and the eventual outcome of the October 1990 elections for the theologically based Assembly of Experts, the body which among other things is empowered to choose the Faqih and, if need be, dismiss him as well, the Leader–President alliance managed to pull the rug from under the feet of the radical clergy opposed to the Rafsanjani government's economic and foreign policies, for the control of this important institution (Malek 1991). Ayatollah Khamenei supervised the implementation of changes to the assembly's election procedures proposed by the Leader–President alliance over the summer of 1990, and as a consequence of the vetting of the 169 candidates under the new rules, the Council of Guardians rejected the credentials of 60 would-be candidates. Notable absentees from this assembly (many of whom refused to take the theological test proposed by Ayatollah Khamenei) included the following individuals: Ayatollah Moussavi Ardebilli, Hojjatoleslam Mohtashemi, Hojjatoleslam Karrubi, Ayatollah Khalkhali, Hojjatoleslam Moussavi and Hojjatoleslam Khoini'a (who refused to participate in the elections in solidarity with the rejected candidates even though his own credentials had been accepted by the Guardian Council). This successful coup of the leadership alliance was interpreted by local commentators as a decisive victory over the Maktabis. Furthermore, the eight-year term of membership of the assembly virtually ensured the position of Ayatollah Khamenei as the Supreme Leader, for as of October 1990 most of the members of the assembly belonged either to his or to President Rafsanjani's faction (*Kayhan* 21 July 1990; *Nimrooz* 14 October 1990; *Tehran Times* 10 October 1990).

It was said in chapter 1 that the Revolutionary Council of the Islamic Republic, which was formed in 1979, has provided the leadership of the republic since its inception. Genuine reformers/liberals like Bazargan, Qotbzadeh and Bani-Sadr rose from that same council to take charge of revolutionary Iran. Rafsanjani, his Vice-President Habibi, Khamenei, Moussavi, Montazeri and Moussavi Ardebelli were also members of the original Revolutionary Council. Indeed, many were also amongst the first Majlis deputies in republican Iran. In the absence of other institutions in the formative years of the republic, the Majlis provided a solid base for the cultivation of individual (as well as collective) political power. To this end, many individuals who later came to hold executive posts in the Islamic Republic sought access to the Majlis. Table 13 illustrates the point. In the absence of the great religious figures of the 1979 Revolutionary Council (Ayatollah Beheshti, Hojjatoleslam Bahonar, Ayatollah Talaghani and of course Ayatollah Khomeini himself) and of the liberals, the inheritors of that great coalition have come to form the leadership of the Second Republic.

Institutional tensions do persist, however. Indeed, the constitution simultaneously generates co-operation between the arms of the state and competition within the system. The Majlis, the original power base of

Table 13 Political figures of the IRI: deputies in the first Majlis

Name	Political office	Number of votes (1980)
Hassan Habibi	Vice-President	1,568,709
Mehdi Bazargan	Former Prime Minister	1,447,317
Hojjatoleslam Khamenei	Faqih	1,405,976
Hojjatoleslam Bahonar	Former Prime Minister	1,375,876
Hassan Ayat	Former presidential candidate	1,364,899
Hojjatoleslam Khoini'a	Former Prosecutor-General	1,248,391
Mohammad Rajaii	Former President	1,224,789
Hojjatoleslam Nateq Nouri	Former Cabinet Minister	1,201,933
Hojjatoleslam Rafsanjani	President	1,151,541
Ebrahim Yazdi	Former Foreign Minister	1,128,304
Ali Akbar Velayati	Foreign Minister	745,110*
Habibollah Asgharouladi	Former Cabinet Minister	704,228*
Assadollah Lajevardi	Former Tehran Rev. Prosecutor	509,939*

Source: The figures for the 1980 election results have been compiled from Abrahamian (1989: 203).

Note: The data refer only to the candidates standing in Tehran.
* Those who qualified for the run-off elections.

Hojjatoleslam Rafsanjani himself, does remain equally influential in the Second Republic, and in the hands of the right individuals can serve as a seat of opposition to the President. The first post-Rafsanjani Speaker of the Majlis followed in Rafsanjani's footsteps in utilising his position as a source of political power. Although he did not use his office to challenge the new administration during his first term, there can be no guarantee that he or the next Speaker may not choose to do so in the future. The important point is that by virtue of this office the Speaker is able to do so. Indeed, Hojjatoleslam Karrubi's re-election as the Speaker of the Majlis in June 1990, with 150 votes in favour out of a total of 229 cast, was an indication that he had begun to consolidate his power base in the third Majlis (IRNA 12 June 1990). Equally, his failure to get re-elected in 1992 and the emergence of the pro-Rafsanjani Hojjatoleslam Nateq Nouri as the Majlis Speaker considerably weakened the radical line in and out of the chamber, an outcome not altogether unexpected as far as the President was concerned (Sarabi 1994).

By the turn of the decade the reformers were in control, although they clearly lacked the 'liberal' credentials of the original 'liberal' reformers of the Provisional Government of Bazargan. The realists/pragmatists have been taking steps to improve the socio-cultural environment in Iran as a factor in the substantive economic reforms. The legalisation of amateur boxing, chess and fencing, the growth of the theatre, and the arts, the revival of traditional Iranian and Western 'classical' music, may appear insignificant developments, but they serve as examples of this trend.

Without the changes in the structure of power in Iran after Ayatollah Khomeini's death the wide-ranging policy changes might indeed not have been implemented at all. Milani has summed up the relationship between changes in the structure of power and policy reforms in Iran succinctly:

> For better or worse, Iran has historically experienced stability and rapid economic growth only when the central government has been powerful. For the first time since . . . 1979, the government is now both powerful and relatively centralized. That the power is centralized [in the executive branch] when Iran needs to begin its reconstruction is not accidental . . . political institutions shape politics and are in turn shaped by politics, history, and the social context within which they operate.
>
> (Milani 1993: 97)

4 The revolutionary state in search of an economic system

The Moussavi years

> To speak of the Islamic Republic's economic policy is to describe a phantom. To some it is a solid, purposeful doctrine, firmly embedded in the Koran, with clear answers for all economic and social problems. To others it is a will-o'-the-wisp which disappears into thin air when one attempts to come to grips with its practical implications.
>
> (Andrew Whitely, *The Approach of the Islamic Republic of Iran to Economic Policy*, Bonn: Neue Gesellschaft, 1980)

It can be surmised from the many policy statements of the Iranian leadership, including Ayatollah Khomeini himself, that the revolutionary Islamic Republic aspired to surpass the capitalist and socialist models of development. But, as will be shown below, to all intents and purposes, by the end of the 1980s the Islamic Republic had managed to create a mixed economic system within which the state sector played the dominant role.

For a fuller picture, however, one needs to examine both the nature of the Iranian economy and the role of the state sector within it during the Shah's reign. One can then proceed to look at the economic policies of the First Republic and the changes which its leadership implemented in this sphere. The impact of the new and earlier strategies of the Moussavi governments on the economy of the republic and its revolutionary, parastatal and institutionalised components will be examined in this chapter with particular reference to the role of the state.

THE RISE AND FALL OF THE PAHLAVI STATE

The early 1960s marked the rise of intensive capitalist development in Iran. The Pahlavi regime's ambitious plans for the future necessitated an expanded role for the state in the economy, one which was to be both interventionist and orchestrating. As a capitalist state, it enabled private accumulation through expanding the market, and it facilitated capitalist reproduction through institutional control of labour and investment in infrastructure and those industries which, for one reason or another, were not attractive to the private sector. But as the state was the promoter of capitalism and because it also had monopoly control (*vis-à-vis* local capital) of the fountainhead of capital accumulation – oil revenues – it attained a certain degree of autonomy in its operations.

As the source of much national wealth, and being external to the structure of society, the oil revenues helped to reinforce the autonomy of the state as well as the supremacy of the Pahlavi court-related state and *comprador* bourgeois factions. (The term *comprador* refers to that faction of the Iranian bourgeoisie whose interests compelled it to co-operate with foreign interests in the national economy in production, the provision of services and exchange; Najmabadi 1987). The internationally linked capitalist strata thrived on the state sector, which in turn legitimised the values and interests of the private sector as a whole.

According to the Second Development Plan (1956–62), 'public sector investment would be limited to a few basic industries' (*Iran Shows the Way* 1976: 84) but, owing to the inability of the private sector to fulfil the obligations assigned to it by the planners, the state became a more active investor. In 1960 the state operated only 75 factories (Chemical Bank New York Trust Company 1964: 6), but as Table 14 illustrates, by the late 1960s the picture had changed and public sector investment was beginning to outstrip private sector investment. Compared with the early 1960s, by the advent of the revised Fifth Development Plan (1973–8), the investment ratio between the public and private sectors had been almost exactly reversed, the public sector being expected to account for approximately two-thirds of total investment in the economy. It may have been intended as a temporary reversal of roles, but public sector dominance was to prevail until the end of the Pahlavi system.

Table 15 depicts the changing relationship between the public and private

Table 14 Investment by the public and private sectors in Iran, 1959–78 (%)

Year	Public sector	Private sector
1959	33.7	66.3
1961	32.3	67.7
1963	32.4	67.6
1965	42.7	57.3
1967	49.0	51.0
1968–72	54.7	45.3
1973–8	66.1	33.9

Source: Iran Shows the Way (1976).

sectors at the macro-economic level. It is interesting to note that while the public sector's share in gross fixed capital formation had overtaken the private sectors contribution by the early 1970s, in relation to consumption expenditures the private sector continued to dominate.

Table 15 Gross domestic fixed capital formation and consumption expenditures, 1967–76 (billion rials)

	1967/8	1972/3	1974/5	1975/6	1977/8
Gross fixed capital formation	151	287	564	1,100	1,075
Public sector	74	146	364	647	663
Private sector	77	141	200	453	412
Consumption expenditure	540	898	1,820	2,277	2,638
Public sector	98	253	581	769	799
Private sector	442	645	1,239	1,508	1,839

Source: Amuzegar (1977); Central Bank (various years).

Note: Figures rounded up for convenience.

Increasing dependence on oil exports in the 1970s, compounded by an acceleration in the direct penetration of the Iranian market by foreign capital, led many analysts to classify the Pahlavi state as 'dependent capitalist' (Thiemann 1983). As such, the locus of power was declared to lie with the capitalist metropole. In the evolving international division of labour, Iran would serve as a stable source of relatively cheap oil and a consumer of Western-supplied goods and services. As a semi-peripheral country (Wallerstein 1979), however, it would also be active in the production and export of some industrial products. Within this arrangement the Iranian bourgeoisie was able to participate in investment as a partner either of foreign capital or of the state, or of both. It can be said with a degree of certainty that the Pahlavi state's monopoly control of the country's hydrocarbon resources gave it the 'edge' over the domestic capitalist class factions, even though at the same time it deepened its exposure to external forces and international market processes. The edge at home at the same time strengthened the state's position *vis-à-vis* foreign capital and the supranational capitalist structures. To a degree, the Iranian capitalist system's relations with foreign capital in the 1970s resembled the 'tripartite' relationship between the state, national capital and transnational corporations which had become a characteristic feature of the Brazilian economic system.

The rising oil revenues, totalling $84 billion in export revenues between

1973 and 1977, from an annual income of $2.8 billion in 1972/3 to $17.8 billion in 1974/5 and to just over $20 billion in 1976/7 (OPEC 1980 and Central Bank of Iran 1983) provided levels of capital accumulation hitherto unimagined by the Iranian bourgeoisie, but the dramatic extension of the state's operations in the economy after 1973 encouraged many owners of private capital to focus only on a few (highly profitable) economic activities, such as construction, some intensive investment in light industry, commerce and real estate speculation, rather than become a substantial and active class of industrialists engaged in large-scale production. Through this process of role change, entrepreneurs became even more dependent on the state 'handouts'.

While the bourgeoisie as a whole was enjoying the economic boom, the Pahlavi court took advantage of the new situation to extend its influence even further and to consolidate its alliance with the *comprador* bourgeoisie as its senior partner (Karshenas 1990). Control of the huge oil revenues offered the bureaucratic elite the opportunity to amass capital and private fortunes of their own. The Pahlavi-linked 'state elite' thus became an important economic partner of the bourgeoisie. In the context of post-1963/4 development of Iran's ruling structures, the state elite was to become the non-royal faction of the ruling bourgeoisie.

Historically, the Pahlavi state has been active in the economy; as early as the 1920s 'the monarchy [had] became the conduit through which all economic development in Iran occurred' (Helfgott 1976: 20). However, before the 1960s its role was rather limited, functioning as a subsidiser of the private sector. The expansion of its role and functions did not signal the establishment of 'state capitalism' in Iran. The relationship between the state and the private sector may have undergone some profound changes in the last 15 years of Pahlavi rule, but the essence of private capitalist accumulation was never in question. Conscious of the implications of this expanding role of the state, the ruling elite was always careful to draw attention to the distinction between state intervention in a capitalist economy (i.e. Iran) and a centrally planned one: '[our economy] is not, repeat not, a socialist economy. Ours is a mixed economy, with a very profound social conscience' (Premier Hoveyda's speech, delivered at the Iran-United Kingdom Financial Conference in Tehran, 12 October 1975). Technocrats were always careful to draw a clear distinction between Iran's development planning, a major function of the state, and socialist planning as practiced by the centrally planned economies. The rapidity of the industrialisation process (squeezing in a short space of time industrialisation and socio-economic development) necessitated enlarged public sector participation in the economy, although by the mid-1960s observers were commenting that in Iran '[h]eavy reliance is being placed on public investment to stimulate private investment' (Chemical Bank New

York Trust Company 1964: 1), with planned public and private sector outlays of 120 billion and 100 billion rials respectively.

In the 1970s, however, the role of the state sector became marked in all aspects of economic activity. For instance, government income from state-owned enterprises rose from 483.3 billion rials in 1975/6 to 1,107.7 billion rials in 1977/8, second only to income from hydrocarbons (1,314.2 billion rials) and about three times the government revenues from taxes (397.6 billion rials) in the latter year (Plan and Budget Organisation 1975 to 1978). To put these figures in perspective, we can note that state revenue from hydrocarbon sales was 310.5 billion rials only four years earlier (Central Bank 1975). Indeed, between 1949 (the year of the launch of Iran's development plans) and the Fifth Development Plan period, state investment in economic development had increased by 1,000 times, from $68.0 million (1949–55 plan period) to $68.6 billion (1973–7 plan period) (*The Middle East and North Africa* various years).

In the view of some analysts, the Fifth Development Plan 'radically expanded the role of the state in the economy. In every sector, oil money was to be spent on bigger projects and more wide-ranging social programs' (Razavi and Vakil 1984: 75). Oil revenue increases provided the *modus operandi* for an expanded state role. Regarding the Iranian economy in the 1970s, another economist has commented that:

> The pattern of the economy is such that if the government does not continue expanding means of communication, electric power capacity, areas under irrigation, water supplies, and other utilities, private investment, particularly outside Tehran, cannot prosper. Far from conflicting with public investment, private investment is dependent on it.
>
> (Looney 1973: 20)

The dawn of huge annual national incomes accelerated the growth and development of the modern, internationally linked strata in comparison to the rest of the bourgeoisie. But, under the tutelage of the Pahlavi elite, and largely through its control of oil revenues, the state was increasingly becoming an accumulator in its own right, all the while that it was serving the specific interests of the large domestic bourgeoisie. In short, the state had become 'the economic prop of the ruling regime' (Muller 1983: 74).

By the late 1970s the state was employing 10 per cent or more of the adult work force of the country and provided some 70 per cent of the total investment funds in the economy. So even though the ownership of Iranian industry and trade was predominantly private prior to the revolution, with about 45 families controlling approximately 85 per cent of the larger (with a capital of more than 10 million rials) privately owned firms, the state and the state sector provided the capital basis of the capitalist economy (Muller 1983:

81). Thus, when the revolution occurred, it had a profound impact on both the political and the economic structures of power. The revolutionary process brought the Pahlavi regime to an end, but it also 'scattered the ranks of the *comprador* and Pahlavi/state segments of Iran's bourgeoisie', as one observer has put it (Cockcroft 1980: 151). The power of the dominant faction of the ruling class, in short, was decimated.

The fall of the Shah created a vacuum at the top of the hierarchy, part of which was filled by the expansion of the 'new' state machinery through its acquisition and control of the assets of the court and its state and '*comprador*' associates. While the revolution failed to turn the social pyramid upside down, it did achieve its more immediate goal of removing the pinnacle of the dependent capitalist structure. With the court-linked faction of the bourgeoisie liquidated or exiled, ideal opportunities for growth presented themselves to the smaller traditional and modern bourgeois forces.

The forces which had conspired and co-operated to put an end to Pahlavi rule were now free to jockey for position within the evolving structures of power as well as to penetrate the crust of the old state. Thus, although the struggle against one source of dominant domestic power had ended, the power struggle for the control of the country had only just begun. In wishing the revolution complete, the functionalist Provisional Government (PG), comprising largely the middle class liberal and non-clerical wing of the anti-Shah coalition, had taken up office to bring 'order' and a modicum of normalcy to civil society. It had sought the re-strengthening and re-legitimisation of the state through the depoliticisation of civil society at the very moment when the latter was radicalising in different and competing directions. It sought, in short, the *status quo*, yet had to face the tremors arising from the end of the *status quo ante*. Amidst the continuity, thus, the state was also changing.

The state needs autonomy from any of the factions of the dominant class in order to express the interests of the dominant class as a whole. The Pahlavi state functioned effectively precisely because the court was the unchallenged nucleus of bourgeois power and the pinnacle of the Iranian capitalist system. The state was autonomous in so far as it created the conditions for the growth of the rest of the bourgeoisie, in line with the Pahlavi regime's scheme. At the birth of the Islamic Republic, on the other hand, state autonomy emerged in the absence of a dominant state/private/court-based class: other factions and capitalist forces (large and small) became more active. Liberated from the pressures of big capital, they struggled to increase their share of power and the economic pie. As none of the factions in the revolutionary coalition at that time was in a position to stamp its own authority on the system and dominate its structures, the state was able to function autonomously.

Paradoxically, when the new revolutionary state did find room for autonomous action it was not in a position to take advantage of it: the Iran–Iraq war had helped in the 'pacification' of society (to use Anthony Giddens's term), thus releasing the regime's energies to deal with the war, but the impact of the war on its resources was such that the state was unable to translate its newly found autonomy into policy initiatives aimed at transforming the country's social structure.

STATE AND ECONOMY IN THE AFTERMATH OF THE REVOLUTION

The fall of the Pahlavi regime was followed by intense competition for power amongst the various bourgeois factions and *petit-bourgeois* factions, but the overthrow of the dominant faction of the bourgeoisie gave the emerging (Islamic) state the opportunity to reshape the structure of economic and political power to fit the new Iran. As it emerged, the new regime set about the trimming and cutting of the state machinery to fit its own shape, size and form. However, it became evident that under the new elite, the Iranian capitalist system was not in danger of extinction; it was merely changing its order of battle.

The new elite did not revolutionise the state and the social relations of production, but actually added new appendages to the former as hallmarks of its own identity. New 'Islamic' institutions mushroomed, each encroaching further on the private domain of social life, thereby adding to the state's control of civil society.

While one can therefore identify an altered state form, this should not be confused with an institutional attempt to revolutionise the economic functions of the state. Despite the fact that the early years of the Islamic Republic were marked by political competition between the dominant anti-Shah coalition forces (the clergy and the 'liberals'), this did not represent a struggle to implement specific or competing economic agendas or to impose them upon the state form. Indeed, in order to fulfil its aim of bringing order to the country's bureaucracy and economy, and in order to mitigate the influence of spontaneously developed revolutionary institutions, the PG was forced to enlist the support of the clerics. Thus the ascendancy of the clerical establishment was assured through the PG's attempts to utilise clerical influence in ending the revolutionary phase of the post-Pahlavi order.

To prevent the economy's collapse, and with Ayatollah Khomeini's personal intervention, workshops and other productive units of the exiled *comprador* class and the substantial assets of the court elite were nationalised, bringing under government control the industrial complexes of the country's 51 major industrialists (see Table 16). Typically affected by these nationalisations were the Lajevardi and Sabet families. At the height of its power in

Table 16 Assets of Iran's major industrialists before the revolution

Name	Main business activities
Akhavan	Majority shareholder in Darioush Bank; General Motors, Iran, car assembly plant; substantial shareholder in other banks
Sabet	Iran representative of Audi-VW group; RCA audio-visual consumer goods factory; Mina bottle and sheet glass-making factories; manufacturer of soft drinks
Farmanfarmayan	Pars oil company, Tehran Siman (cement), Soufian Siman, Pars paper-making and paper products factory; substantial shareholder in Iran National car assembly plant, and in one or two banks and construction companies
Rezai (two brothers)	Shahriar industrial group (five major factories); Ama industries; Skol brewery; a number of mineral mines; owner of a number of large mines; Arak heavy agricultural machinery and road construction equipment
Arieh	Ariana industrial group; shareholdings in financial houses and mines
Vahabzadeh	Pakdis distillers; Iran representative of BMW and Caterpillar corporations; shareholdings in major banks
Khayami (two brothers)	Koroush superstores; Asia Insurance Company; Jamco, Iran Mobl and Belerian furniture-making factories and stores; Iran National vehicle assembly group; Reza industrial complex (Mashad); financial institutions shareholdings
Yasini	Abgineh sheet glass-making factory; Momtaz textile and yarn factory
Irvani-Motaqi	Melli industrial group (36 production units)
Barkhordar	Pars Electric Industries; Kerman Siman; Iran Metal Industries; Iran Batri (vehicle battery manufacturing); Iran Kompresorsazi (compressor manufacturer); Iran representative of Toshiba; mechanised carpet-weaving factory
Lajevardian	Kashan textile factory; Isfahan textile and nylon yarn factory; mechanised carpet-weaving factory; Ama industries
Lajevardi family	Kashan textile and silk yarn factory; Behshahr industrial group; packaging factory
Payravi	Owner of chromite mines
Mahdavi	Khorasan food-processing units and industrial factories; shareholdings in some major banks
Ebtehaj family	Shomal Siman; shares in many banks and enterprises; shareholdings in industrial groups and large construction contractors; subcontracting businesses
Daneshvar	Ekbatan new town; shareholdings in Iran National vehicle assembly group
Alikhani	Isfahan Navard metal works; Isfahan brick-making factory

Table 16 continued

Name	Main business activities
Javaheri	Major shareholdings in a number of industries
Isfahani	Major shareholdings in a number of industries
Akhavan-Kashani	Great Iran superstore; Sa'adi tile and ceramics factory; Kashan textiles; Shilat supermarket
Shekarchian (two brothers)	Zeeba thread and weaving factory
Mazinrad	Major shareholdings in a number of large industrial units
Alam	Tehran Siman; Kermanshah sugar-beet processing factory
Mirashrafi	Tehran Taj textile and weaving factory
Harandi	Barak garment-making plants
Hedayat	Naqsh-e Jahan sugar-beet processing factory; Ahvaz metaltube foundry
Abunasr-Azad	Ahvaz sugar-beet works; writing paper-making and paper products factory
Omidhuzoor Bros.	Bells shoe factories (12 industrial units); shareholdings in banks
Harati	Isfahan brickworks; Shomal Siman
Rahimzad-e Khoi	Soufian Siman; Tabriz Industries; industrial cable manufacturing
Qadimy-e Navayi (two brothers)	Neyshabour sugar-beet processing; Naqsh-e Jahan sugar-beet processing
Boushehri	Pak dairy products; Organisation of International Gatherings; four small factories
Panahpour	Many factories making intermediate industrial goods; construction companies
Assadi	Iran industrial group; Leyland Motors
Ziyaii	Fars and Khouzestan Siman; other shareholdings
Hajtourkhani	Shahid sugar-beet processing factory
Behbahani	General household appliances conglomerate; motor cycle and bicycle works
Khosrowshahi (two brothers)	Pars factories; Alborz Investment Company; Tidi industrial units; Mino biscuits and food-processing factories
Fouladi brothers	B. F. Goodrich, Iran; Kiyan Tyres
Namazi	Iran Buick car assembly corporation; textile and fibre manufacturer; shareholdings in some large industries
Rashidian	Ta'avouni and Touz'i Bank; shareholdings in many industries

Sources: Ehteshami (1993a); *Iran's Who is Who* (various years).

1978 the Lajevardi empire owned the Behshahr Industrial Group, which comprised 20 wholly-owned companies and 26 partnership ventures, in addition to having substantial stakes in the International Bank of Iran and Japan and in the Iranian Development and Investment Bank (Thurgood 1978:

17). In the late 1970s the group had 12,000 employees and just one of its products (detergents) controlled about 30 per cent of the domestic market.

Similarly, the Sabet empire spanned many fields of economic activity. Habib Sabet, the main figure of the Sabet corporate structure and founder of more than 40 enterprises (in manufacturing, refining, assembly plants and the service sector), was also vice-chairman of the Industrial and Mining Development Bank of Iran and a member of the board of directors of the Iran–British Bank (Muller 1983).

The nationalisations gave the state direct control of between 80 and 85 per cent of the country's major production units. In a parallel development, the Pahlavi Foundation, the court's holding company, gave way to the Foundation of the Deprived (springing out of the revolutionary process, this foundation was said to be ready, as early as 1983, to return some of the companies under its control to their former owners) (*Financial Times* 6 May 1983). It embraced some 600 companies (including 150 factories, 200 trading houses, and 80 per cent of the country's cinemas), a number of 'five star' hotels, hundreds of agribusinesses and mechanised farms, private properties and dwellings, and real estate in New York (*Financial Times Survey* 1985).

In due course other foundations and Islamic organisations were formed to act as holding companies for the huge abandoned wealth, or for channelling resources to the regime's most ardent supporters (these included the Martyr Foundation, the 15 Khordad Foundation, the Foundation of Life Sacrifices and the Foundation for the Imposed War Refugees. Many of these foundations have been active in industry, engaging in various aspects of low-level and non-technology-intensive production).

The initial 'nationalisations' should be understood not as a deliberate move to transform the economy in the interests of the 'deprived', but as a stop-gap measure motivated by the urgent need to bring back productivity as well as order and management to a large and abandoned section of the economy.

This policy of confiscation was soon to be formalised, however, with the following government directives:

1 The nationalisation of those properties owned by the court and its close associates.
2 The nationalisation of those properties whose owners had fled.
3 The nationalisation of any firm which owed more than half its assets to the banks.

Clearly, of the three, the last measure was an attempt at providing a rescue package for those firms in deep financial difficulties. Assumption of ownership by the state, therefore, was a pragmatic rather than an ideologically motivated move.

Other sectors brought under state ownership or control were the banking sector and insurance companies. Some 37 private banks (14 of which had foreign partners) and 10 insurance companies were nationalised as a result of an order issued by the Revolutionary Council (Economist Intelligence Unit 1979). In doing this the clerical establishment was removing the remaining influence of the former elites in the financial sector, while at the same time providing the state with the mechanisms for bailing out Iran's troubled industrial sectors. During the last years of the Shah's rule, industrialists and others with capital had been removing an average of $2 billion to $3 billion a year from the country, draining it of industrial investment and private savings. Data are sketchy, but some sources have mentioned figures in excess of $15 billion having left Iran during the revolutionary period alone (Ehteshami 1992). As far as the new regime was concerned, therefore, it was imperative that it should take charge of the abandoned assets, prevent the collapse of the economy, and find some way of injecting funds into an industrial sector which was not immediately profitable or attractive to private investment. The state sector after the revolution was thus not only to become a direct subsidiser of the private sector but also acquired the potential to become an 'independent' accumulator of capital in its own right. This latter potential of the state sector was reinforced by the 1979 constitution, which gave the state the leading role in the economy and in the control and direction of the country's natural resources and assets.

The net result of the nationalisation of the country's major industrial and financial corporations, and many other economic activities, in addition to the extension of state control over all the country's mines and mining activity (and the country's natural resources), was an overwhelming state presence in almost all aspects of economic activity. Although the sanctity of private ownership was never questioned in the Islamic Republic, three issues – all arising from the revolutionary process itself – remained unresolved and problematic: redistribution of wealth in favour of the 'deprived', land reform, and the control of foreign trade. Being of immense political significance in the new Iran, these issues also had an ideological dimension.

Prolonged disputes over these issues point towards an absence of overall economic direction in the Islamic Republic, even though substantial progress had been made in terms of bringing much of the *comprador* class's activities under state control. What was as yet undetermined was which forces would have ultimate control of the state, and to what specific end. Political instability and economic uncertainties during this period merely postponed the resolution of this question.

The struggle between the *kolahis* and the liberal factions (and their allies) and their Hezbollahi and clerical counterparts (which ended with the defeat of the former in 1981) had two related outcomes for the system: on the one hand it extended the power of the clergy and its allies to the far reaches of the bureaucracy and the state, but on the other the open struggle resulted in the physical elimination of many of the committed individuals in the clerical faction, including many of Ayatollah Khomeini's own (senior) clerical allies. The initial task of the first Moussavi government, therefore, was to restore political stability to the country. In so doing, however, the government also sought to introduce a substantial populist economic and socio-economic reform programme (which one may term 'radical' in the Islamic Republican political context).

ECONOMIC DEBATE: POLICY AND DIRECTION, 1982-8

At the heart of the economy debate in the republic was the question of ownership. Should state ownership be consolidated and even extended further, in accordance with the provisions of the constitution, or should clear and legal frameworks which would give the private sector confidence and an important and legitimate role in the economy be introduced in order to offset the negative dimensions of the constitution? The revolutionaries, many from the Islamic camp and virtually all the leftist groups were in favour of almost complete state control of the economy. They equated private ownership in the economy, whether of factories, land or natural resources, with imperialist domination of the country. Others, particularly those in executive posts, tended to express views ranging from support for a full-scale command economy to those who advocated a free market system, in accordance with Islamic values. To say that the debate remained inconclusive is perhaps to underestimate the depth of the problem, particularly for a reformist government which not only had to run a war and sanction-ridden economy but also to develop a truly just and Islamic socio-economic system in Iran. Seven years after the revolution the issue was still a live one. Note the words of a Majlis deputy (Assadollah Badamchian):

> Let us make it clear what we really want to do in this country. Do we want factories or not? If not, let us say that being an industrialist is an offence and anybody who has a factory should turn it over to the government. If we say large factories should be held by the government and the rest as co-operatives let's say so . . . For God's sake, let us give a clear definition of a capitalist.
>
> (*Arabia* March 1986: 67)

Article 44 of the 1979 constitution envisaged three economic sectors: state, co-operative and private. Reflecting the revolution's spirit, the constitution gave pride of place to the state sector, intending to bring under its jurisdiction all strategic, large-scale and 'parent' industries, foreign trade, major minerals, banking, insurance, the broadcasting media, postal, telegraph and telephone services, aviation, shipping, roads and railways, power generation, dams and large-scale irrigation networks. The constitution thus anticipated a secondary role for the private sector: 'The private sector consists of those activities concerned with agriculture, animal husbandry, industry, trade and services which complement the government's economic activities' (Business International 1991: 164). In theory, at least, the private sector in the Islamic Republic was not to lead the economy but to be led. Although some thought had clearly been given to the organisation, the distribution of power and the structure of the economy in the new order, it is important to point out that by the time the first authoritative government of the republic finally came to power (in February 1982, three full years after the revolution) many of the *ad hoc* decisions and haphazard policies of the previous governments had already begun to give some character to the nascent system. The first Moussavi government, therefore, was not dealing with a 'clean slate' as far as economic policy formation was concerned.

Formal recognition of the state's leading role in the economy, coupled with its full control of the oil revenues, merely reinforced the relative autonomy of the state *vis-à-vis* the dominant and subordinated social classes. In consort with its expanded role, the 'Islamic' state machinery was well placed to implement the new elite's emerging national economic blueprint. While previously the government had relied on its coercive powers to counter the violence which is a by-product of any revolutionary change, after 1982 the regime was able to move towards fuller control of civil society by strengthening its 'infrastructural' power, to borrow a phrase from Mann (Mann 1986: 109). This was a major element in the legitimisation of the regime after the violent episodes of the previous three years. Only now could it attempt to redefine its relationship with foreign capital and re-examine its trading links. But as we shall see below, other factors were to prejudice the implementation of any comprehensive socio-economic reorientation package which may have been contemplated by the new government.

Bearing in mind the Western-imposed embargo and the pressures associated with running a war economy, the new government's policies had to be based on securing the flow and sale of hydrocarbons and on expanding industrial and agricultural output. As neither task was possible without an intimate relationship with the international capitalist system, the fulfilment of these objectives in turn meant the continued binding of the Islamic Republic to that very system. Even measures such as the rationing of essential goods, controls on imports and food subsidies owed little to the introduction of any new redistributive economic strategies, but much to a pragmatic set of policies which aimed to minimise the impact of the war and of the embargo on society as a whole.

Even though much economic activity had by now come under central government control, the debate on how to construct an 'Islamic' economy raged on. Apart from vague notions pertaining to the promotion of economic self-sufficiency and self-reliance, the re-distribution of income and wealth in favour of the deprived and a reduction in the country's dependence upon international capitalism, the government's initial economic policies in fact helped the interests of the strongest remaining bourgeois faction, the bazaar. State control of the economy limited the scope for private investment in large-scale industry and as the former extended its power over the industrial sector it weakened the power of the small, but influential, non-*comprador* 'national' bourgeoisie.

Under these conditions the commercial bourgeoisie became the most active faction of the ruling class. Imports of intermediate industrial products (58.7 per cent of total imports in 1987, compared with 54.1 per cent of the total in 1977), capital goods (23.6 per cent, compared with 27.5 per cent in 1977) and consumer goods (17.7 per cent, compared with 18.4 per cent in 1977) (Central Bank various years) continued unabated, but the government's attempts to insulate the economy from external forces and pressures during the war brought the prospect of a clash between the commercial bourgeoisie and the étatist wing of the government that much closer. The existing system of checks and controls on foreign trade (80 per cent of which was in government hands by the mid-1980s, according to the Prime Minister; *MEED* 1 March 1986) operated through various Ministries, the state-controlled banks, the Procurement and Distribution Centres and finally the customs administration, were to be augmented by the government's proposal for the nationalisation of foreign trade, as stated in the constitution. Although the role and place of the commercial bourgeoisie in the evolving class structure of the Islamic Republic were never seriously challenged (nor indeed was the bazaar's importance as an important distribution network and source of funds for the state), many government policies and proposals during the 1980s did concern the bazaaris.

The Council of Guardians' (the council functions as an upper parliamentary chamber, empowered to veto legislation passed by the Majlis which does not stand up to scrutiny in terms of its own interpretation of Islamic law) interventions against the direction which government policies were taking, specifically opposition to further nationalisations, to other basic economic reforms such as land reform and the sequestration of property, to high taxes and to further limitations on the activities of the private sector on religious grounds, had two important implications. Firstly, as many of the Council of Guardians' members seem to have identified with the bazaar and other propertied classes (Ja'far and Tabari 1984), their opposition to government legislation represented the resistance of those classes to further encroachments by the state. Secondly, the Islamic basis of the council's opposition was indicative of the problematic nature of the constitution itself, which rather eclectically (but consistently with Islamic principles) had recognised the sanctity of private property while simultaneously endeavouring to impose limits on the extent of its activities (Akbari 1990). As far as the Council of Guardians was concerned, new government legislation was in fact questioning the very basis of private ownership in the Islamic Republic, going far beyond the premises of the constitution. The thrust of the council's views was strongly and openly endorsed by influential voices from within the business community, as can be seen from an article which appeared in the October 1985 issue of the *Journal of the Iranian Chamber of Commerce*:

> [T]he private sector, despite all its interest and keenness to invest and expand its activities, has not been provided with the necessary opportunities to do so . . . This is mostly due to the fact that despite the more than six years that have passed since the . . . revolution, the private sector does not yet enjoy any security or guarantee, nor has it been provided with correct directions. The excuse generally put forward – that laws in this field have not yet been framed – is not plausible because the country has the Islamic law which does not impose any limitations on sound private sector activities . . . Hence there is no need to fix a limit to the activities of the private sector. If anything, one needs to limit the activities of the public sector precisely, so that the private sector could operate in all fields which do not fall under the purview of the public sector.
>
> (Quoted in *Arabia* March 1986: 67)

Two prominent schools of thought regarding the direction which the economy should take were now clearly discernible. One, the Hojatieh faction, was composed of passionate free-marketeers who opposed radical socio-economic legislation, high taxation and statist policies, advocating instead a more cautious and traditional 'Islamic' approach. Particularly effective was their protest that high taxation and efficient collection of taxes by the government might in fact undermine the authority of the religious establishment and reduce the flow of annual revenues to the mosque. One government official, opposed to this line of thinking, was to say, 'those who argue against taxes are the same people who believe we should privatise oil pipelines and mines' (Minister of Heavy Industry Behzad Nabavi, quoted in Ehteshami 1987). In other words, the disputes over taxation represented only the tip of the iceberg: above all else, much of the debate related to the overall direction of the economy and the nature of the system under the Islamic Republic.

The second trend, the Maktabis (also known as the Followers of the Imam's Line), believed equally strongly in the politics and economics of the 'dispossessed', advocating centralised economic planning, higher taxation, substantial material support for the poor, the confiscation of land without compensation and its redistribution in favour of the peasantry. Although the Hojatieh's power in the government was effectively on the wane in the mid-1980s, the radical agenda of the Maktabis was continually stymied by the pragmatic elements in the regime and by the intervention of the Guardian Council. Despite the official demise of the Hojatieh Society, many in the regime continued to press the case for a strengthening of the private sector. Even Ayatollah Khomeini himself spoke on more than one occasion in favour of the bazaar and the private sector: 'we promise that as long as there is Islam there will be free enterprise also' (*The Sunday Times* 10 January 1983). His 'eight-point decree' issued in 1982 was also seen as making the basis for private sector investment more secure (*Arabia* March 1986: 67).

It was in this environment that the government's industrial policies began to take shape. In general terms there were four aspects to this. Many of the major projects started under the *ancien régime* were to continue or be restarted. All necessary intermediate goods were to be imported to supply the old assembly plants. The government embarked upon the construction of intermediate industries in Iran to supply the existing assembly plants. Finally, and as a strategic objective, the state sector was instructed to build chains of industries from basic petrochemicals and mineral resources in order to achieve *khod kafai* (self-sufficiency) in the economy, and thus reduce the country's overall dependence in the future. In all this, the thrust of practical policy-making was, as Rafsanjani was to put it, that 'the Islamic government has to lead the private sector' rather than necessarily to replace it (*The Middle East* 1985: 52). The corollary of this approach was, as Nabavi said, 'We are not communists and ideologically we believe in private ownership. On the other hand we don't believe in the total dominance of the private sector. We are not going to allow entrepreneurs to run our government' (cited by *Financial Times Survey* 1985: IV).

Paradoxically, in view of the expansion of the state, but not so surprisingly when one considers this 'pragmatism' of policy-making and the removal of the power of the '*comprador* bourgeoisie', the revolution sparked off an unprecedented development of small-scale private industry, largely financed in the initial stages by soft government loans. According to official statistics, the number of new factories and workshops employing over 30 people during the period 1979 to 1985 may have been as many as 14,000 (*The Middle East* 1986). Government encouragement was reflected in approximately $2.5 billion worth of industrial investment commitments by the private sector in 1983 alone, involving 6,804 proposals and licences (*MEED Special Report* 1984).

Despite this demonstration of economic activity, however, the economy as a whole was becoming increasingly crisis-ridden throughout the Moussavi premiership (1982–9). Rising food imports (compounded by the needs of the rapidly growing population – over 3 per cent per annum on average) testified to the continuing deficiencies in agriculture, and stagnation was evident in the manufacturing and industrial sectors. Industry was said to be running, at best, at 50–60 per cent of capacity and many of the state-owned establishments were running at a loss. Significantly, the Industrial Development and Renovation Organisation's losses in 1983 were estimated at $3.5 billion (ibid.). This organisation, which had held a stake in over 100 companies in the late 1970s, including a majority interest in 55 of them, had grown substantially after the revolution, so these losses represented a substantial blow to the economy as a whole. By the middle of the decade, only 10 major concerns were consuming nearly 70 per cent of the foreign exchange allocated to heavy industry (*MEED Special Report* 1984). In effect the Islamic government had become the subsidiser of the Shah's 'white elephant' and other industrialisation projects, but in the process had lost the economic muscle of his regime.

A clear indication of the regime's economic failures was that, during the 1979–87 period, the gross domestic product of Iran averaged a growth rate of −0.7 per cent, or a 15.7 per cent decline in GDP compared with the average annual GDP for the 1976–8 period (Amirahmadi 1990). Thus, according to the Central Bank's data, real *per capita* incomes (at 1982/3 prices) had fallen from 292,000 rials in 1977/8 to 151,000 in 1988/9 (Central Bank of Iran various years).

As Table 17 shows, despite all the expectations and the government's commitment to turning the 1986/7 oil crisis, in Prime Minister Moussavi's words, into an 'opportunity to achieve self-sufficiency' (*MEED* 10 May 1986 and 19 July 1986), the Islamic government had managed neither to change the structure of the economy nor to reduce in any meaningful way the country's dependence on oil revenues. The 'blessing in disguise', as the Industry Minister interpreted the government's financial crisis (*MEED* 10 May 1986), failed to clear the path for the implementation of more autocratic economic strategies and merely deepened the general crisis engulfing the country's war economy. The government's problems were magnified in the second half of the1980s with the substantial drop in oil prices and the subsequent decline in Iran's revenues (oil income in 1986 dropped to $7.2 billion, compared with an anticipated $18.5 billion) (*MEED* 10 May 1986 and 14 June 1986; OPEC 1988), compounded by Iraq's increasingly successful attempts at hampering and paralysing Iran's oil-exporting capabilities. Iran's sustainable oil production capacity had fallen from 5.5 mb/d in 1978 to around 2.5 mb/d in 1988 (OPEC various years).

The crisis is evident in the budget allocations of some of the most

Table 17 Oil and the economy

Measure	1974	1977	1980	1982	1984	1985	1986	1987	1988
Crude oil exports (mb/d)	5.27	4.86	0.79	1.62	1.52	1.56	1.45	1.69	1.71
Value of oil exports ($ billion)	20.9	23.6	13.3	19.2	12.3	13.1	7.2	10.5	8.2
Oil exports (as % of total)	97.0	97.3	94.2	99.0	98.7	98.4	96.3	90.0	89.9
Oil revenue *per capita* ($)	653	674	366	457	266	273	143	206	150

Sources: OPEC (various years); Central Bank of Iran (various years).

important Ministries. The foreign exchange allocation for industry in 1985/6 was set at $2.5 billion in that year, less than half the amount needed to keep industries operating at full capacity (*MEED* 11 January 1986), and the foreign currency allocation to the Heavy Industries Ministry was down from $2.4 billion in 1983/4 to $1.62 billion in 1985/6 and, because of the expected low income from oil exports, it was scheduled to be as low as $1.35 billion for the following year, according to the Minister (*MEED* 1 February 1986).

To make matters worse, the Majlis, with the Council of Guardians' approval, actually increased (for the first time in five years) the government's budget for the Iranian year starting in March 1986 by about $2.5 billion (IR 200 billion), even though many MPs and economists regarded the government's oil revenue projection as unrealistic (*MEED* 15 March 1986). The Energy Minister, Taqi Banki, reported in 1986 that as government revenues had been falling in the previous three years it was likely that the development budget for 1986/7 would be cut by 38 per cent (*MEED* 26 April 1986). All this time, moreover, the government had remained committed to providing 80 per cent of the foreign exchange needed for imports of essential supplies, and maintaining the subsidies on foodstuffs, fuel and many other essentials, even though in the first three quarters of 1986 its foreign currency earnings had reached their lowest point since 1973/4 (*MEED* 3 January 1987).

More alarmingly still, from the mid-1980s the government's commitment to economic development began to show signs of wavering. As official allocation figures indicate, in real terms the share of the development budget in total government budget had dropped significantly by the 1988/9 budget, from $12.1 billion in a total budget of $41.5 billion in 1982/3 to $12.5 billion in a total budget of $66.2 billion, having reached its highest point in the 1984/5 budget ($15.2 billion in a total budget of $48 billion) (*MEES*; *MEED*; *EIU*). By the end of 1987, government development expenditures stood at only 18 per cent of the general budget, whereas current expenditures absorbed 82 per cent of the total (Amirahmadi 1990). Thus the development of the Iranian economy, regarded as a major goal of government policy, had been subordinated to the immediate needs of the war economy. In addition, unemployment, never really brought under control since the mid-1970s, began to rise more steeply in the mid-1980s. In 1984/5 it stood at about 2 million (approximately 15 per cent of the work force of 12.5 million) (*MEED* 19 March 1986) and reached 3.8 million by the end of 1986 (of a total work force of 13.3 million) (*MEED* 28 March 1987), continuing to rise in the remaining period of the Moussavi premiership (Amuzegar 1993).

ECONOMIC CRISIS AND THE NEED FOR ECONOMIC POLICY CHANGES

Despite the government's apparent ability to keep the economy from total collapse, the combined effects of mismanagement, lack of clear direction in the economy (even the republic's first Five Year Development Plan, set to start in 1983/4, formulated by the first Moussavi government, had to be shelved indefinitely), war with its associated physical destruction, shortage of expertise, inefficiency (even sheer neglect), coming at the same time as a relatively sharp decline in oil revenues (Amuzegar 1992), meant that by the second half of the 1980s the government had little choice but to turn to the private sector and the nationalised banks for assistance in embarking on a programme of national economic recovery. A broad debate about the liberalisation of the economy ensued following Ayatollah Khomeini's statement on 9 June 1986 (and not for the first time) that 'The government . . . should give a role to the people in all [economic] affairs, give them a role in trade' (*MEED* 14 June 1986), which prompted Ayatollah Imami Kashani (Tehran's substitute Friday prayers leader) to interpret the Imam's words in the following fashion: 'the people should be allowed to participate while the government should supervise' (*MEED* 28 June 1986).

Although as early as 1982 the government's proposed Bill on Private Sector Activities had envisaged a fuller role for the private sector in the economy, and in 1985 a 'denationalisation plan' had been prepared – geared to transferring non-basic industries to the private sector – it was not until July 1986 that the government announced it was seeking private sector involvement in certain sectors, most notably in mining, and was considering offering incentives in order to attract private sector investment (*MEED* 26 July 1986). Export licences for some 90 varieties of goods were also dropped at about the same time, and plans for the establishment of a limited free port on Kish were even unveiled (*MEED* 20 September 1986). A year later (August 1987), new measures for the promotion of exports were announced and tariffs on exports of fruit, vegetables and some other goods were lifted (*MEED* 22 August 1987).

The oil crisis of 1986/7 caused major financial problems for the government. As it had promised to maintain its existing levels of subsidies for essential goods (approximately $1.3 billion for that year), and external sources of funds were drying up, the government turned its attention to the generation of revenues from the national economy itself. The most obvious source of funds in the domestic economy was to be realised through taxation. First, taxes due had to be more efficiently collected and, secondly, new taxes had to be imposed. As the second option would have involved a lengthy process of negotiation with the Majlis and the Council of Guardians, the government concentrated its efforts on the more efficient collection of taxes. Thus the government's tax revenues rose by 4 per cent in the second half of 1986 (to $9.2 billion), the direct taxation component of which reached $5.2 billion (*MEED* 28 February 1987): for the year 1987/8, it claimed to have collected nearly three times that amount in taxes (*MEED* 13 May 1988). By the middle of 1987, income tax revenues were said to have risen by 40 per cent, for the first time outstripping government income from indirect taxation (*MEED* 12 September 1987).

The end to hostilities with Iraq in August 1988 promised the commencement of an era of economic reconstruction and industrial rejuvenation in Iran. Developments in this period can be divided into two phases: the twilight of the Moussavi premiership and the rise of the Rafsanjani presidency. The political crisis, stemming from the differences between the government and the Majlis on the one hand and the Guardian Council on the other over economic policy and the role of the state, had continued unabated and, by 1988, had reached an impasse. A new body (the Council for the Determination of Expediency) had to be formed in February 1988 to mediate between the Guardian Council and the Majlis/government, but this by no means facilitated any meaningful change in policy or helped the government's cause. Indeed, when help did come, as it did in the form of Ayatollah Khomeini's comments about the absolute authority of the Islamic regime to override all other matters of religion and state, it was to help not the Moussavi government but its successor. In a response to Hojjatoleslam (as he was then) Khamenei's Friday prayer speech of 1 January 1988 the Faqih gave the government a virtually free hand in conducting the affairs of the state, declaring that the government was a 'primary rule in Islam', an 'institution ordained by the Almighty and founded with absolute authority entrusted to the Prophet' (*Kayhan International* 9 January 1988).

ECONOMIC POLICY CHANGES OF THE MOUSSAVI GOVERNMENT

Moussavi's tenure of office upon re-election as Prime Minister in May 1988 was to be short-lived. By the following August the constitutional reforms would sweep him and his office away, leaving eight years of ambiguous government in its wake. Unable to reduce or limit private ownership of land and capital, and faced with an inefficient and overblown bureaucracy, his government eventually resigned itself to an expanded role for the private sector. After a decade of state intervention the 'radical' government of the previous eight years indicated its preparedness to reduce the state's economic activities.

The new policy was signalled by the Prime Minister in his government's 1988 Five Year Plan proposal to the Majlis, which envisaged substantial levels of investment by the private sector (*MEED* 11 November 1988), and his 1989/90 budget speech in which he stated that the aim of the government's economic policy was not to destroy the private sector (*The Echo of Iran* 12 January 1989 and 19 January 1989). The Heavy Industries Minister indicated that, as part of the reconstruction policy, there was a 'strong' disposition in the government to involve the private sector in a greater share of the economy (SWB, ME/W0077, 16 May 1989) (see *MEED* 12 May 1989). 'There's high temperature to privatise', he was to say.

The first concerted move towards economic liberalisation and deregulation was to be found in the government's lifting of restrictions on the importation of many essential and 'luxury' items by the private sector. This was to be followed by a comprehensive privatisation policy, announced in April 1989, based on the transfer of ownership of all 'non-essential and non-strategic' profit and loss-making companies to the private sector (*Resalat* 26 April 1989). The Tehran stock exchange reopened formally on 6 September 1988 with an offer of shares in state-owned industries, including sales of shares in nine big enterprises (*MEED* 16 September 1988).

On the major issue of foreign borrowing, his government continued to hold out – for a time. 'Foreign loans', the Deputy Prime Minister Hamid Mirzadeh stated, 'would in the long run make the country dependent' (SWB, ME/W0074, 25 April 1989). As the pace of reconstruction accelerated, however, and the demands on resources multiplied, so the government began to reassess the value of retaining even this sacred cow. The Economics and Finance Minister, Mohammad Iravani, boldly stated that the Islamic Republic should borrow from abroad for investment purposes (*Eqtesad* July 1989). The holder of the influential office of Chairman of the Majlis Commission on Planning and the Budget, Morteza Alviri, entered the debate on foreign participation in the economy in January 1989 by lending his support to those who argued in favour of foreign loans and direct foreign investment in Iran. 'About foreign participation, the experiences have been positive', he remarked in a speech:

> and if I am asked that foreign participation and use of foreign sources were beneficial to the country, I will respond clearly that they are. Because, the existing experiences show that the countries which did not explore these grounds were remorseful some years later . . . Use of foreign sources can basically benefit us at the service of the development of the country, provided that it is not approached carelessly and negatively.

> (*The Echo of Iran* 2 February 1989: 18)

In the end even on this issue the government had to compromise its long held principles and accept project-based foreign borrowing: it was announced in early 1989 that the government had approved foreign borrowing of $2 billion to $3 billion for the next five years (*MEED* 3 March 1989).

Overall, however, little of substance was achieved in this period. The initiatives were too little too late as far as the survival of the Moussavi government was concerned. The Moussavi government's indecisiveness throughout its eight years at the helm had reflected the same tensions within the elite as existed in society as a whole. Lack of direction in economic planning had left a large public sector in charge of the country's productive activities while the private sector had been confused by contradictory policies. As indicated above, a lack of commitment either to full central planning or to a dominant and unhindered private sector meant that the resulting mixed economic system tended to bring out the worst in both sectors. By the late 1980s, not only had the main economic problems which had fuelled the 1979 revolution not been resolved, but with the ending of the Iran–Iraq war a number of new problems, many of them structural, had also surfaced.

As for policy choices open to the government, Patrick Clawson's observations are instructive:

> The prospect of a long period of austerity makes the need to adjust the structure of the economy even more compelling. The possible policy choices are essentially two – either make more room for market forces or increase state control of the economy. Any middle path would combine the worst of both, with the private sector too suspicious of government intentions to invest, while controls that are not universal in coverage would lose effect because they leave too many opportunities for evasion.

> (Clawson 1988: 388)

In other words, a decade after the revolution the Islamic government could contemplate the implementation of only two macro-economic policy options: to privatise or to centralise. As we have seen, direct control of the economy by the state was the instinctive thrust of the Moussavi governments' policies, evolving as these had with the revolution itself; yet, as Prime Minister Moussavi himself had to acknowledge, to get out of its current predicament, structural adjustment policies, or to 'make room for market forces', as Clawson puts it, were the only realistic policy choices remaining open to the government.

In the end, even though the revolution had broken the power of the Pahlavi ruling class and of its Western economic partners in the Iranian economy, the successive Moussavi governments had not managed to create an alternative economic system to that founded by the Shah and were passing on to the Rafsanjani administration an economy still very much dependent on the West and featuring the same ills as other medium-size Third World economies.

5 State and economy under Rafsanjani

For the sake of the reconstruction of this vast country and for the renovation of damages we are prepared to accept the participation of friends and
governments who will deal with us . . . without any expansionist and
colonialist motives.

(Hojjatoleslam Rafsanjani, February 1989)

The new administration of President Rafsanjani took over executive responsibility for the republic amidst grave economic problems, coupled by
enormous pressure from the populace for economic rejuvenation and an end
to austerity. Many of the regime's economic difficulties on the eve of the
Iran–Iraq war cease-fire were outlined in the previous chapter and do not
require further attention here. However, for the sake of gaining a perspective
on the task facing the Rafsanjani administration let us bear in mind that during
the period 1977/8 to 1989/90 income per head of population dropped by
nearly 45 per cent (Nakhjavani 1992: 14), from 107,042 rials (in 1975 rial
prices) to 58,560 rials, and that the supply of food for the population had
become a major issue for the government. During the same period, imports
of wheat had gone up from nearly 1.2 million tons to 5.3 million tons, while
consumption had increased from 5.9 million tons to 10.6 million tons.
Domestic production of wheat in 1989/90 (having increased substantially in
the preceding three years) was virtually the same as it had been in 1977/8,
almost exactly 5.5 million tons (Haqvoroody 1993: 99).

The Islamic Republic under the executive leadership of President Rafsanjani tried to put an end to the search for revolutionary alternatives in economic
development strategies, and opted instead to pursue economic restructuring
policies consistent with those of the capitalist Western and Third World
countries. Thus, if there ever existed an 'Islamic' model of development in
revolutionary Iran, it was shelved after 1989. In the words of Foreign Minister
Velayati, 'economic considerations overshadow political priorities' (*MEED*
14 June 1991). As will be shown later, Hojjatoleslam Rafsanjani's govern-

ment has tried to put behind it the populism of the 1980s, and has opted for tighter integration into the world capitalist system, aiming to reconstruct the shattered economy in the context of greater private domestic and foreign participation. In essence, the new policies are deepening the capitalist enterprise, and fuelling the profit-making 'spirit' of private entrepreneurs. This, of course, has an equally significant impact on the balance of power among the social classes comprising the Iranian 'community' – a reference to the combination of all Iranians living in and outside Iran.

As will be illustrated below, the economic reforms proposed and implemented by Rafsanjani's first administration have been significant and are likely to continue in his second term of office. Although the economic policies of the Second Republic are consistent with international trends towards economic liberalisation, in the case of Iran the mix of political and economic, domestic and international inputs provide a useful backdrop for theoretical construction in conjunction with empirical analysis of economic reform and political change, not purely because the Islamic Republic has claimed to be revolutionary in North–South terms, but also because the revolution was meant to be unique in its blend of Islamic political and economic development.

On the constructive side, the continuing presence of the private sector, in the light of public sector failures, meant that when the need for reconstruction was recognised in the late 1980, a radical change in elite thinking could develop which determined to utilise the potential of the private sector as the instrument of recovery, in the process swinging economic policy in favour of the free-market alternative. As Rafsanjani had identified in December 1988, while the Moussavi government was still attempting to resolve the economic crisis,

> To face these difficulties, we have to take certain measures. First, to increase the country's production and in order to implement this we should inject the capital which is at present accumulated in the private sector. However, these people have no confidence; most of them are afraid to show their wealth.
>
> (*The Echo of Iran* 5 January 1989: 15)

The potential for redirected economic policy which emerged in the post-war period was recognised, again by Rafsanjani. He said then: 'The concentration of affairs within the state was a necessity during the war, a necessity which does not exist any more' (SWB, ME/0341, 22 December 1988). Rafsanjani's rise to executive power in August 1989 was to provide the opportunity for him to adjust economic policy to suit the new circumstances. This necessitated a greater role for the private sector (*Abrar* 7 December 1992). In the words of Ali Naqi Khamoushi, head of the Iran

Chamber of Commerce, Industries and Mines: 'The economic policy of the government is based on its five-year development plan and is designed to encourage the private sector to make more investments than the public sector' (SWB, ME/W0194, 27 August 1991). Rafsanjani's choice of Ministers indicates his administration's strong tendency towards technocracy, but it also highlights a measure of continuity with the past. Many of the individuals chosen to serve in the 'reconstruction Cabinet' of Rafsanjani had held Ministerial or similar posts under Premier Moussavi. The point is illustrated in Table 18. Such continuity could provide underlying executive stability while he pursued policies of economic innovation.

Table 18 Continuity in government: a comparison of personnel, 1984 and 1989

Name	Government	
	Moussavi's 1984	*Rafsanjani's 1989*
G. Aqazadeh	Supervisor, PM's Office	Oil Minister
H. Habibi	Justice Minister	Vice-President
M. Khatami	Islamic Guidance Minister	Islamic Guidance Minister
B. Namdar-Zanganeh	Construction Crusade Minister	Energy Minister
M. Nezhad-Hosseinian	Roads and Transport Minister	Heavy Industries Minister
M. Reyshahri	Intelligence Minister	Prosecutor-General
A. Velayati	Foreign Minister	Foreign Minister

Sources: MERI Report (1985); IRNA.

A combination of factors, including the death of the patriarch, the institutional weakness of 'radical' factions and the emergence of a united leadership around the Rafsanjani–Khamenei axis, allowed the exploration and implementation of a radical economic strategy by the new government which replaced the spasmodic economic liberalisms of the last decade with a policy of economic liberalisation, privatisation and deregulation. The strategy was also to include private and public bilateral and multilateral foreign participation as sources to be tapped for Iran's economic recovery (as embodied in the new Five Year Development Plan, which was approved by the Majlis on 11 Bahman 1368 Iranian calendar and when after consideration by the Council of Guardians, became implementable at the end of 1368) (1989/90).

The plan forecast an average annual GDP growth rate of 8.1 per cent (about 7.9 per cent per year excluding hydrocarbons) and a *per capita* production increase of 4.9 per cent a year on average (Business International 1991). In terms of sectoral expansion, mining was projected to lead all other sectors, with an average annual growth rate of 19.5 per cent, followed by construction

Table 19 Government revenue and expenditures under the plan (billion rials)

Period	Budget deficit	Government revenue	Government expenditure
1989/90	1,298	3,150	4,448
1993/94	92.5	6,442	6,535

Source: Plan and Budget Ministry (1989).

(14.5 per cent) and manufacturing (14.2 per cent) (ibid.). On investment and employment the plan envisaged dramatic growth. An average annual investment growth rate of 11.6 per cent during the plan period was designed to reverse the total investment-to-GDP ratio of the last Moussavi government, raising the investment component from 14.5 per cent in 1989/90 to 17 per cent in 1993/4. According to the plan's predictions, by 1994 private sector investment would account for 52.8 per cent of total investment in the country (ibid.). On employment too, the plan forecast major developments: the creation of 394,000 new jobs annually (a total of two million new jobs) and an average annual increase of 5.2 per cent in per capita labour productivity. Per capita income was planned to reach 543,000 rials by 1994, an annual rise of 4.9 per cent. As another of its main objectives, the government set itself the task of reducing its budget deficit from 51 per cent to 1.5 per cent by the end of the plan. Though the Rafsanjani plan drew heavily on the Moussavi development plan of 1989, the new plan was much more ambitious in scope and bolder than the revised, original Moussavi plan of 1983/4–1988/9.

As mentioned earlier, as the main plank of its policies towards fulfilling the plan's objectives, the government advocated, and indeed presupposed, an active role for the private sector; hardly surprising, in view of Tehran's new priorities, but again reference to just one fact should make clear the necessity for the government to divest itself of some of its economic responsibilities if the reform package was to prove effective. By 1989, on an annual basis, the large public sector companies had come to account for around 20 per cent of the country's GDP and approximately 60 per cent of the government's receipts and payments (Business International 1991). These enterprises' inefficiency, their lack of profitability and continued dependence on (expensive) intermediate imports acted as a constant drain on government resources and tended to reduce the latter's power to deal with the economic crisis which it had inherited from the Moussavi government.

ECONOMIC REFORM STRATEGY OF PRESIDENT RAFSANJANI

The President's strategy was a complex one. It aimed, first and foremost, at economic reconstruction and expansion of output. His government was aware, however, that in order to achieve these goals it would need to release the private sector's energies and resources. Economic liberalisation and the retraction of the state were now regarded as the keys to economic renewal. The strategy was the releasing of Iranian private sector resources (estimated at billions of dollars in 'hoarded' capital) and allowing capital to flow into activities so far forbidden to it. The share of the private sector in the country's economy was projected to rise from the 25–30 per cent in the late 1980s to 75–80 per cent in the course of the 1990s, thus reversing the trend prevalent in Iran since the first oil boom of 1973. Under a plan drawn up by the first Rafsanjani government, some 800 publicly owned enterprises were earmarked for privatisation. A number of serious problems, however, had to be overcome before privatisation and liberalisation could take effect. In the words of an official report

> many of the firms [with the potential to be transferred to the private sector] have weak management structures and too many employees . . . which because of the current [labour] laws cannot be sacked very easily, and this problem, irrespective of their potential profitability, reduces the attraction of these firms to the private sector . . . Therefore it is essential that before privatisation of such firms, some changes to their structures be carried out.
>
> (Economic Affairs Secretariat 1991: 52)

It is possible to identify the main features of the administration's open door policy. In total, there are 11 elements to the economic reform process:

1 Privatisation of industry, mines and other industrial and non-industrial productive activities.
2 Deregulation of economic activity and of banking and financial services.
3 Activation, expansion and modernisation of the Tehran stock exchange.
4 Encouragement of inward direct foreign investment.
5 Foreign borrowing.
6 Establishment of free trade zones across the country.
7 Devaluation of the rial.
8 Gradual reduction of subsidies.
9 Liberalisation of trade and returning it to the private sector.
10 Freeing of prices; and last but not least.
11 Return of exiled capital and (not inconsiderable) expertise.

The main planks of the reform process will be examined in some detail here and the process of policy changes outlined. The final part of this chapter analyses the impact of these reforms on the Iranian state and its profile, as well as on the social structure of the country and on the economy as a whole.

The revival of the Tehran stock exchange was one of the main components of the liberalisation strategy. It aimed to raise investment capital as well as to encourage private sector participation in the country's reconstruction efforts. The Economic Council thus directed public organisations to offer more shares on the exchange in the units affiliated to them. At the same time, it began considering reforms of the taxation system, and of the commercial, accounting and legal regulations, to ease the increased transactions taking place on the stock exchange (SWB, ME/W0106, 5 December 1989). Any company with more than a hundred shares was allowed to register on the stock exchange under an Economics and Finance Ministry directive in 1988.

The number of transactions on the stock exchange began to rise in 1984, reaching 10 billion rials in 1988. In 1989/90, 11.13 billion rials' worth of stock was traded – still only a fraction of the highest recorded value of transactions, totalling 44 billion rials in 1977 (SWB, ME/W0106, 5 December 1989). The number of companies offering their shares went up from 39 in 1988 to 54 a year later, and by the end of 1991 the number had reached 121 (SWB, ME/W0124, 17 April 1990; SWB, ME/W0210, 17 December 1991). To encourage further trading, the Central Bank offered 100,000 of its shares in the National Iranian Investment Company on the exchange in December 1989. It was announced in November 1990 that 49 per cent of the shares in the industries affiliated to the National Iranian Industries Organisation were to be sold off in the form of securities and bonds. 365,000 shares in 13 industries, worth 1,128 billion rials, were by then already denationalised (SWB, ME/W0153, 6 November 1990). Shares of 14 other units were to be sold off in the same fashion.

The speed of denationalisation accelerated in 1991 and 1992. It was announced in May 1991 that the NIIO would sell 100 billion rials' worth of shares in state-owned companies to the private sector (SWB, ME/W0180, 21 May 1991). It was further announced in August 1991 that 120 billion rials' worth of shares in firms and factories controlled by the NIIO would be put on sale through the stock exchange by the end of March 1992 (SWB, ME/W0193, 20 August 1991). By the same date, the stock exchange was to handle 200 billion rials' worth of shares, including 120 billion rials' worth owned by the NIIO: the 1992/3 budget envisaged that the NIIO and the Organisation for the Promotion and Renovation of Industries would be selling 154 billion rials' and 127 billion rials' worth of their shares respectively through the stock exchange, a total of 281 billion rials for the Iranian year beginning March 1992 (SWB, ME/W0209, 10 December 1991). During 1992/3 the Bank of Industry and Mines planned to turn 35 of its affiliated

factories over to the private sector through the stock exchange, and to sell
direct to private sector interests another 60 such production units (SWB,
ME/W0228, 28 April 1992).

The net result of these developments was that total stock exchange
transactions for the year March 1990–March 1991 reached 65 billion rials,
the highest figure recorded since its operations began in 1967 (SWB,
ME/W0193, 20 August 1991). Figures for 1991 show that by October some
150 billion rials' worth of shares had changed hands (though in his budget
speech President Rafsanjani put the March-to-November figure at 301 billion
rials), 102.1 billion rials of which were from public sector companies and
government organisations (a total of 16.2 million shares) (SWB, ME/W0199,
1 October 1991). Some 50 per cent of all the shares made available on the
stock exchange belonged to companies formerly controlled by the NIIO. By
the end of March 1991, 77 factories had been sold to the private sector, from
which the government had earned some 37 billion rials (SWB, ME/W0195,
3 September 1991). It is perhaps a measure of the weakness of private capital
formation in Iran during the 1980s that throughout the activation of the stock
market in the early 1990s it was government and parastatal agencies which
were the most active in offering shares on the stock exchange. Indicative of
this trend are the data in Table 20: during 1991/2 millions of tradable shares
on the bourse were offered as part of the denationalisation process, belonging
to firms formerly under the control of various Ministries, state-owned banks
and holding companies and revolutionary foundations.

Table 20 Shares offered on the stock exchange by the state sector, 1991–2

Offering agency	No. of shares offered (millions)	Value (billion rials)
NIIO	28	201
State banks	16	103
IDRO	3.4	29
Disabled and deprived foundations	0.61	4.6
Martyrs' foundation	0.19	1.7

Source: Statement of the Central Bank Governor (SWB, ME/W0228, 28 April 1992).

Sales of other government assets have included the privatisation of all
mines except those regarded as holding 'strategic reserves'. To encourage the
private sector the Supreme Council of Mines extended the time limit on mine
extraction from six to 15 years. In addition, Iran's National Steel Company
announced that it was willing and prepared to give financial assistance to the
private sector with regard to the exploitation of mines. In this way the state

is subsidising the re-entry of the private sector into large-scale mining and mining-related operations. Within the first 17 months of this policy, over 150 mines extracting coal and various minerals were transferred to the private sector (SWB, ME/W0161, 8 January 1991). All disused copper mines and identified copper seams were to be likewise transferred, and all coal, industrial dolomite and chalk mines to be privatised. In total, more than a billion rials had been invested in mining by the private sector by the end of August 1991 (SWB, ME/W0193, 20 August 1991). By May 1991, 4.4 billion rials had been raised by the Ministry of Mines and Metals through transferring a large number of mines to the private sector (SWB, ME/W0181, 28 May 1991). By July 1992 as many as 1,400 operational mines (out of 2,100 mines in the country) had been transferred to the private sector, and the remaining 700 mines were in the process of being privatised.

The trend was to continue in the transfer of heavy and other industries to the private sector. Vice-President Zanjani announced in December 1989 that the government should handle only big strategic industries, thus indicating that the rest of the industrial sector was to be made open to private investment and control. By the end of 1990 the status of some 800 manufacturing and industrial companies was being studied by the Economics and Finance Ministry, with a view to offering them to the private sector (SWB, ME/W0149, 9 October 1990). A major development in this process was the Cabinet decision of 30 January 1992 to privatise Iran's main car-making and car assembly industries, and a number of other heavy industries nationalised in 1979. The pre-revolution shareholders in these concerns were to receive compensation from the government (*MEED* 14 February 1992). The 10 car makers to be privatised (virtually the entire national capacity) were: Iran Kaveh, Iran Khodrow, Iran Vanet, Khavar, Khodrowsazan, Moratab, Pars Khodrow, SAIPA, Shahab Khodrow, and Zamyad. The four heavy industries were named as: Ahvaz Rolling Mill, Arak Aluminium Rolling Mill, Arak Steel Company, and Iran Marine Industries. In April 1993 two important companies owned by NIIO, Pars International Products (valued at 11.5 billion rials) and Hakim Pharmaceutical (valued at 7.5 billion rials), were sold to private investors (*MEED* 7 May 1993). During the first plan period a number of large industrial projects initiated by the public sector were also to be handed over to the private sector upon completion, in addition to nine petrochemical projects. As another part of this process the private sector was encouraged to take over the national electricity distribution system and to invest in power generation as well (*MEED* 21 May 1993).

In addition, the private sector was being encouraged to undertake further investments in new construction and industrial plant. According to Minister of Industries Nematzadeh, 38,000 agreements in principle had been reached with the private sector by mid-1990 (SWB, ME/W0134, 26 June 1990). In

1990 private sector investments in heavy industry reached 300 billion rials, indicating the rapid response of the private sector to these opportunities and the sheer scale of private capital which had previously lain unutilised (SWB, ME/W0173, 2 May 1991); by March 1992 the Heavy Industries Ministry had received some 1,416 applications (with a projected investment value of 1,364 billion rials) from the private sector for investment in heavy industry (SWB, ME/W0229, 5 May 1992).

It was announced in November 1991 that the Iranian fisheries industry was to be privatised as well, including the catching, packing and export of all types of edible and non-edible fish (SWB, ME/W0206, 19 November 1991). Some months after this announcement the Construction Jihad Ministry expressed its readiness to transfer to the private sector some of its considerable assets, including milk and meat production industries, haymaking, livestock breeding, farms and pasture land, forestry resources and fisheries (SWB, ME/W0239, 14 July 1992), the total value of which could run into many billions of rials. In addition, the Supreme Administrative Council pressed ahead with encouraging private sector participation in many other fields hitherto regarded as being within the exclusive domain of the state sector. Activities such as road and railway construction, oil refining, the building of airports, the running of ports and handling their operations were new areas opening up to the private sector.

Monetary reform, a cornerstone of government policy and the objective of improving Iran's international competitiveness were to be reached through the formulation of a three-tier flexible foreign exchange rate policy (with a view to establishing a single 'realistic' exchange rate before the end of the plan period) and the eventual abandonment of government subsidies, estimated at \$4 billion in 1990 (*MEED* 2 August 1991). During 1992 much of the monetary strategy debate focused on the utility of the three-tier exchange rate system ('official' rate: 70 rials = \$1; 'competitive' rate: 600 rials = \$1; 'floating' rate: 1,600 rials = \$1), the implications of the *de facto* devaluation of the rial for the economy as a whole and for producers in particular, and the need for the introduction of a single exchange rate. From mid-1992 the plan for a single (market-derived) exchange rate for the rial was unveiled and on 21 March 1993 the rial was officially devalued, by 95.6 per cent (*MEED* 23 April 1993), and a single floating exchange rate was introduced. The national currency became fully convertible on 13 April 1993. One link in this chain was forged on 23 October 1991, from which date it became possible for branches of Iranian banks in other Persian Gulf countries to accept the rial as a creditworthy currency (SWB, ME/W0201, 15 October 1991).

It was argued by many government and Central Bank officials and Iranian economists at the time of devaluation (*Kayhan International* 29 March 1993) that an overvalued rial and the existence of the multiple exchange rate system (a government-controlled rate for essential and agricultural goods, a second for transactions in the production sector and a floating rate for trade and services) had not only caused investors confusion about government policy but had also caused bureaucratic corruption in the machinery of government. Furthermore, officials argued that the creation of a single rate was likely to increase competitiveness and end 'irrational support of the [inefficient] domestic producer' (in the words of the head of the Plan and Budget Organisation) (SWB, ME/W0265, 19 January 1993). It would furthermore absorb some of the excess liquidity in the economy and accelerate the fulfilment of the plan's objectives in that it would enable further privatisation and economic liberalisation and attract foreign investors.

However, devaluation was likely to increase unemployment, cause tremendous hardships for those on fixed and low incomes (including the 2 million in the bureaucracy) and fuel inflation. That it would enrich the government at the expense of the private consumer (as the government was the main source of foreign exchange, which was now to be sold at the market rate) was not overlooked by the critics of the policy. Some of the devaluation policy's pitfalls were recognised as long ago as 1980. The main concern then was that 'a major devaluation of the Rial, as is logically demanded, would only raise the cost of imports and be of little value for exports, considering the strength of demand for oil and the small trickle of non-oil goods involved' (Whitely 1980: 157). This reality has not changed a great deal since and the view that devaluation was likely to cause great problems for the economy was forcefully expressed by many in and outside Iranian government circles.

In conjunction with the above policies, the government sought to improve the economy's international competitiveness, as well as to ease foreign trade by the private sector, in the first instance by easing restrictions on imports, thereby developing domestic competition and providing the raw materials and intermediate goods necessary for expansion of Iranian manufacturing and industrial productive capabilities. In addition, private sector involvement in importing essential and consumer goods was seen as an efficient means of alleviating shortages in the economy. To this end, some $1.6 billion worth of permits to import basic goods was given to the private sector in 1990 alone (SWB, ME/W0159, 18 December 1990). Exporters were also offered a variety of direct and indirect incentives. The establishment in 1991 of a new export promotion bank was another feature of the export drive. With an initial capital of 50 billion rials (raised to 100 billion rials in July 1993), the bank's brief included providing facilities for foreign buyers of Iran's commodities and to use the expertise of 'international banking consultants to advise [Iranian] exporters' on ways of improving their products (SWB, ME/W0194, 27 August 1991).

As well as emphasising Iran's traditional exports, the government sought to encourage private sector participation in new areas of exports. Incentives included the return of up to 11 per cent of foreign exchange designated for exports to the exporter, securing foreign exchange for private sector industrialists (on the same basis as for the public sector), and giving priority support to those industries which export their products (in exchange for machinery and industrial raw material) (SWB, ME/W0205, 12 November 1991). The Heavy Industries Minister encouraged Iranian private sector contractors, producers and contract engineers to take part in international tenders, both at home and abroad. They were also encouraged to participate in joint ventures with foreign firms engaged in projects under the Five Year Development Plan.

The international competitiveness strategy envisaged direct foreign investment in the economy. The government planned to raise $20 billion in foreign capital investment in the course of the Five Year Plan, later readjusted to $27 billion in foreign finance and investment, including $3 billion of foreign investment in heavy industries during the plan period. To facilitate this, restrictions on direct foreign investment in key sectors (like petrochemicals, power generation and distribution) were lifted and the country's foreign investment law was reformulated to allow up to 49 per cent equity holding by the foreign partner (from the 35 per cent ceiling allowed under the Pahlavi regime), an historically unprecedented level for Iran. Dr Nourbakhsh, the then Economics and Finance Minister, stated quite unequivocally that in the country's foreign investment law 'no limits exist' on the level of foreign investors' equity holding and that 'this level is set by the Supreme Council for Investment, which is comprised of a few Cabinet Ministers' (in other words, the setting of levels for foreign investment is an executive decision and not a matter for the Majlis, nor is it to be determined by the constitution) (quoted in *Ayneh Eghtesad* September–October 1992: 11). As we have seen, even the 49 per cent ceiling on foreign equity holdings was being questioned by the executive branch. Dr Mohammad M. Navab-Motlaq, head of the foreign investment division in the Ministry of Economics and Finance, said in this regard, 'if, under present conditions and in view of our foreign currency needs, we try and impose the 49 per cent [legal limit] on foreign partners involved in investment projects, we would probably not be able to fulfil the country's total investment requirements' (quoted in ibid.: 12).

In this endeavour the executive found powerful allies from within the business community and among their allies in the regime. One such ally has been Mr Khamoushi, an MP and president of the Iran Chamber of Commerce, Industries and Mines since 1981. He stated in 1991 that 'shortage of domestic capital and the absence of essential technology [in Iranian industry] are the most important factors in making the need for foreign investment essential' (ibid.). The republic's ambassador to Germany, Hussein Moussavian, went a step further and announced that not only did no legal limits exist on foreign investment in Iran, but 'many provisions for such investments, such as unlimited transfer of annual profits in hard currency, unlimited transfer of capital in hard currency' and legal protection and rights equal to those offered to domestic investors were being formulated, in addition to the right to full compensation in hard currency in the event of nationalisation of assets (ibid.).

Despite Article 81 of the constitution, banning the establishment of companies and institutions by foreign interests in Iran, the government was determined to bring Iran's foreign investment law and attitude towards foreign capital in line with other medium-sized industrialising economies. The executive tried to accomplish this by bearing the onus of interpretation and determination of a coherent policy about direct foreign investment on its own shoulders and attempting to establish good relations with foreign interests. Under the foreign investment law adopted by the government, investments which are registered with the foreign investment office at the Ministry of Economics and Finance will enjoy full government protection. However, this office will only register and protect those investment projects which give the Iranian partner a 51 per cent holding. That said, the government has also been encouraging foreign investors who do not seek registration at the foreign investment office and prefer 100 per cent ownership of their assets. These investors also will be permitted to transfer their assets and profits overseas in hard currency (determined by the 'floating rate', which existed before the rationalisation of rates and devaluation of the rial). Much of the investment in Iran's newly established free trade zones (FTZ) were envisaged as of this nature (see below).

The internationalisation of Iran's industry and economy received another boost through the establishment of two free trade zones in the Persian Gulf and a number of others in the north, west and south-east of the country, though this measure did not receive unqualified support from the law-makers: the FTZs were not put on a proper legal footing until the summer of 1993 and even then the Council of Guardians objected to them (on constitutional grounds), passing the matter back to the Majlis for amendment (*MEED* 16 July 1993). The Bill was finally ratified in September 1993. President Rafsanjani reflected the views of his administration in saying that the FTZs 'can serve as a bridge between domestic and foreign industries' (SWB, ME/W0149, 9 October 1990). The Kish island FTZ is Iran's first experiment with control-free offshore economic activities.

Like FTZs elsewhere in the world, the Kish FTZ is designed to attract Iranian and foreign investment for both industrial and non-industrial activities. It offers income tax exemptions, customs duties holidays of 20 years, subsidies towards residents' utility bills, and expenses for transport and other public facilities. Qeshm, the other important FTZ, is also receiving attention.

The former director of the Qeshm FTZ was particularly active in trying to attract foreign investment to Qeshm. In a meeting with 60 German industrialists in January 1992, Shams Ardakani listed the advantages to German investors of investing in Qeshm. These included: low energy costs ($0.02 per kWh), no income tax and no duties on imports and exports, and the bonus of a 30 per cent reduction in the profit tax. He added: 'Through the Qeshm FTZ international industrialists and traders can reach the markets of Iran, Pakistan, Afghanistan, the former republics of the Soviet Union and also the Arab states of the Persian Gulf in the shortest time and with minimal expense' (*Kayhan Havai* 29 January 1992). Heavy industry activity had already begun by 1991, with German, Italian and Japanese companies leading the way. Five other FTZs, Sirjan, Sarakhs, Chah Bahar, Jolfa and Sofian, became operational in 1993, and the oil city of Khoramshahr joined the list of FTZ cities in early 1994, most aiming initially to act as a focal point for through traffic and storage of cargo and facilitating trade.

A final point regarding the integrationist moves of the Iranian government is the boosting of Iran's IMF quota to 360 million SDRs ($850 million), said by the then Governor of the Central Bank, Mohammed Hussein Adeli, to have the advantage of improving Iranian voting rights (and influence) in the IMF, until then regarded as a bastion of the 'satanic' powers. Related to this is Iran's application in 1993 to join one of the most important institutions of the international capitalist system, the General Agreement on Tariffs and Trade.

Two other aspects of the economic liberalisation drive in Iran need further comment. In the first instance, unlike economic liberalisation attempts in the West and elsewhere in the developing world, under the first Rafsanjani administration tax reductions were not considered at the outset as an essential part of the package in Iranian policy reforms. On the contrary, the government has emphasised the importance of taxes, (estimated at 11 billion rials in the Five Year Development plan), as a source of revenue (even more important than hydrocarbon exports) for its activities and has been keen to bring a more efficient tax collection service into being. According to official figures, taxation income was to rise from 986.2 billion rials in 1988/9 to 3,180 billion rials in 1993/4 (see Table 21). Figures since 1989 point to the seriousness of the government in pursuit of this policy and its successes: between 1989/90 and 1991/2 taxation revenues as a proportion of current government expenditures had risen from 28.8 per cent to 40 per cent (SWB, ME/W0225, 7 April 1992).

In planning to raise taxes, the government risked its friendship with the 'Islamic free-marketers' and some alienation from business and private taxpayers, but nonetheless has been trying to fulfil its stated objective of maximising the use of domestic resources for reconstruction. Bearing in mind

Table 21 Government revenues from taxation (billion rials)

Year	Tax revenue	Year	Tax revenue
1973/4	132.6	1985/6	1,035.5
1975/6	273.4	1989/90	1,150.0
1977/8	449.2	1990/1	1,688.0
1980/1	340.4	1991/2	2,097.0
1982/3	614.7	1992/3	2,592.0
1984/5	900.1	1993/4	3,180.0

Source: Economic Affairs Secretariat (1991).

Note: Revenues for 1989/90–1993/4 are the plan projections.

the nature of the system as it exists in Iran, to the extent that the government has sought to raise the private sector's stake in the well-being of the republic, representation through taxation appears a logical position to adopt. Again, a combination of political considerations and economic factors seems to have played their part in formulating policy objectives in the Islamic Republic; policies which, I would argue, in reality tend to contradict the conventional wisdom about the 'global mechanisms' of economic liberalisation and deregulation strategies. For instance, tax reforms were introduced some two years into the plan period and then only in stages: a new law on direct taxes (enacted to take effect from 21 March 1992) raised exemption ceilings quite substantially for public and private sector employees (from 70,000 rials to 200,000 rials per month for public sector employees) and for married couples and unmarried individuals (SWB, ME/W0219, 25 February 1992). Other changes to the fiscal regime included the raising of tax exemption thresholds to stand at annual income levels of up to 300 million rials, the lowering of taxable income rates (from 75 per cent for the top rate to 54 per cent) and reductions in inheritance tax (SWB, ME/W0223, 24 March 1992).

The second additional aspect of the liberalisation process needing comment is the position of banks and the banking sector. The state seems reluctant to denationalise the financial sector, taken over in 1979. This is partly because it can use the banking, insurance and other financial institutions to exercise some control over the activities of the expanding private sector. Since the banks are heavy investors in industry, state control over them lends the government a backdoor influence upon the direction of private sector investment and other economic activity in the country. In the absence of other mechanisms, and as the pace of deregulation accelerates, retaining control of the economy through finance capital has become an increasingly attractive option for the government. Significant deregulation in the operation of banks, however, has already been introduced. From 23 October 1991 banks have been authorised to open foreign currency accounts in both their national and their overseas branches, and pay interest (called 'profit' locally) on all such accounts. The rate of interest is set on a daily basis by the Central Bank, according to the deputy director of the bank (*Kayhan Havai* 30 October 1991). Customers can also switch money between their rial and foreign currency accounts without prior permission, without forfeiting the interest due on such transactions.

The drive to attract private resources has led Iranian officials to encourage the return to Iran of capital-rich and technocratic exiles. In effect, the first post-Khomeini government has envisaged the return of the former *comprador* bourgeoisie and its technocratic facilitators. This may be because foreign capital would also prefer to have the *ancien* class back. The retrenchment of the state continues with the promise that much of the former owners' assets and property will be returned to them when they undertake to invest in economic reconstruction. Many of these assets were placed under the control of revolutionary organisations and foundations back in the early 1980s. What impact this will have on the nature of political power in Iran and on the country's class structure remains uncertain. What is clear, however, is that the return of capital-laden exiles and a large section of the Western-oriented middle class will have a direct impact on the economy, the direction of economic growth and the satisfaction of luxury and consumer demand as opposed to essential goods. After a decade of active state intervention in the economy, the government policy of privatisation and deregulation has thus shifted the balance of power in the economy decisively away from the deprived and towards the bourgeoisie and its middle class allies. This trend is reinforced through deregulation of the prices of foodstuffs and other goods and services.

The removal of barriers to capital accumulation can and does lead to the emergence of new capital. If, therefore, the exiled bourgeois class and its entourage do not heed the government call and stay away, and the privatisation strategy continues, then in essence the state will be midwife to the birth of a new industrial bourgeoisie. Rising in part from the ranks of the rich and highly successful commercial bourgeoisie, this faction of the capitalist class would probably be the closest to what could come to be regarded as 'national' in a country such as Iran. If all does not go according to plan, in other words, the Islamic state, with its economic liberalisation and deregulation policies, could be laying the foundations for the rise of a new ruling class. It is quite clear, therefore, that in the dynamic and fluid social structure of Iran (and many other late-industrialising countries besides), the state – even in its efforts at minimalism – is not a neutral instrument. At the very least, it will continue to shape the politico-economic structures of Iranian society even as its own form is changing.

The implication of this argument is not only that the 'Bonapartist' state can behave in ways hitherto regarded as contradictory to its nature, but that the Third World state is not the domain of one type of property only, even though it may well be 'representing' particular interests. Indeed, the Iranian state has shown that it can forge new alliances with an exiled and disregarded ruling class, besides being able to facilitate the germination of a new one. At critical junctures, furthermore, we can see that the state acts against specific interests in order to secure the well-being of the entire system.

ECONOMIC DIFFICULTIES AND ACHIEVEMENTS, 1989–94

Few Iranian policy-makers, least of all President Rafsanjani, had expected the economic reform process to be painless and without pitfalls. Despite the guarded warnings, however, few were prepared for the economic difficulties that accompanied it, worsened by the drastic decline in oil prices after Operation Desert Storm. By the third year of the plan it was clear that the government had a long way to go to surpass the economic development figures of the 1970s (Lailaz 1993). This was recognised by the President himself, when he stated (in 1993) that Iran's problems could only be solved within a 10–year time-frame, starting in 1989 (SWB, ME/W0276, 6 April 1993). Nonetheless, economic growth was rapid in the early 1990s, standing at 8 per cent on average during the First Five Year Plan period. A growth rate of 3 per cent in 1989/90 was followed by a 12.1 per cent growth rate in 1990/1 and 9.9 per cent in 1991/2, according to the President (SWB, ME/W0277, 13 April 1993). This put Iran amongst the top five countries in terms of GNP growth rates in the early 1990s (*Kayhan Havai*, 19 January 1994). Additionally, the government was successful in reducing the population growth rate from over 2.3 per cent a year to around 1.8 per cent by the mid-1990s.

Other areas of success were the government's ability to generate revenues to meet its expenditures. Its income has risen from 49.4 per cent of expenditures in 1988/9 to 86.9 per cent and government borrowing from the banking sector dropped from 47.7 per cent of expenditures in 1989/90 to 11.8 per cent in 1991/2. Furthermore, current expenditure dropped from 80.6 per cent of total expenditures in 1988/9 to 68.4 per cent in 1991/2, and in the same period development expenditures rose from 19.4 per cent to 31.6 per cent of government outlays (*Resalat* 30 March 1992). Record output levels in agriculture were also set (in 1992/3) and non-oil exports reached $3 billion to $4 billion by the end of March 1993 (SWB, ME/W0276, 6 April 1993; *Kayhan Havai* 16 February 1994). In addition, the government had managed to reduce the unemployment rate to 11.4 per cent of the work force by the last quarter of 1993 (*Kayhan Havai* 29 September 1993), and to under 10 per cent by the end of 1994. Under the First Five Year Plan unemployment was targeted to come down from 15.4 per cent of the work force to 13.4 per cent. Finally, in the course of the First Five Year Plan the government met one of the main planks of its reform strategy: its current deficit was reduced to only $756 million in 1992, from $7.1 billion in 1991 (IBRD 1993).

Iran's economic problems began to mount from 1991, however. Although total oil export income during the first 52 months of the First Plan period stood at $61.7 billion, higher than the target of $60.2 billion (*MEED* 27 August 1993), the crisis was triggered by high imports (totalling $47 billion to $50 billion between 1989/91 and 1992/3) (*MEED* 23 April 1993) and the unexpected drop in the oil price, particularly as in the aftermath of Operation Desert Storm Tehran had calculated its expenditures on an oil price of about $30 per barrel (*The Middle East* January 1994). In the event oil prices dropped sharply from 1992 onwards, hovering at around $14 per barrel towards the end of 1993, as against the OPEC target price of $21 per barrel.

Currency devaluation in 1993 and sharp tariff cuts began hurting local industry and brought protests by many industrialists and even the Minister

Table 22 Iran's vital economic statistics, 1989–91 ($ billion)

(a) *Foreign trade*

	Exports	Imports
1989/90	13.0	14.7
1990/1	18.8	20.5
1991/2	18.4	28.5

(b) *Foreign currency income*

	Planned amount	Actual
1989/90	17.2	11.9
1990/1	17.8	17.5
1991/2	21.0	16.1

Source: Iran Farda (January–February 1993).

of Heavy Industry (*MEED* 23 July 1993). To put the devaluation in perspective, it was calculated that, owing to devaluation of the rial, an Iranian investor would have needed to find 1,400 million to 1,500 million rials for $1 million worth of industrial imports, compared with 70 million to 80 million rials before devaluation (*Iran Farda* November–December 1992). A sharp drop in imports, to no more than $10 billion in 1993 (*Nimrooz* 31 December 1993), also adversely affected the country's productive units (which are extremely import-dependent) and consumers in general. With devaluation, factories began facing acute shortages of cash and raw materials; factory shutdowns have in turn led to workers being laid off and have caused severe hardships among the low-income strata of society.

By mid-1992 Iran found itself in unfamiliar territory: receiving substantial loans from the World Bank and carrying a high foreign (short-term and medium-term) debt and falling in arrears with its repayments. Iran's total foreign debt was about $30 billion by the end of 1993, according to the Ministry of Economics and Finance (*MEED* 24 December 1993). Another source of concern relating to the debt problem was the need for extra foreign currency in order to meet the debt interest. In 1992 the servicing of Iran's debt of $14.2 billion (according to World Bank estimates) stood at $810 million (IBRD 1993). A debt of $30 billion, however, Azimi estimates, would cost Iran about $4 billion a year in debt servicing (Azimi 1992). Debt servicing thus became a major drain on the government's dwindling financial resources.

The crisis attained such proportions that towards the end of 1993 the rial was devalued by more than 8 per cent, to stand at $1=1,730 rials (*MEED* 3 December 1993), reaching a record low of 1,920 against the dollar by the end of November. In mid-December another record low was set when the value of the rial dropped to 2,190 against the dollar (*MEED* 24 December 1993). The currency crisis compelled the government to reintroduce limits on the banks' hard currency sales in order to stabilise the rial and conserve foreign exchange. At the same time, a number of development projects were also suspended (*MEED* 10 and 24 December 1993). The deepening currency crisis had a knock-on effect on the rest of the economy and fuelled inflation.

Additionally, inflation was running at around 35 per cent a year in 1993, higher than expected by the government (*The Middle East* January 1994) and was acting as another squeeze on salaried and low-income households. Inflation was partly fuelled by government expenditure on capital projects (which had not yet become productive yet) and rises in consumption, which grew at 10 per cent per year between 1989 and 1993, twice the government's anticipated rate, according to the Economics and Finance Minister (*Kayhan Havai*, 19 January 1994).

To rub salt into the wound, it had become apparent by 1994 that the FTZs, a feature of the reform process, had failed not only to attract foreign investment in productive activities and encourage technology transfer but had also failed to generate any income through exports, according to Morteza Alviri, head of the FTZs administration (*Farhang-e Towsee* December–January 1993/4). Far from acting as a window of opportunity for exporters, the FTZs had become a channel for imports of (mostly) non-essential consumer goods.

The debt and currency crises were the key concerns of Rafsanjani's second administration on the eve of the Second Five Year Plan. Saeed Lailaz noted that as a result of the drop in incomes, tax revenue would fall short of its target by some 1,000 billion rials in 1994/5. Foreign currency earnings of the government were estimated not to exceed $10 billion in 1994/5 (*Kayhan Havai* 26 June 1993). Crude oil revenues decreased to about $13 billion in 1994 (*Nimrooz* 31 December 1993) and showed no prospects of rising substantially in the immediate future. The oil price situation and its impact on the Iranian economy was so serious that President Rafsanjani felt compelled to telephone King Fahd and Shiekh Al-Sabah in September 1993 in order to arrive at a common policy on OPEC oil output and the raising of oil prices (*Kayhan Havai* 6 October 1993). Alarm bells were also sounding in Washington about the implications of the low oil price on Persian Gulf security. According to one scenario being developed in Washington, the oil price crisis might lead to direct confrontation in the Gulf:

> President Rafsanjani, if he remains unable to attract western investment, will try to increase his [oil] revenue by turning up the heat on his OPEC colleagues, threatening them with unfortunate consequences if they do not cut production sharply enough to raise oil prices to about $30 [per barrel].
>
> (Stelzer 1994: 7)

These economic difficulties were compounded by the human and economic costs of a series of natural disasters (earthquakes and floods; the 1990 earthquake alone caused over $7 billion worth of damage: *MEED* 13 July 1990) in the early 1990s and the arrival of a large number of refugees from neighbouring states. Playing host to over 4 million refugees (the largest number in the world), without receiving much international support for this humanitarian effort, has acted as another drain on the fragile economy.

Despite these economic setbacks, the administration is to push ahead with the reform process, much of which will be implemented through the Second Five Year Plan (based on state expenditure of $121 billion and oil revenues

Table 23 Countries with substantial refugee populations, 1992

Country	No. of refugees	Country	No. of refugees
Iran	4,150,000	Kenya	401,000
Pakistan	1,629,000	Zaire	392,000
Malawi	1,580,000	Mexico	361,000
Germany	827,000	Tanzania	292,000
Croatia	648,000	China	288,400
Ethiopia	431,000	Azerbaijan	246,000

Source: United Nations Commission for Refugees (1993).

of $77.6 billion) (*MEED* 17 December 1993). In broad terms, the second Rafsanjani administration has been plannning the reduction and eventual scrapping of government subsidies (standing at $1.2 billion for essential goods in 1993/4; SWB, ME/W0276, 6 April 1993); completion of the privatisation programme and continuation of structural reforms (*MEED* 2 July 1993), banking reform (including privatisation and further commercialisation of the banks and wider acceptance of internationally recognised credit and debit cards such as Visa and Master Card; *The Middle East* January 1994) and the extension of the privatisation programme to the 'strategic' economic sectors were given as the main priorities (SWB, ME/W0285, 8 June 1993). As the Second Plan period did not envisage further large-scale investments by the government (*MEED* 29 January 1993), it was assumed that the administration's main priority would be to complete the structural reform process. The government did, however, plan to increase Iran's oil production capacity to 4.5 mb/d (*Kayhan Havai* 6 October 1993) and to raise the country's non-oil exports to between $10 billion and $12 billion annually in the course of the 1990s (*Kayhan Havai* 16 February 1994).

THE IMPLICATIONS OF LIBERALISATION

The government is seeking a new relationship for Iran with the current international division of labour. As the Heavy Industries Minister commented in January 1992: 'we must find our own place in industry [international industrial division of labour] and in the international market place' (*Kayhan Havai* 29 January 1992). Having remained bound to the world capitalist market through exports of its hydrocarbons, imports of industrial and semi-industrial products and consumer goods and affiliation to various capitalist multilateral institutions, the republic under the Rafsanjani government has been attempting to revise Iran's status by expanding the country's industrial activities and exports. It is, in short, aiming to turn Iran into another successful newly industrial (or semi-peripheral) country. This had always been one of the objectives of the *ancien régime*. The Shah's plan was to have borne fruit by the early 1980s, but, while the international environment at the time was conducive to such transformation, it is not at all clear that such is still the case. The 'market' for semi-peripheral states may already be saturated and the Islamic Republic may have a difficult time proving to international capital that, beyond its hydrocarbons, location and labour power, it has anything unique and marketable to offer in terms of the international division of labour. Furthermore, as a research document published by the Iranian National Industrial Investment Company highlights (Research Report No. 25),

Under present conditions . . . one cannot expect a great volume of inward foreign investment in order to alleviate [Iran's] foreign exchange short-ages, help meet the planned levels of investment [in the economy] and of transfer of technology, particularly as . . . in addition to the existence of some legal obstacles [in the way of foreign investment], no specific legal framework to deal with foreign investment activity has been created.

(*Ettela'at Siasi-Eghtesadi* February–March 1993: 60)

The report also reminds Iranian decision-makers that in any case the attention of foreign investors is no longer focused on West Asia and the Middle East, but is seeking opportunities in the former Soviet Union and its erstwhile Comecon partners in Eastern Europe.

In addition, it is difficult to see how the maintenance of a neo-import substitution industrialisation (ISI) strategy, which is usually conducted at the planning and implementation level by the state, will fit into the new scheme. In so far as the goal of economic self-sufficiency through the implementation of an ISI strategy remains a government priority, it is hard to envisage complete state withdrawal from active participation in production, the direc-tion of resources, etc. The role of a market-oriented private sector, thus, in an economy where the state not only continues to depend on hydrocarbon exports but also pursues a pre-ordained economic goal remains unclear. But even if ISI is abandoned and the state reduces its economic exposure to a minimum it will remain a significant social force, particularly as it will, at the very least, continue for the foreseeable future to be an allocative mecha-nism, supervising the distribution of state-accrued oil rent in society.

Indeed, it is here, at this juncture of changing policies and priorities, that the long-term structural problems which haunted the Pahlavi regime in the 1970s may emerge to haunt Iran's post-Khomeini leadership, for, as Looney notes (of pre-revolution Iran),

no single raw-material industry can be expected to lead a country all the way through diversification and industrialisation. The production and consumption linkages of a series of vigorous raw materials are required before the capacity to absorb is great enough to avoid the instabilities of an export economy. The fiscal linkages of a single raw material in general are not large enough to foster the transformation of the entire economy.

(Looney 1985: 63)

In the same vein, Yaghmaian notes that the republic seems to have been unable to resolve both its short-term problems and the more deep-seated structural imbalances arising from Iran's position in the international division of labour since the 1940s. Yaghmaian's 'triangle crisis' (relating to Iran's place in the international division of labour, the oil market and the Iran–Iraq war), although now reduced to a 'biangle crisis' (since the 1988 cease-fire), continues to haunt Iran's post-revolution leadership (Yaghmaian 1993).

On the other hand, the revival of the country's fortunes, based on its huge oil resources and labour power, will have a direct impact upon its relations with international capital. Paradoxically, as the state retreats from economic intervention, it strengthens and revives itself *vis-à-vis* foreign capital. Indeed, its autonomy will then depend not on its control of economic activity but on its encouragement of an independent private sector. The retraction of the proprietor state, therefore, ought not to be confused with a contraction or weakening of the political state in social terms (particularly *vis-à-vis* social classes at the top). In fact, one can foresee the state's revitalisation as private sector efforts move the economy from the red into the black.

The same pragmatism that led previous governments to intervene in the economy has led Iran's post-war governments to try and free the country's owners of private wealth. The fact that the market as a mechanism was never extinguished in revolutionary Iran means that the steps towards economic liberalisation have entailed not a transformation of the entire class structure, as might have been the case in Eastern Europe and some other Third World countries, but rather a reinforcement of the bourgeoisie. In the late 1980s the top 10 per cent of households received nearly 42 per cent of the national income and the bottom 20 per cent only about 4 per cent, indicating that real economic power still lies with a minority at the top of the social pyramid. In seeking to improve the economy, therefore, Rafsanjani's policies have naturally sustained, even advanced, the position of these strata.

According to neoclassical economic theory, economic liberalisation and deregulation must be accompanied by the 'rationalisation' of the bureaucracy. But in societies such as Iran the bureaucracy is very much a symbol of the revolution, and its expansion owes much to the corporatist pull of the regime (in Iran the bureaucracy grew from 800,000 individuals in 1977/8 to

Table 24 Distribution of total national income, selected countries

Country	Share of lowest 20%	Share of highest 10%
Iran	3.8	41.7
Turkey	3.5	41.5
Egypt	5.8	33.2
Israel	6.0	22.6
United States	4.2	28.2
France	5.5	26.4
United Kingdom	5.8	24.8
Japan	9.1	22.7

Source: Encyclopaedia Britannica (1988).

stand at 2 million in 1992/3; *Iran Farda* January–February 1993). Under these conditions tinkering with the bureaucracy would be politically suicidal for the Rafsanjani leadership. Firstly, the leadership cannot afford to risk losing its institutional power base. Secondly, President Rafsanjani recognised that without the bureaucracy's blessing the new government policies would not reach fruition. Hence the government chose not to risk 'civil service reform' at the beginning of the reform process and contented itself with a rapid reform of economic organisation. But in order to produce results, in terms of expanded economic activity by the private sector, a reduction in state activity must entail a reduction in the size of the bureaucracy and the elimination of red tape. So it was that – in 1991, over a year after the formulation of the Five Year Plan, government departments and Ministries were told to improve efficiency and make savings. They were advised to do so by transferring 'various affairs to the private sector' and reducing 'the existing inflation in manpower' (SWB, ME/0968, 12 January 1991).

Another initiative aimed at the rationalisation of the bureaucracy was the proposal to merge a number of ministries. Although one such merger had already happened (that of the Pasdaran with the Defence Ministry), controversy continued to surround these proposals, which were seen by many government employees not only as a denial of the regime's revolutionary spirit, but as a sure way of causing large redundancies. Government critics in the Majlis and elsewhere, moreover, maintained that such mergers would also lead to greater inefficiency and disrupt capital investment projects already undertaken by each Ministry. Despite these reservations, however, in 1993 the administration initiated public discussion of the proposed mergers, and by April 1994 had managed to secure the Majlis's approval for the merger of the country's three industry Ministries (the Ministries of Industry, Heavy Industries, and Mines and Metals). Another proposal aimed at the merger of the Construction Jihad and Agriculture Ministries was also said to be in the offing.

The total impact of these reforms is difficult to calculate. While it is true that the mergers will streamline the government's operations and allow some savings to be made on expenditure, politically the administration is taking chances both with the loyalty of the bureaucracy in relation to its stated economic and public policy goals, and with its continuing support for the regime as a whole. The reduction of five independent ministries to two is a big step, and if completed in the course of the Second Development Plan will mean major labour and capital displacement. To put the employment impact of the proposed mergers in context, it suffices to note that the three industry Ministries employed at least 35,000 people in 1992 and the Construction Jihad and Agriculture Ministries another 150,000 personnel (Plan and Budget Organisation 1993). The major redundancies that will inevitably follow these mergers is seen by some insiders as destabilising, threatening to unravel the regime's inner government network and cause a general deskilling of the bureaucracy. It is clear that most of the Ministries' employees see themselves as fulfilling a vital 'technical' function in the administration of the country, a perception that is reinforced when they compare their work with the Presidential Bureau's largely 'non-productive' staff of nearly 16,000.

In addition, as all but one (Construction Jihad) of these Ministries are also big spenders and investors in capital projects, any short-term government savings on personnel would have to be balanced by the probable medium- and long-term harm that the mergers could cause to the country's development ambitions. On the other hand, slimmer government is increasingly being seen by many social scientists as a prelude to less political repression and more economic freedom – the loosening of Big Brother's grip. While the international jury's verdict is still not final on this issue, though, the implications of these developments in Iran would have to be viewed not purely in economic or domestic terms; the analysis needs to be broadened to take account of the eventual effect of administrative reform on the country's political health and its general socio-economic direction.

Whether or not the case of Iran provides support for Alavi's contention that 'structural imperatives' eventually reorient state policies in the developing countries (even revolutionary or 'disjunctioned' ones) 'into line with the requirements and demands of peripheral capitalism' (Alavi 1985: 296), one still has to consider the power and influence of the ruling elite in concrete terms. In charting new paths the elite in Iran is at the same time changing and attempting to stabilise the system. Herein lies the risk: change and stability are not Siamese twins. The success of the reforms could bring prosperity and stability to the system, but the same success could put an end to the Islamic Republic as we know it if the ex-class returns to Iran *en masse*. A failure of the reforms on the other hand could lead to the alienation of the current ruling coalition and drastically undermine the legitimacy of the entire regime. It is in this context that I consider the relationship between economic and political liberalisation in the Iranian Second Republic.

Within weeks of the passing of the December 1988 political parties legislation, 29 groups and societies applied for registration and expressed willingness to comply with the guidelines set by the Interior Ministry, thus aiming to legalise their activities. None of them was among the militant and armed opponents of the Islamic Republic. The new government, however, has been reluctant to implement the law, as it will enable the opposition forces to organise and challenge the Rafsanjani–Khamenei coalition. The challenge comes from a number of quarters, including the 'radicals' within the power structures of the republic. Opening up the political system would carry risks, without necessarily ensuring support for the instigators of political reform.

Gorbachev's experience has been noted by the Leader–President coalition. The Rafsanjani government, therefore, has been reluctant to legalise channels of political opposition, content with the belief that if economic channels of self-expression exist the need for political reform diminishes. The emergence of new class factions at the ruler level, or a return of the old ones, will, however, increase the pressures for political reform. Indeed, if economic reform does not bear fruit, then pressure for change at the political level may become overwhelming.

It appears to be the belief of the current government that it can rely on the support of the middle classes so long as the only political alternative remains the hard-line Maktabis. In this perception lies the ruling alliance's intolerance of opponents – leftist, monarchist, 'liberal', nationalist and others – acting as alternatives to the regime. Whether they maintain a presence in Iran, or operate from beyond the political arena at home, their mere existence has the potential to undermine the legitimacy of the current rulers. Political reform in Iran, thus, has not gone hand in hand with economic liberalisation and market-oriented policies, because it poses a threat to the entire system. In the Islamic Republic, at its inception at least, the two processes of economic and political liberalisation were mutually exclusive.

The economic policy metamorphosis of the Islamic Republic outlined in this chapter, coupled with the anticipated return of some members of the exiled bourgeoisie, indicate that the class structure of society is in a process of flux so that in due course it may well begin to reflect that of the Pahlavi regime pyramid, ultimately raising the question as to whether the (Iranian) Islamic economy is in reality any more than a mythical concept, advanced more as an alternative to revolutionary economic policy than as its result.

One final word on the process of economic reform in post-Khomeini Iran is needed before we leave the subject. It has been made clear in this and the preceding chapter that the Islamic state has been and remains fully committed to the private sector, legally and ideologically. Although the First Republic's economic policies were leaning towards populism, nonetheless the state sector was not designed (in an ideological sense) to take over the national economy and regulate its existence. Massive state intervention after the revolution arose from the needs of capital at the time, but inevitably that same need and process gave rise to those political forces that welcomed and wished to push further the boundaries of state ownership and control. The so-called economic radicals belong to this trend, whose position was enthusiastically supported by the Tudeh party and its leftist allies. For them, the *petit-bourgeois*-dominated Islamic Republic was ready to leave the 'imperialist orbit' and adopt as its economic strategy the Soviet-favoured 'non-capitalist path to development' (Saadatmand 1993: 59). However, as was argued in chapter

4, nationalisation of industry and services and state control of the economy were not – at least not at the outset – motivated by an ideological mission.

By the same token, when economic reform became the order of the day it was pursued partly because of the deep economic crisis the Moussavi government had left in its wake. As the private sector had always been an integral part of the Iranian state, its return to centre stage in post-war and post-Khomeini Iran was perhaps more a matter of course. Furthemore, as has been shown in this chapter, far from displaying an ideological commitment to denationalisation across the board and at all costs, the government has been pursuing a sectoral economic liberalisation strategy whose future direction is likely to depend on the impact of the process already under way rather than on the fulfilment of an abstract economic ideal. Introduction of some restrictions, including a degree of price controls, trade regulations and currency transfer restrictions in 1993 and 1994 in response to economic difficulties, at the same time as pushing ahead with privatisation, are quite indicative of government attitudes towards economic reform and the high level of autonomy the state continues to enjoy: in the last analysis, the Iranian government has shown that it can adopt short-term policies that may run counter to its reform strategy, without necessarily changing direction completely or indeed halting or reversing the process.

6   Iran's post-revolution regional policy

> Oil has drawn the world's attention to the Persian Gulf, an area in which, after a period of deceptive calm following the British military withdrawal at the end of 1971, local rivalries have now emerged. There are many potential causes of unrest, both internal and inter-state, and a build-up of modern weapons is taking place on a very considerable scale.
>
> (IISS, *Strategic Survey* 1973)

It has come as no surprise to observers of Iran that the revolution brought with it profound changes in the country's regional and foreign policy. These were inevitably in part shaped by the war with Iraq, which challenged the republic so early in its life. As Chubin and Tripp stated before Iran's acceptance of a peaceful resolution to the conflict:

> Whatever the future of the Islamic republic, there can be no disagreement on the degree to which the war has shaped its language and institutions and conditioned its influence abroad and also how much it will continue to condition and constrain its future course at home.
>
> (Chubin and Tripp 1989: 255)

The Islamic leaders were faced with a dual challenge – to provide immediate policies in reaction to events in Iran's regional environment and to develop longer-term foreign policy strategies to encompass relations with the world beyond the war. During the period when the war raged, it was inevitable that attention should be focused on the first of these, with the result that wider issues were often reduced to rhetorical and ideological gesticulation. Since the war ended, however, the republic has been forced to finally come to grips with the need to formulate coherent and functional strategies for its foreign relations which enhance its domestic political and economic development. Within this context, it becomes clear that this has been made possible as much by the institutional readjustments within Iran for which I have coined the term

Second Republic as by the international environment in which Iran now finds itself.

This chapter aims to examine the first phase of the republic's foreign policy, between 1979 and Iranian acceptance of the SCR 598 in July 1988. Such an examination cannot, however, be isolated from the preceding period, simply because many of the imperatives of foreign policy, geo-strategic position, historical relations with neighbours, and so forth, had existed before the republic and continued to act upon policy-makers thereafter.

IRAN'S REGIONAL POLICIES BEFORE THE REVOLUTION

The creation of the state of Israel in 1948 was regarded as calamitous by the Arab world. Although Iran voted against both the plan of partition that emerged from the work of 'Sub-committee 1' of the UN Ad Hoc Committee (25 November 1947) and the General Assembly Partition Plan for Palestine resolution (29 November 1947), there were soon signs that a strategic alliance was evolving between the newly created Jewish state and Iran, especially after the reinstatement of the Shah in 1953. This development was seen to pose a tremendous strategic problem for the Arabs. Loss of Arab territory (and, associated with it, the Palestinian diaspora) was compounded by the enlargement of the non-Arab Middle East and an apparent commonality of purpose between two of the latter's component members.

When Iran joined the Baghdad Pact in 1955 (revamped as CENTO after Iraq's departure following the revolution in 1958) tying it into a strategic alliance with, amongst others, the other non-Arab Middle East state, Turkey, the mould of Iran–Arab relations was apparently set. Tehran's departure from its traditional policy of neutrality between the great powers, at the height of the Cold War, not only signalled its siding with the West, but also delineated the boundaries of Iran–Arab relations as reflected in the prevailing East–West divide of the Middle East sub-system itself. As John Marlowe has stated: 'Thus Iran became a kind of country member of NATO and an associate of a Western system which sought to contain communism by a mixture of military deterrent and economic betterment' (Marlowe 1962: 211).

On 23 July 1960 the Shah publicly confirmed that Iran had recognised the existence of Israel, prompting serious disruption in Iran–Arab relations thereafter and confirming Arab fears that Iran was central to a Western-originating anti-Arab campaign. The radicalisation of the Arab world and the emergence of nationalist Arab regimes in the Middle East served ironically to bring Iran and Israel only closer. Yet in spite of Arab reservations towards Iran, the latter was able to exploit the differences among the Arab regimes by siding with the moderates. As well as developing close alliances with non-Arab states, therefore, including Israel, Pakistan and Turkey, substantial ties were forged with the monarchies of the Persian Gulf: Jordan, Egypt, North Yemen, Morocco and Tunisia.

Iran's swift recognition of Kuwait in 1961 against Iraqi threats, its leading role in raising the price of crude oil in the 1970s, its armed forces' involvement in the defence of the Sultan of Oman against his internal enemies in 1974, its condemnation of Israeli 'excesses' in concert with the international community, its conclusion of a 'peace treaty' with a hostile Iraq in 1975 (under some degree of military coercion), and the continuity of its politico-military and economic ties with the non-Arab Middle Eastern states (including Israel) as well as with the influential extra-regional powers, all pointed to the existence of a strong and confident power broker in the shape of Imperial Iran, whose regional force and status were such that even its unilateral actions could affect the political and military balance of the entire region. Iran's own dramatic military build-up and its active role in regional forums and in OPEC were the material manifestations of Tehran's expansionist stance, it was argued, buttressed by the Nixon/Kissinger Doctrine from the late 1960s (regional policeman policy), and the impotence of the moderate Arab states themselves in dealing with the Soviet-supported Arab regimes.

Not surprisingly, the conservative Persian Gulf states were rather alarmed by the Shah's grand designs in the Gulf and the Indian Ocean regions, treating his regime with caution (Cottrell 1975). In general, however, so long as Iran's orientation remained essentially pro-Western and pro-*status quo* they had little reason to argue with the Iranian regime over details.

The 1970s saw the accentuation of rivalry over OPEC oil policy between Iran and Saudi Arabia and, by association, over the control of the affairs of the increasingly wealthy and strategically important Gulf region. Both Iran and Saudi Arabia were determined to employ their newly found financial wealth to curry favour with other states in the region. Security and strategic considerations formed the basic determinant of Iran's economic aid policy. By 1976 Iran was disbursing $752.5 million in economic aid to other developing countries, up from $408.3 million only two years earlier (OECD 1983). The main beneficiaries of Iranian economic assistance at this time were India, Pakistan, Egypt, Afghanistan and Morocco (ibid.). To ensure maximum political return on the aid investment, Iran ensured that much of it was disbursed through bilateral channels. According to the OECD, as much as 75 per cent of Iran's aid was bilateral.

As the military expenditures of Iran and Saudi Arabia in the 1970s show (*The Military Balance* various years), both countries were in fact aiming for military domination of the Persian Gulf region (in Iran's case with significant spill-overs into the Indian Ocean, and in Saudi Arabia's case with reference to its Red Sea coastline), oblivious to the implicit threat they were posing to the moderate camp's position in the regional balance of power. The policies pursued by the two states were inspired partly by competition with each other, partly by competition with Iraq, and partly in conjunction with the 'twin pillar' strategy developed in Washington.

Imperial Iran's role in supporting President Sadat of Egypt's endeavours, in the face of a rare show of unity among the Arabs in opposition to the Camp David process, may have brought condemnation from his neighbours but also served to impose some degree of stability and security upon the moderate Middle East under the umbrella of Saudi, Egyptian and Iranian like-mindedness.

The Iranian revolution of 1979 was to alter this balance of forces dramatically, breaking in the process the deadlock between the moderate and the radical camps in the Arab world, and forging a realignment of Arab forces. Other events of the late 1970s also played a role in reshaping the region, combining to thrust change on to the finely balanced equilibrium of forces in the Middle East.

THE REVOLUTION AND ITS IMPACT ON THE MIDDLE EAST

The Iranian revolution brought to an abrupt end the politico-military alliance of Egypt, Iran and Israel which the Camp David process had promised to develop under American patronage. The revolution appeared initially to offer great potential for Israel's chief enemy, the PLO, as the re-occupation of Jerusalem (Al-Quds) for the sake of Islam (as the Islamic revolutionary leadership in Iran saw things) was taken as evidence of a common purpose. It was not until September 1980 that the two paths were seen to lead in opposite directions. Both the Iran–Iraq war and the ideology of the Islamic Republic itself forced the redefinition of Arab and Islamic identities in a manner that was to run through the veins of the Palestinian movement – the epitomy of Arabism – as well as the region at large. The Iran–Iraq war gave material substance to the competing visions of change for the Muslim Middle East: while Iran's Islamic revolutionaries pointed to a new (Islamic) realignment of forces, the 'progressive' Arabs were keen to maintain the course sought at the Baghdad summit. Meanwhile, as the hitherto rather loose Arab poles of moderacy and rejectionism became virtually set in stone with the emergence in the late 1970s of the Steadfastness Front (Algeria, Iraq, Libya, South Yemen, Syria and the PLO), the delicacy of regional relations was deeply affected by the isolation of Egypt and the defection of Iran from the moderate camp. Add to this Tehran's potent and all-encompassing militant Islamic ideology, as well as its still fearful military potential, and the die seemed cast for further antagonism between Iran and its former Arab allies and friends – those in the Gulf in particular. So when war broke out between

Iran and Iraq, it is not difficult to imagine the conservative Persian Gulf states rubbing their hands at the prospect of a conflict on the northern shores of the Gulf which clearly had the potential to weaken both their 'northern devils' simultaneously.

THE EVOLUTION OF POST-PAHLAVI POLICIES

In the immediate aftermath of the revolution, until the final victory of the FIRs over their liberal and secular competitors for power, foreign policy was defined largely by the requirements of the internal consolidation of power (Ramazani 1985). Talk of the export of the revolution and the negative balance strategy of 'neither East nor West' was as much directed towards the ideological mobilisation of the people behind the regime as it was intended to serve as foreign policy. Both elements of this, naturally enough, caused a not inconsiderable degree of alarm amongst Iran's Persian Gulf neighbours (Chubin 1987), even as they reflected an internal power struggle inside Iran itself.

It seemed in 1980 that Iran was demonstrating undisguised hostility towards the conservative Persian Gulf states, Iraq and the moderate Arab countries (Gurdon 1984). Meanwhile Tehran went out of its way to appease other (politically radical and ideologically secular) Arab states. If the intention was a realignment with the 'progressive' Arab forces, then the alienation of (equally) radical Iraq – a powerful and useful Gulf partner for an unwelcome government such as Tehran's – signals a contradictory strategy. Throughout this early period (and beyond), Iran maintained close ties with its non-Arab Muslim neighbours, despite its defection from CENTO and the latter countries' close association with Western economic and politico-military pacts. In fact, after a short freeze, the Regional Development Co-operation Organisation (set up in 1964, renamed Economic Co-operation Organisation in 1985) resumed its former activities, substantially expanding the number and extent of trading ties and exchanges between Iran and Turkey, and Iran and Pakistan – both major non-Arab regional allies of the United States.

It emerges, therefore, that the new regime's regional strategy was not confined to siding with the radicals in the puritanical radical–moderate poles of the Arab world. Tehran's regional policy reflected a complex outlook and the application of a set of principles designed to satisfy the republic's more immediate needs rather than the adaptation of an unitary yardstick for displaying the country's new revolutionary Islamic attitudes.

In practice, the new Iranian leadership had initiated a multi-dimensional regional policy, based on four principles:

1   Close collaboration with selected members of the Arab Steadfastness Front.
2   Correct and pragmatic relations with Turkey and Pakistan, based on mutual respect, non-interference in each other's internal affairs (particularly as far as the common 'Kurdish problem' of Iran and Turkey was concerned) and fruitful economic relations.
3   Opposition to the Gulf Arab monarchies and the moderate Arab camp.
4   Rhetorical opposition to Israel but practical collaboration (particularly in the military field) with the Jewish state so long as the war with Iraq lasted.

Adjustments to the country's international relations also occurred. By the end of 1980 Iran had cancelled $9 billion worth of arms contracts with Western countries; severed its formal diplomatic links with Israel and South Africa; left CENTO; and became a full member of the Non-aligned Movement. As early as February 1979, Iran established diplomatic relations with communist North Korea, and had expressed its desire to expand trading ties with the Third World countries in general. According to Foreign Ministry information, Iran had established 17 new diplomatic missions between 1979 and 1986, 12 of which were in Africa. By contrast, it had broken off diplomatic relations with Egypt, Jordan and Morocco and had revised Tehran's policy towards Oman shortly after the revolution.

THE ENTRENCHMENT PERIOD

Once the FIR forces in Iran had secured control of the revolution, they embarked upon a period of entrenchment in their regional agenda. To some extent, this 'digging in' was forced upon them by a combination of events apparently beyond their control. Most notable of these was the Iraqi invasion of Iranian territory in September 1980. The essence of the entrenchment period was captured by Ayatollah Khomeini in the following terms;

> We should try hard to export our revolution to the world, and should set aside the thought that we do not export our revolution, because Islam does not regard various Islamic countries differently and is supporter of all the oppressed . . . If we remain in an enclosed environment we shall definitely face defeat. We should clearly settle our accounts with the powers and superpowers and should demonstrate to them that . . . we [shall] confront the world with our ideology.
>
> (Khomeini's first Iranian New Year speech, FBIS, 24 March 1980)

These two notions, the export of the Islamic revolution and the scope of its particular message, found substance and vigour in the conflict with Iraq (Ramazani 1985). The victory route to Al-Quds, it was claimed by Tehran, runs through Baghdad. That apart, the peoples of the Gulf Arab countries, maintained the ruling Iranian theocrats, would turn to 'our Islam' and against their own rulers once Ba'thism and its regional supporters had been defeated and the Islamic Republic of Iraq had been founded. Along with Iraq, Lebanon, with its majority Shii population, was regarded as the territory most receptive to Tehran's 'exporting' of the 'Islamic' revolution strategy. By 1978 the Iranian clergy had already recognised the potential base of support that existed for its Islamic revolution among the Shii populations (and many others, it must be said) of the Arab countries. The ruling Iranian FIR forces' explicit aim after the Iraqi attack on Iran in 1980 was to galvanise the Shii of Iraq, Bahrain, the United Arab Emirates, Kuwait and the Lebanon into subverting and destabilising their own regimes to the point of replacing them with like-minded Islamic republics (Ramazani 1986).

In the case of Lebanon at least the destabilisation strategy had already been activated in late 1979. In December 1979, for instance, Abbas Mohammad Montazeri (the son of Ayatollah Montazeri) tried to send a force of 10,000 revolutionaries to the Lebanon, ostensibly to join the Palestinian fighters (*International Herald Tribune* 10 December 1979). So it is no coincidence that, of the 13 'liberation movements' holding a conference in Iran in 1987, eight had Lebanese or Gulf Arab connections and one Palestinian connections. Of the eight, six were fronts representing one or more of the Gulf Arab states (*MEED* 12 December 1987).

The opportunity for 'export', however, did not seriously arise until the summer of 1982. The commencement of successful Iranian counter-offensives against Iraq, and the inevitable penetration of Iraqi territory by the regular and irregular armed forces of the republic, appeared in the eyes of Iran's leaders to provide the moment for the message to be relayed. Unfortunately for Tehran, by this time the Arab world had recovered sufficiently from the crises of 1979 to react cohesively to this direct threat to 'Arab territory'.

The creation of the Gulf Co-operation Council in May 1981 had been in many ways a direct response to the challenges of the day in the region, chief amongst which were the influence of the Steadfastness Front, the weakening of the moderate camp, the Soviet invasion of Afghanistan, the Iran–Iraq war, the powerful Israeli war machine and of course the Iranian revolution. Despite its many weaknesses, the GCC had soon become a strategic reality of the Arabian peninsula, giving voice to the conservative Gulf Arab states' collective security interests in the Persian Gulf region and providing a mechanism for a co-ordinated response.

In rallying round the Iraqi war effort, the GCC states gave vent to their fears over the expansionist character of the Islamic revolution (Ramazani 1986; Gurdon 1984). Their new-found resolve to defend their 'patch' was in tune with the responses to the war not only of moderate states like themselves but also of 'radical' actors like the PLO. Jordan led the way in open support of Iraq in November 1980, followed by Egypt, Morocco, Tunisia and the PLO. Syria, however, condemned King Hussein's call for volunteers to fight on Iraq's side as 'a worthless political stunt designed to distract attention from the Arab–Israeli conflict' (*The Guardian* 1 February 1982). The radical Arab camp, the potential supporter of Iran, had been weakened by the split between Syria and Iraq at the beginning of the Iran–Iraq war, reducing the clout of the Steadfastness Front as well as the potency of the moderate–radical divide among the Arabs. The support of Syria, Libya, Algeria and South Yemen for the 'Persian Shia aggressor' against 'radical Iraq' pulled the rug from under the feet of Arab nationalists.

By 1982 the radical Arabs' problems in the context of the crisis in the Persian Gulf were to be superseded by a more fundamental challenge to their zones of influence when Iran's militants embarked on systematic encroachment of the main domain of the radicals' Arab policy; Palestine (and associated with it, the Lebanon).

THE ISLAMIC REPUBLIC AND THE LEVANT

The Iran–Iraq war put an abrupt end to the Iranian–PLO honeymoon of 1979–80. Just two weeks after the Iraqi invasion of Iran, Yasser Arafat was in Baghdad warmly embracing President Saddam Hussein and publicly praising his role in regional matters, a fact not lost on the Iranian leadership. Nor had the Iranian rulers overlooked the PLO's close relations with the Islamic Republic's domestic secular and Islamic leftist enemies, or its primary position in Lebanon (particularly in the country's predominantly Shii districts).

The PLO was unhappy to see a conflict (involving its closest ally, Iraq) in the region which attracted attention away from its own Arab–Israeli struggle. The war would inevitably lead to further divisions within the Arab world, and would reinforce the coincidence of interests between Tehran and Damascus, both of which had already shown a desire to marginalise Arafat's leadership and the role of the mainstream PLO. Iranian support for anti-PLO Palestinian factions and the arming of Lebanese groups in strategic parts of the Lebanon convinced the Fatah leadership that their movement's salvation lay in opposition to the Irano-Syrian designs and unconditional support for Iraq and its supporters in the war. The rupture in PLO–Iranian relations was confirmed when the IRI refused PLO representatives visas to attend the celebrations for the sixth anniversary of the revolution. In a short statement, Iran accused the PLO of taking 'an unprincipled position' on Iran (*MEED* 22 February 1985). Some five months later leaders of the three prominent

Syria-based anti-PLO Palestinian factions (Said Abu Musa of the anti-Arafat Fatah faction, Ahmad Jibril of the PFLP–GC and Farhan Abu Haja of SAIQA) arrived in Tehran on an official visit (IRNA 5 and 6 July 1985; *MEED* 22 February 1985 and 10 August 1985).

Two important events in the early 1980s marked the involvement of Iranian forces in Lebanon: the Syrian military confrontation with the Israeli-backed Christian Phalange, and the Israeli invasion of Lebanon in 1982. Iranian Revolutionary Guards were dispatched to the Syrian-controlled Bekaa Valley to train and provide support for the (Muslim) forces opposing the PLO, and the Israeli-backed Phalangists. The mainstream Amal organisation of Nabih Berri was soon overshadowed by more militant Lebanese Shii groups that were trained, financed and supported by their Iranian co-religionists. The Hezbollah, Islamic Jihad and the Islamic Amal Organisation all reflected Iran's uncompromising line in both local and regional matters. High on the agenda of these new organisations was the following: opposition to the PLO under Arafat's Fatah, opposition to Saddam Hussein, and support for a Lebanese Islamic Republic modelled on the Iranian master plan. Internationally, they were committed to Iran's foreign policy objectives *vis-à-vis* the West.

While Damascus and Tehran could see eye to eye on the first two counts, the third objective threatened to dissolve the alliance, for it directly and blatantly challenged Syrian authority in its own 'back yard' (Hunter 1990). However, economic considerations and geopolitical concerns prevented the alliance's dissolution. Continued political and military support from Syria was essential for Iran to counter the criticism that its regional diplomatic campaigns and military strategies were overtly anti-Arab. Secondly, Syrian support for Iran meant the unhindered progress of the war, providing the necessary assurance for the republic's Arab supporters of the potency and militancy of the Iranian programme of action. The Syrians, on the other hand, financially bankrupt and under pressure in the Lebanon, needed both Iranian petro-dollars and oil as well as revolutionary armed manpower for the success of their Lebanese campaign and their proxy war against Israel. The possible overthrow of the competing Ba'thist regime in Iraq was an attractive added bonus.

By 1987, however, the complexities of Lebanese politics were working against the alliance. Syrian-backed Amal (and Phalange) forces had come into head-on confrontation with the militant and heavily armed Iranian-backed Shii groups in Beirut and elsewhere in Lebanon (Vaziri 1992). The reasons for this were multi-faceted. As the threat of PLO dominance in Lebanon had subsided after 1983 so too had the domestic motive for co-operation between these disparate Lebanese groupings. Syria, having suffered numerous international and regional setbacks, had decided to clamp down heavily on the Islamic revivalist irritants who were by now eroding Damascus's influence in the Lebanon and threatening the tacit and fragile cease-fire between Syria and Israel. Iran, under mounting economic pressure at home, and with substantial difficulties on the war fronts, was unable to react to the Syrian exercise of power and reservedly submitted to Syria's will. Although Iranian ambitions in Lebanon remained great, the Lebanese Islamic Republic experiment had to be postponed indefinitely. A similar fate had also befallen the republic's Persian Gulf policy in the entrenchment period.

IRAN'S PERSIAN GULF POLICY, 1980–8

The outcome of the Amman Arab League summit of November 1987 is probably the most emphatic testimony to the failure of the Iranian–Syrian anti-Iraqi strategies. The offer of Egyptian security guarantees to the GCC states reinforced the marginalisation of Syria and highlighted the failure of Iran to cow the conservative Gulf states into abandoning Iraq. It was obvious even before the Amman summit that the deep internal cracks in the Steadfastness Front would prevent the extension of unreserved extensive diplomatic and military support to Iran: Algeria and South Yemen were both cooling towards Iran, as was illustrated when they declined an Iranian invitation to attend the meeting of Foreign Ministers of the Steadfastness Front in January 1985. Only Syria and Libya sent their Foreign Ministers to the meeting, PLO representation not even having been considered.

The participants in the Amman summit not only invited Egypt back into the Arab fold and called for an increase in Cairo's politico-military role in the Persian Gulf, but impressed upon Syria the need to join in the official condemnation of Iran, as well as to endorse the explicit support given to the GCC states against Iran. This was recorded by the communiqué issued at the end of the conference:

> The conference condemned Iran's occupation of part of Iraqi territory and its procrastination in accepting UN SCR 598. They [*sic*] called on Iran to accept the resolution and implement it according to the sequences of its operative paragraphs . . . The conference declared its solidarity with Kuwait in confronting the Iranian regime's aggression, and denounced the bloody criminal acts perpetrated by the Iranians in the vicinity of the Holy Mosque in Mekkah.
>
> (*MEED* 14 November 1987)

The strategic slogan 'War, war until victory' had left Tehran little room for manoeuvre and compromise. In spite of this, Iran was pursuing a complex carrot-and-stick policy with its conservative Gulf Arab neighbours – the closest and main supporters of the Iraqi war effort. In this context one can note the different points of emphasis in the following statements, made by Iran's top political figures. President Ali Khamenei's statement seems to be seeking to put pressure on the GCC states:

> We urge them [the GCC states] to put pressure on Iraq to stop its warmongering in the Gulf – or stop supporting Iraq if it will not listen. We have nothing against them and do not wish to fight them . . . [Iran] would not be indifferent if they helped Iraq.
>
> (*The Daily Telegraph* 9 June 1984)

Prime Minister Moussavi had emphasised a month earlier that:

> Our policy is to deal a stronger blow against any blows. We have repeatedly warned the Persian Gulf states against linking their fate with that of Saddam. We issue the very same warning right now.
>
> (*The Guardian* 21 May 1984)

Speaker Hojjatoleslam Rafsanjani, on the other hand, attempted to placate the Gulf Arab states and inform them of Tehran's intentions:

> Mister Fahd asked the Syrian Vice-President to visit Tehran to learn about Iran's attitude to the two countries [Saudi Arabia and Kuwait] and whether Iran really intended to expand the war to engulf the two states as well. Our answer was a definite no.
>
> (*The Guardian* 26 May 1984)

Three years later and after the passage of SCR 598, Foreign Minister Velayati showed a change of tack and issued new threats to the Gulf states:

> Any country which supports Iraq is subject to our retaliatory measures, [including] certain areas in Kuwait.
>
> (*International Herald Tribune* 29 July 1987)

In the same month the Iranian Foreign Minister sought to justify the Iranian position in broader regional and strategic terms by stating:

> We have successfully defended ourselves and pushed the Iraqis back. Do you think it is enough? If we accept a cease-fire now, men like Saddam Hussein would try to attack us again in future . . . [A]t the beginning of the war Saddam said Iraq had signed the treaty with the Shah in 1975 because the Shah was strong and Iraq was weak, when Iraq was strong and the Islamic Republic of Iran was weak; that treaty was no longer valid . . . Who can guarantee that he will not attack us again when he feels strong enough to do it? We want to fight against our enemy deeply – not superficially – and eradicate his roots . . . Such a man cannot follow a

normal policy. Why should we leave the future in the hands of such a man? Why?

(*The Middle East* August 1987)

The formulation of a 'back door' (exit) policy to get Iran out of the war was never seriously considered in Tehran, for two main reasons: the domestic political repercussions of such a strategy would have been enormous, particularly in terms of the regime's general standing at home and of undermining the moral of the Islamic revolutionaries engaged in battle; furthermore until the spring of 1986 the Iranian leaders were convinced of their eventual victory over Iraq.

A NEW BEGINNING

Iran's unconditional acceptance of SCR 598 has been shrouded in controversy, not least because of the debates within Iran which seem to have raged around that one decision (Menashri 1989). Many of the top Iranian leaders publicly declared that the republic should look towards reform as well as closer contacts with the outside world in its second decade.

At least a month before the Iranian acceptance of the cease-fire many of the high-ranking politico-religious figures in the republic were endorsing the realist (or pragmatist) line as the best means of confronting all Iran's ills. After Iran's acceptance of SCR 598, they proposed a critical reappraisal of the country's domestic and international policies since the revolution. Their apparent aim was to highlight publicly the setbacks and mistakes of the first decade and, on this basis, to push their agenda through on the back of popular approval and, while it lasted, the Ayatollah's explicit support. Ultimately, they hoped, such a strategy would unavoidably open society up to the outside (mainly Western) world.

A similar spirit of pragmatism was also vividly demonstrated by Ayatollah Khomeini's former heir, Ayatollah Montazeri. Recognition of the need for a transition from confrontation to compromise, from expansionism to coexistence, is marked by the substance of his speech only four days after Rafsanjani's new appointment as the acting Commander-in-Chief. Ayatollah Montazeri, who in 1979 had been at the forefront of calls for the export of the revolution through any means (*Iran Times* 21 September 1979), explicitly questioned the value of the main external manifestation of the revolution: its exportability. In contrast to Ayatollah Khomeini's well known position, Ayatollah Montazeri stated that if political and economic freedom were to be guaranteed for the people then:

> the country would become an example to others and no doubt it would influence all the Third World countries and Islamic states, and willingly

and unwillingly they would follow our example. That is all we have to do
. . . to make our country a model . . . This is the meaning of exporting the
revolution. You do not need to export the revolution.

(SWB, ME/0172, 8 June 1988)

The new strategy envisaged by the Faqih-designate would be internal change
based on reforming the system and avoiding catalytic external engagements.

The cease-fire itself promoted the line that wished to effect these changes
through a conciliatory foreign policy (Hunter 1990). The cease-fire thus
accelerated the demise of the First Republic. Even before the official implementation of the cease-fire, the realists were busy mending fences with many
of those countries that they had managed to alienate (Ramazani 1989). Three
developments in August 1988 illustrate the urgency of the need for reform
felt by some elements of the Iranian leadership. On the 7th ex-President
Bani-Sadr was approached by Islamic Republican functionaries inviting him
to participate in a government of national unity. Other 'liberal' exiles were
also approached in this period: on the 10th the Omani Foreign Minister paid
a one-day visit to Tehran, meeting Rafsanjani and the Prime Minister to
discuss regional security and post-war relations between Iran and its southern
Gulf neighbours; on the 15th Iran announced that it would welcome GCC
assistance and participation in the clearing of Iranian-laid mines in the Persian
Gulf.

By the middle of September Iran had upgraded its diplomatic relations
with both Kuwait and Bahrain and had held extensive secret discussions with
Saudi officials about improving bilateral relations and other regional issues.
A month later, Iran normalised relations with 'Little Satan' Britain, and had
accepted equal OPEC production and export quotas with its erstwhile enemy,
Iraq. Between September and December, high-level Foreign Ministry officials paid at least three visits to the smaller GCC states, meeting the rulers
and other officials of these sheikhdoms. Deputy Foreign Minister Dr Mohammad Ali Besharati met the Emirs of Bahrain and Qatar in September and
Foreign Minister Velayati visited Dubai and Sharjah (the UAE) in December.

In a low-key statement in December, Rafsanjani set out Iran's new strategy
towards its GCC neighbours. On relations with Saudi Arabia he said: 'we and
they both have the desire to resolve problems pertaining to bilateral relations.
In my opinion, our relations will be normalised in the not too distant future'.
More generally:

> We did not have expansionist intentions from the beginning, just as our
> southern neighbours do not have aggressive designs . . . We urge our
> southern neighbours . . . to co-operate with us in order to resolve existing

issues concerning the oil market, maritime laws and Resolution 598 [i.e. relations with Iraq].

(SWB, ME/0341, 22 December 1988)

During this period the 'pragmatists' were careful to obtain Ayatollah Khomeini's support for their integrationist strategy, including the creation of a post-Khomeini agenda for the reformed Islamic Republic. Whether he was aware of it or not, the appointment of Rafsanjani to the post of acting C-in-C was the most practical dimension of the Faqih's support for the changes entailed in the transition programme. Throughout this period Rafsanjani had been careful to link his own position with Khomeini's, a sound insurance policy for himself, the same as virtually guaranteeing the supremacy of the line he championed.

The balance of forces in Iranian domestic circles inevitably influenced the foreign policy of the country. As always, the domestic dimension became externalised to influence Iran's foreign relations; conversely, external factors and developments were utilised by competing factions in the domestic arena to advance their own agendas. This point is illustrated below by a considera- tion of the Islamic Republic's condemnation of the author Salman Rushdie in 1989 on religious grounds and the imposition of a death sentence on him.

At first glance, one is struck by the ease with which the Rushdie affair was used for the reinforcement of the regime's Islamic revolutionary and rejec- tionist credentials, marking a downturn in the general reconciliation with the outside world. Radical elements among the FIRs pounced on the Rushdie affair, apparently in an effort to derail the multi-faceted integrationist strategy of the realists. The pronouncements of Ayatollah Khomeini on *The Satanic Verses* and the Islamic Republic's characteristically aggressive general line did indeed strike a blow against the integrationist programme of the reformers in the system.

The crisis also highlighted the differences of opinion at home about the future direction of the republic's energies in the absence of war. A careful reading of the late Faqih's judgement on the achievements of the republic, its experiences and future direction has thrown some light on the deep-rooted divisions within the leadership's outlook at the end of the 1980s decade. His condemnation of the reformers just prior to his death, and his rejection of the integrationist option, left little doubt as to the Faqih's anxieties over the identity of his Islamic Republic – his fears of its losing its uniqueness on the global scene. In the end, the clergy-dominated reformist groups were treated by the Faqih in the same accusing way as the secular liberals of the *kolahi*– clergy coalition had been. It must be borne in mind here that on other occasions too Ayatollah Khomeini had used popular issues to consolidate his standing both on the domestic scene and on the international front.

It was also apparent, however, that the seeds of change had already been released and had been spreading rapidly, permeating through the entire system. It is noteworthy that the worsening of relations with the European Community in 1989 did not affect the regime's *rapprochement* with the conservative Gulf Arab states. Nor indeed did it meaningfully darken Iran's relations with other Muslim countries – despite the cool response of the Islamic Conference to the Ayatollah's anti-Rushdie *fatwa*. In fact, simultaneously with the increased tensions with Western Europe, Tehran demonstrated its pragmatic streak yet again by positively warming to the calls for co-operation from the communist countries of Europe and Asia.

It can be said that in the last analysis, and in the event of failure of the reformist alliance, history may show that Ayatollah Khomeini was indeed the 'modern' Islamic Republic's worst enemy. His final word on the changing nature of the Islamic Republic is worth quoting at length:

> It is not necessary for us to go seeking to establish extensive ties, because the enemy may think that we have become so dependent and attach so much importance to their existence that we quietly condone insults to beliefs and religious sanctities. Those who continue to believe that and warn that we must embark on a revision of our policies, principles and diplomacy and that we have blundered and must not repeat previous mistakes; those who still believe that extremist slogans or war will cause the West and the East to be pessimistic about us, and that ultimately all this has led to the isolation of the country; those who believe that if we act in a pragmatic way they will reciprocate humanely and will mutually respect nations, Islam and Muslims – to them this is an example.
>
> (*The Echo of Iran* 16 March 1989: 24)

It is perhaps ironic, therefore, that since Ayatollah Khomeini's death Iran's new leaders have sought to re-establish as far as possible the economic (as well as some of the politico-military) ties that existed between Iran and the West during the Shah's reign. The republic's new leaders have found no realistic alternative to rethinking their foreign policy, particularly in its regional context. The exchange of letters regarding mutual relations between the two Presidents of Iraq and Iran, Hussein and Rafsanjani, in the spring of 1990, the holding of the first direct talks, under UN auspices, between the two countries' Foreign Ministers in Geneva in July 1990, and the formal visit of Foreign Minister Velayati to Kuwait in the same month all indicated that the pragmatist line was to prevail.

Foreign Minister Velayati's overtures to Egypt and the talk, since the summer of 1990, of restoring diplomatic relations between the two countries at the earliest possible opportunity, as well as the forcefulness of the new administration's arguments against the continuation of the republic's Lebanon policy under the Mohtashemi–Moussavi era, further indicate that the new leaders were prepared to minimise their unyielding support for the Lebanese Hezbollah and to push for the release of Western hostages held by their Lebanese allies in exchange for better relations with the outside world. Iran's relations with its Syrian ally continued to be problematic and are indeed likely to remain a source of tension even if Iran opts for the unlikely policy of abandoning its erstwhile Islamic allies in Lebanon. Tehran's reaction to the military confrontations between the PLO, Amal and the Druze on one side and the Hezbollah and their Iranian Revolutionary Guard allies on the other in southern Lebanon in July 1990 show that while the Hezbollah remained the republic's 'favourite son' and while, to the annoyance of many of Lebanon's groups, Iran continued to meddle in Lebanon's internal affairs, it no longer felt inhibited about talking to some of the republic's former enemies resident in Lebanon, such as the PLO. The exchange of messages and the verbal extension of some support for the PLO's position (in the context of 'containing Zionism', and resolving Lebanon's problems 'peace-fully' and in a 'brotherly fashion') could be seen as marking a qualified turning point for Iran's overall Arab policy.

On the Palestinian issue, the differences between Iran and Syria have become more marked since the commencement of the US-instigated Arab–Israeli peace process in Madrid in October 1991. Syria's endorsement of and involvement in direct discussions with Israel, as well as its support for the PLO in these talks, could impair the Iranian–Syrian relationship. For the moment both Iran and Syria have opted to extend assistance to the anti-September 1993 accord Palestinian and Islamic groups, although Syria's offers are as likely as ever to be more restrictive than enabling for the groups concerned.

The general reduction in the Second Republic's hostile and anti-Arab propaganda since September 1989 has opened many doors to Tehran, but it has so frustrated the Iranian hard-liners that they have sought their own independent avenues of criticism of the new policies. Mohtashemi's line has remained powerful and vocal both in and outside the republic's corridors of power. In his maiden speech to the Majlis, for instance, Mohtashemi strongly attacked the new leadership and its policies, branding them as the 'new hypocrites' whose real aim was to re-establish relations with the 'American lackeys' in the region and to 'weaken the policies defined by Imam Khome-ini' (SWB, ME/0821, 20 July 1990). He has also condemned the July 1990 talks between Velayati and Aziz in Geneva, referring to Iran's position as 'conservative and cowardly'. In his monthly magazine, *Bayan*, Mohtashemi continues to attack both President Rafsanjani and his Cabinet as well as the Leader by name, and provides ample space for the condemnation of the 'Leader–President' line by the leading Maktabis.

All this means that Iran's 'Islamic' foreign policy (and the exporting of the Islamic revolution), regarded by many as the most significant feature of the revolutionary transformations in Iran, have been subject to 'modernisation'. Nonetheless, the possibility remains that an unforeseen event or unforeseen forces in Iran could yet set the whole process back. Judging by developments since June 1989, total reversal can be considered unlikely but deviation is not. The uninterrupted unfolding of the current strategy could ultimately mark the real 'turning point' for the entire Islamic Republican system.

Regionally, the legacy of the revolution and the very existence of the republic as overtly 'Islamic' have meant that Islam and Islamic issues continue to play a major role in Iran's foreign policy formulation. As imperatives of strategy, however, they have been matched in recent years by a need to make up for the diplomatic losses of the Iran–Iraq war and the harmful effects of the early strident rhetoric of the regime, by the real need to reaccommodate Iran to its regional environment and by the imperatives of good-neighbourly relations.

7   The foreign policy of the Second Republic

In the process, international politics – the interaction and struggle among nation-states – are being transformed into a more organic process of global politics. That process tends to blur the distinction between domestic and foreign priorities. It enhances the importance of internal economic and political well-being in determining the conduct and the relative importance of individual states in the world arena.

(Zbigniew Brzezinski, *The Consequences of the End of the Cold War for International Security*, Adelphi Paper 265)

Observers of international relations maintain that foreign policy theory must have an empirical basis if it is to serve any purpose. Yet, while a factual and largely empirical study of any state's behaviour could be regarded as useful in deepening one's understanding of that particular state, without a theoretical framework the collection of facts and data will not necessarily offer perspective, nor help in explaining the underlying reasons for the state's behaviour and the evolution of its policies. To satisfy both criticria one must understand the linkages between the domestic and the external, the objective and the subjective.

In analysing the foreign policy behaviour of Arab states, Korany and Dessouki have developed a dynamic framework of analysis which can be adapted usefully to offer new insights to the study of the foreign policies of developing countries in general (Korany and Hilal Dessouki 1991). In the first instance, the model visualises foreign policy output as a role. Role theory empowers the analyst to look at foreign policy behaviour in two integrated but distinct dynamic realms: role conception (general orientation and foreign policy objectives) and role performance (specific actions and foreign policy behaviour). The separation of foreign policy outputs into general objectives and concrete behaviour serves as the departure point for the analysis of four sets of factors.

The 'domestic environment' component of the proposed framework, comprising geography, population and social structure, economic capability, military capability, and political structure, falls within that part of the discipline traditionally known as capability analysis. It is, one might say, the sum of the input variables. In determining the impact of these sub-criteria on the foreign policy behaviour of developing countries one need not give them equal weight. With these categories in mind one can proceed to deal with the remaining core factors: foreign policy orientation, the decision-making process, and foreign policy behaviour.

Aspects of the Korany and Dessouki conceptualisation are employed here as the most relevant framework with which to account for the foreign policy behaviour of the Islamic Republic. By employing the role model the analyst is able to explain the behavioural changes in Iran's foreign policy since 1988, and gauge any changes in its orientation. The domestic component of this analytical framework is seen as a crucial dimension of the discussion, accounting for the changes in the political structure of the state, the way in which the country's military capabilities were affected by the Iran–Iraq war, and the importance of economic policy to the post-Khomeini leadership. Consideration of geopolitical factors is seen as an essential component of the analysis too. In Iran's case such factors have played an important part in the reformulation of foreign policy. A firm grasp of the interaction between the domestic and the external is crucial in understanding post-revolution Iranian foreign policy behaviour, particularly since the end of the Iran–Iraq war.

In broad terms, the foreign policy of the IRI has gone through three distinct phases since 1979; the first, which was identified in the previous chapter as the consolidation phase, comprised the initial overhaul of Iran's foreign policy away from proximity to the West and towards non-alignment, Third Worldism and a populist 'anti-imperialist' strategy. Islam as an infrastructural element of foreign policy surfaced at this early stage, unambiguously depicted as such in the constitution of the republic, which was drawn up soon after the revolution.

The second, entrenchment, phase also referred to in the previous chapter, began with the ousting of the 'liberal' wing of the revolutionary coalition from the power elite, and lasted until 1988, with an increasing degree of pragmatism in evidence after 1985. The essence of orientation during this period was political de-linking from the capitalist and socialist systems and the pursuit of populist economic policies. The revolution's slogan of *esteqlal* (independence) permeated the ideology of the republic. During this phase the new orientation of Iran's foreign policy spread roots. The entrenchment phase is perhaps best encapsulated in five strategic slogans of the time: 'War until victory', 'War is a blessing', 'Down with the Satanic powers', 'Export the Islamic revolution', and 'Neither East nor West'. Generally speaking, in regional terms, the orientation was both anti-monarchical and anti-secular.

The basis of policy, thus, was to try and change the regional map, rather than to coexist with the given regimes (and state forms) of the post-colonial Middle East.

The third phase was inaugurated by the decision of Iran's rulers to accept SCR 598. This marked the beginning of the transition era which would lead to attempts by the republic's first-generation post-Khomeini clerical leadership at the reintegration of Iran into the international order. The emphasis of the executive leadership from July 1989 was on constructive diplomacy. Hence, in objective terms, the new orientation in the IRI's foreign policy increasingly resembled that of the *ancien régimes*. The 1990/1 crisis in the Persian Gulf happened just as Iran, under the Rafsanjani presidency, was accelerating its attempts to normalise its relations with the regional actors (with the exception of Israel) and the West (with the exception of the United States). As this chapter will demonstrate, the end result of this reorientation has been that the Islamic Republic has demonstrated the potential to move away from being a major regional *actor*, which had been its status prior to the revolution and throughout the 1980s, and towards becoming a major regional *power* in the 1990s.

THE TURNING POINT, 1988

The string of Iranian military defeats from April 1988 onwards illustrated the malaise and vulnerability of Iran's armed forces. The decline in the military's performance, compounded by the loss of morale and an appreciable drop in revolutionary zeal, merely helped to advance the reformist path advocated by the pragmatist alliance.

Two important historical features of the late 1980s had a profound impact on the Islamic Republic. First, the rise of Gorbachevism, and the sea-change in the world order which followed, transformed Iran's geopolitical environment. Second, the death of Ayatollah Khomeini in June 1989 provided increased opportunities for fuller implementation of new regional and international strategies by that same pragmatist alliance in Tehran, not least by offering it the opportunity to marginalise the Maktabi forces.

The end of the war seemed to erase many of the old imperatives of Iranian foreign policy. In a 'natural' sense, the end to a confrontational position necessarily entailed some change in posture! However, the road towards reintegration was not smooth. Although a particular conciliatory path had been visible since the second half of the 1980s, its emergence as a comprehensive reintegration strategy, the basis of which was to be 'peaceful coexistence' and economic co-operation with the advanced capitalist countries, had to await the rise to executive power of Hojjatoleslam Rafsanjani as the new President of the Republic and the installation of a new Faqih,

Ayatollah Khamenei. Together they set about de-ideologising both policy and policy-making, and proceeded in a systematic fashion to challenge many of the sacred cows of the First Republic, not least in foreign policy.

The essence of the new policies has been the restoration of stability to the Persian Gulf region, further and faster reintegration into the world capitalist system (President Rafsanjani specifically named South Korea and Turkey as the success stories of the Third World and possible models for Iran to follow in the post-war period; *Kayhan Havai* 13 December 1989) and greater participation in regional and global organisations such as the United Nations and the Islamic Conference Organisation (ICO). In this context, it is noted that Iran, for the first time, appointed a permanent envoy (S. Zanganah) to the ICO (in October 1991) and the Economic Co-operation Organisation (ECO). Satisfactory fulfilment of these objectives is considered essential to the economic well-being and security of the Second Republic. Collectively they aim to find a counterweight to an unrivalled US presence in the Middle East and West Asia, to improve Iran's economic position in international terms, and to accelerate the regional search for a viable 'non-aligned' substitute for the underperforming Non-aligned Movement.

Broadly speaking, President Rafsanjani's foreign policy strategy for Iran can be discerned in the context of two overriding domestic policy objectives. These are the aspiration of the republic to recover ground lost in the debilitating war and, in doing so, to reassert its influence in the region. To recover economically and militarily entails the ending of Iran's regional and international isolation. Prior to his election as President, Hojjatoleslam Rafsanjani had already stated his conviction that there existed direct linkage between economic prosperity at home and politico-military stability in the Persian Gulf region:

> The pressures of war, the psychological problems caused by the war, boycotts and sieges created these [economic and social] difficulties. But now things can be different, up to an extent. And I especially emphasise peace. We should strive seriously for peace to be established in the region. If there is no peace in the region, then I do not think that matters can progress as they should . . . Trust among neighbours and a calm situation in the region can automatically solve many problems for us.
>
> (*The Echo of Iran* July–August 1989: 19)

The legacy of the war left military reconstruction and rearmament as the main priority in the initial months after August 1988. President Khamenei stated in the spring of 1989 that the 'strengthening of the Islamic Republic's defence capabilities is one of the major tasks we face during the reconstruction period' (*Gulf Report* May 1989: 41). Ayatollah Khamenei further stated that: 'we need to strengthen our defence and expand our capacity for further military production. In fact, the development and expansion of our arms production industries should be a foremost goal of the Islamic Republic's reconstruction policy' (*Iran Times* 2 October 1988).

Realising the slow nature of the rearmament process, however, the post-Khomeini leadership changed the focus in the early 1990s to emphasise the need for economic reconstruction and to divert more resources in that direction. A diplomatic charm offensive was launched to improve Iran's regional influence, and to help bring about an environment in the Persian Gulf conducive to economic reconstruction and unhindered development of the country's armed forces.

Rafsanjani's policies have been formulated, however, in global and regional environments that have been deeply affected by factors external to Iran's own domestic imperatives. Gorbachevism ultimately engendered the demise of the entire Soviet system in the 1990s, with the resultant discrediting of Marxist-derived alternatives to US hegemony. At the regional level, Iraq's military defeat of 1991, the disarray in Arab state ranks since August 1990 and the emergence of new republics in the Transcaucasus and Central Asia on Iran's northern doorstep have all impacted upon Iranian policy-makers' perceptions of their national interest.

IRAN'S FOREIGN POLICY BETWEEN THE TWO GULF CONFLICTS

The 'pragmatism' in Iran's regional and international policies from the summer of 1988 found substance in the attempts to restore and improve relations with its neighbours and the West. An improvement in relations was seen as a precondition to the ending of Iran's diplomatic isolation, and the return of stability to the Persian Gulf region. The return to normality, of course, would indeed also remove the need for a high-profile Western military presence in the region, which in turn was vital to the strengthening of Iran's regional position and its ambition to be the regional replacement of the West. Without the Western military presence in the Persian Gulf Iran could again attempt to reassert its authority (challenged by both Iraq and Saudi Arabia after the fall of the Shah) as the dominant power, and the only one equipped to ensure tranquillity in the immediate future and the medium term. Thus what may have started as a short-term Iranian policy of isolating Iraq through *rapprochement* with the West and its Gulf Arab allies was to blossom into a new framework of reference to guide Iran's foreign policy after the cease-fire.

The initial reassessment of policy in the 1986–8 period had been triggered by a number of factors, foremost of which were the following: the rapid Western naval build-up in the Persian Gulf, Iran's naval defeats at the hand of US forces, the Mecca riots and the breakdown in relations with Saudi Arabia (Iraq's most influential Gulf state backer), increasing strains in Tehran's relations with Kuwait, its isolation from the Arab world (as illustrated by the anti-Iranian statement of the 1987 Amman Arab summit), its isolation in multilateral organisations and agencies and the tone and tenure of the UN Security Council Resolution 598 threatening an arms embargo on the party not accepting a negotiated settlement.

In the course of a flurry of diplomatic activity, including visits to a number of Gulf Arab states by high-level delegations, Iran's announcement in November 1988 that it was working on a plan that would guarantee the security of the regional states provided the first concrete evidence of a change in thinking and attitude at the highest decision-making levels in Tehran (*Gulf Report* December 1988). By the end of the year correct and cordial relations with all Persian Gulf states (with the exception of Iraq and Saudi Arabia) had been restored. To reinforce its new position, Iran withdrew all the 20–5 armed speedboats based on the southern Gulf island of Abu Musa which had been used to lay mines and in attacks on shipping in the Persian Gulf (ibid.).

Having embarked on the resolution of one conflict on its borders, Iran continued with the spirit of reconciliation and compromise in its relations with the Soviet Union, and in its attitude towards Afghanistan.

The cease-fire facilitated closer bilateral relations between Tehran and Moscow. The Soviet Union's position as a (neighbouring) superpower, its close ties with the Iranian Communist (Tudeh) party, coupled with its role as Iraq's main arms supplier during the war, had militated against warmer Soviet–Iranian ties since the early days of the republic. By 1989 no vestiges of the earlier difficulties and differences remained. Gorbachev's New Thinking helped the process immensely. The Soviet withdrawal from Afghanistan enabled Iran to exert influence on its Afghani Mojahedin allies to look for a peaceful resolution of the conflict (Rais 1992). Hojjatoleslam Rafsanjani and Foreign Minister Velayati attempted to arrange a peaceful transfer of power from the Soviet-installed government to a Mojahedin-dominated government of 'national unity' as early as January 1989. This in fact was the message of the conference on Afghanistan hosted by Iran in the same month. According to one observer, the January conference in Tehran embodied the change of Iranian policy towards Afghanistan: the Iranian-backed Shii groups were presented not as the vanguard of the Afghani Islamic revolution but as a minority community with specific rights in the proposed Islamic regime (Roy 1990). That peace in Afghanistan might also bring about a speedy return of the Afghani refugees to their own country was not overlooked. Although Tehran's views were still tinted by its competition with Saudi Arabia for control of the Islamic agenda in Afghanistan, it continued to seek the return of order to its eastern borders by advocating an alliance between the competing Mojahedin groups, and by endorsing UN support for a peaceful dialogue with the Najibollah government. Iran's continuing support for its Afghani allies (eight largely Shii groups), however, prevented an early resolution of the Afghan problem. Lack of progress on this front continued to fuel Saudi–Iranian rivalry in Afghanistan.

Improvements in Iranian–Soviet relations received a further boost in early 1989 with Foreign Minister Shevardnadze's visit to Iran and his audience with Ayatollah Khomeini, and with Rafsanjani's arrival in Moscow in June 1989.

The renewed importance attached by Tehran to the three-member-state Economic Co-operation Organisation in the late 1980s was in part a direct response to the emergence of two Arab clubs (the Gulf Co-operation Council in 1981 and the Arab Co-operation Council in 1989) which encompassed all its Arab neighbours. The ECO, of course, has since grown into a 10-member organisation and has the potential to become a particularly important regional body, and potentially a powerful diplomatic tool in Iran's hands (Green 1993).

In the past, the Shah had exploited the non-Arab status of Turkey and Pakistan to Iran's advantage, forging close economic and military ties with both states. One might have expected his fall to put severe strains on the relationship, but the war and the associated military and economic needs of Iran militated against a complete break. Indeed, the ECO continued to survive, and was increasingly seen as providing Iran with both economic and military support, and potentially as the body able to resist, in geopolitical terms, the onslaught from Arab-based regional forums in the Persian Gulf and the Mashreq regions.

The Lebanon policy of the Islamic Republic was also under review by the new leadership. President Rafsanjani's taking charge of IRI's Lebanon policy stemmed partly from domestic considerations. In order to minimise the influence of the Maktabi clerical factions, co-led by Hojjatoleslam Mohtashemi, the former Iranian ambassador to Syria and a key figure in the Lebanese Shii Hezbollah movement, on the affairs of the country his ties with the Lebanese factions (which possessed the potential to disrupt and hamper the reforms of the new President) had to be severed. Mohtashemi's diminishing influence within the ruling elite in Iran, on the other hand, enabled President Rafsanjani to take direct control of IRI policies in Lebanon, including the hostages issue, to renew the IRI's relations with the mainstream Syrian-supported Lebanese Shii Amal movement, and to moderate Iran's policies towards the Palestinians in Lebanon. The presence in Tehran of Nabih Berri, the leader of the moderate Amal movement, during the official mourning ceremonies for Ayatollah Khomeini, prior to Rafsanjani's election, was the clearest indication that the 'pragmatic' factions in the elite regarded the First Republic's policies in the Lebanon as damaging to Iran's interests. Once in power, the new government proceeded to marginalise the influence of the radical factions within the regime, and accelerated secret negotiations with Western powers (largely through the United Nations in 1991) for the release of all hostages. Iran's problems with its Lebanon policy were in effect turned into serving and advancing the domestic needs of the Second Republic!

Iran, in short, had embarked on the road to recovery by the end of 1989. Under the guidance of a new spiritual and executive leadership, its efforts to rebuild the weakened and exhausted army and to reconstruct the shattered economy were beginning to show positive signs. On the diplomatic front, Tehran had either restored full relations or had managed to reopen channels of communications with most of its former antagonists (including the United States, Iraq, Saudi Arabia and Egypt), and was well on the way towards reintegrating Iran fully into the regional and international order.

A number of external events in 1990, however, heightened Iran's concern with stability in its geopolitical environment. An on-going consideration was the lack of any substantial progress in the peace talks with Iraq, and the potentially destabilising impact of the 'no war, no peace' stalemate. This factor, added to the rapidity with which Iran's only influential Arab ally, Syria, was being sucked into the pro-Western Arab camp further heightened Tehran's anxieties.

Although close contacts between Tehran and Damascus were maintained, the *rapprochement* in Syrian–Egyptian relations in 1990, and the successes of the Saudi–Syrian-endorsed Taif process for the return of peace to the Lebanon raised the prospects of a re-emergence of the same Arab alliance which existed in the mid-1970s. The danger from Tehran's perspective was that the presence of such an Arab alliance could only lead to the marginalisation of Iran in regional affairs. Without diplomatic relations with either Saudi Arabia or Egypt, and unable to offer new incentives to Syria, Iran was acutely aware of its vulnerability in this area.

On another front, the resurgence of nationalist movements on Iran's northern borders offered the Maktabi adventurists new opportunities to attempt to radicalise Iran's foreign policy by forging an 'Islamic' alliance with the Muslim republics of the USSR. For the pragmatists in charge of Iran's foreign policy, however, instability on the Soviet side of the long shared border offered only more problems. Apart from the fact that the nationalist sentiments of Soviet Azerbaijanis, Turkmans, Tajikis, Kurds, etc., could influence and raise nationalist aspirations of the same ilk in Iran, preoccupation with events in the north had the potential to divert central energies and resources away from the (reconstruction and renewal) *bazsazi* process, seen by the leadership as the necessary precondition of Iran's recovery in regional terms. But even the reformists could not ignore the speed with which Saudi Arabian resources (money as well as Saudi-printed Qurans) had entered these territories. A repetition of the decade-long struggle between the two Persian Gulf powers for the minds and hearts of the Afghani and Pakistani Muslims was in evidence, but this time the prize was influence in a vast area known as Muslim Central Asia.

The worsening of Iraqi–Western relations in 1990 was another setback for Tehran's attempts to return stability to the Persian Gulf region and its own immediate environment. Although initially the verbal attacks on Iraq were seen by Iran as a sophisticated Western plan to bolster the Iraqi regime's (a Western pawn in Tehran's eyes) 'anti-imperialist' and 'radical' regional standing, Tehran was ultimately convinced that the United States and its allies were actually paving the way for the return of their forces to the region.

Tehran's problems multiplied as new evidence indicated that Iraq had indeed been attempting to manufacture devastatingly powerful new weapons, including nuclear ones. The republic's concern was whether it should seek to match or, alternatively, to slow down Iraq's military build-up. Potential Arab allies were focusing their attention on the immigration of over 200,000 Soviet Jews to Israel as well as on their own domestic problems. Islamic Iran had to show solidarity with the Arabs over the impact of Jewish immigration on 'al-Quds' and the fate of the 'Muslim Palestinians', and therefore could not raise the issue of Iraqi militarisation as the main regional concern. Indeed, the prevailing sentiment indicated that Arab posturing at this time would be conditional on a militarily superior Iraq, regardless of the reservations of many (and influential) Arab forces (Ehteshami 1993b). Iran was in no position to challenge this conventional wisdom. For the emergence of a viable counterweight to Iraq's militarisation, therefore, Iran had little choice but to be passive and to rely on the West.

For Tehran, the Western position on Iraq was a double-edged sword, although an unexpected event in 1990 – the invasion of Kuwait – was to come to Iran's aid (albeit indirectly), changing the face of the Middle East sufficiently for Iran to present and test its new regional policies vociferously. In so doing, it could stamp its renewed authority on matters pertaining to its regional interests, and seek the fulfilment of its fundamental domestic needs by pursuing its desire for stability in the Persian Gulf.

In short, while Iraq embarked on a strategy of regional domination through a military build-up after the cease-fire, Iran launched its own diplomatic offensive aimed at enhancing and consolidating its regional influence through the isolation of Iraq and the opening of hitherto closed Arab doors. Having already transformed the antagonistic basis of its relations with the Gulf Arab states into accommodation and co-operation, Iran was well placed to take advantage of the new crisis to advance its own interests. The significance of friendly Iranian overtures was not lost on the moderate Gulf states: provided that its tendency towards co-operation was not a temporary development, Iran under its new leadership could once again act as an effective counterweight to Iraq in the Persian Gulf region. Concomitantly, the emergence of a moderate line from Tehran removed the need of the Gulf Arab monarchies to rely on a protector such as Iraq. They were not, however, prepared to relinquish their military alliances with the Western countries, and this latter point has since tended to complicate Iranian–GCC discussions about regional security and Iran's role within any formal structures, even though Kuwait, Oman and Qatar have all welcomed Tehran's overtures and have spoken warmly of the republic's potential contribution to any Persian Gulf security arrangement.

THE KUWAIT CRISIS AND AFTER

Although littered with dangers for Iran, in the last analysis Baghdad's adventurism helped to improve Iran's fortunes. The invasion of Kuwait immediately raised Iran's regional profile and brought to the fore the importance of its stabilising influence upon the region. The fact that the invasion also offered Iran opportunities to end its predicament as the only pariah Persian Gulf state, however, were tempered by the presence of over 500,000 Western and other foreign troops on its doorstep (Ramazani 1992).

Iran's position during this crisis stood in sharp contrast to its interventionist and adventurist policies of the Iran–Iraq war years (Mohtashem 1993). Tehran's neutralist stance and support for the UN position, accompanied by its vociferous condemnation of the Iraqi invasion of Kuwait, was calculated to accrue maximum benefits from the crisis to the Islamic Republic (Bakhash 1993). The crisis, of course, did also contain risks for Iran and the Second Republic's leadership, offering the Maktabi forces a chance to challenge the virtues of the government's neutralist position at home, and signalling the return of substantial Western military forces to the Persian Gulf region so soon after the Iran–Iraq war.

By supporting and implementing the successive UN resolutions Iran demonstrated its desire to avoid any regional and international measures that represented an attempt to monopolise the Persian Gulf region under a unilateral US-imposed regime, or to pursue a way out of the crisis through securing an Iraqi withdrawal from Kuwait by offering it a territorial compromise. The United Nations was regarded by Tehran as a preferred, if still unsatisfactory, forum for the resolution of the crisis. In 1990, thus, Iran stood on the side of the West and for Kuwaiti sovereignty and the right of its Emir to rule the sheikhdom, when just a few years earlier it had not only tried to secure the demise of the ruling Al-Sabah family through support for Islamic dissident forces in Kuwait, but had played a significant part in escalating regional tensions.

While Iran's position on the invasion of Kuwait was unambiguous, its views on the use of force to secure an Iraqi withdrawal remained unclear. To begin with, as Iran had not offered any military assistance to the anti-Iraq coalition and the Arab and Muslim forces stationed in the Persian Gulf, it could claim, in the spirit of 'Islamic brotherhood', to act as the only effective peace broker between the warring Arab parties – a role which the United Nations also welcomed. With Turkey, as the other influential non-Arab Muslim actor directly affected by the crisis, already committed to a 'Western' solution by the virtue of its NATO membership, the field was left open for Iran to demonstrate the power of its 'constructive diplomacy'. In practice, however, the successful fulfilment of this role would have necessitated a much smaller Western military presence in the region than in fact materialised. In the end, short of joining the Iraqi camp, Iran's position left it with little choice but to support the UN-sanctioned war for the liberation of Kuwait.

On the other hand, while Iran did not actively encourage the war against Iraq, it did expect such a war to weaken significantly its most stubborn regional competitor. Iran's pragmatic foreign policy behaviour dictated that it should assign to the allies the role of exterminator. In the words of President Rafsanjani: 'The Iraqis must definitely pull out ... Here, we have no objection to them [the 'foreign forces'] obstructing aggression; anybody may help in any way' (SWB, ME/0853, 27 August 1990). What was initially interpreted by the Islamic and secular opponents of the government as inability to respond to a major crisis on its doorstep was in fact a shrewd game of patience being played by the administration, designed to extract maximum benefits for the Second Republic.

As a direct consequence of the Iraqi invasion of Kuwait, Iran was to win the victory over Iraq which had eluded it for the duration of its own war with the Iraqi regime. Iraq capitulated to Iran fully, and accepted the full implementation of SCR 598 and the 1975 Algiers Agreement concerning their border dispute. The then UN Secretary-General's (Javier Perez de Cuellar) statement on 11 December 1991 naming Iraq as the 'aggressor' (the party responsible) for starting the Iran–Iraq war was icing on the cake for the government, vindicating, in its eyes, Tehran's new regional strategies and international behaviour since 1989. Holding Iraq responsible for starting the war may have substantial financial rewards too. The guilty party will have to pay war reparations (over $300 billion, Iran calculates) according to the SCR 598 cease-fire resolution. Iran's position, thus, had been enhanced without an Iranian shot being fired. Its restraint and neutrality also obtained for Iran renewed diplomatic relations with Jordan, Tunisia and Saudi Arabia, and some positive contacts with Egypt and Morocco, the latter restoring diplomatic relations with the Islamic Republic on 18 December 1991. The war also brought an unexpected gift from Iraq: an assortment of Soviet-made military aircraft which included a number of advanced fighters and fighter-bombers.

Beyond the region, by capitalising on Iraq's isolation, Iran was able to draw closer to the European Community and encourage further Western participation in the reconstruction of the economy. Paradoxically, the escalation in regional tensions after August 1990 and the uncertainties surrounding the outcome of a coalition war against Iraq's occupation of Kuwait brought into sharper focus the importance of Iran's newly found moderation in the conduct of its foreign affairs. Furthermore, so long as Iran remained neutral it could afford to sound militant and act moderate. This was particularly important in the Leader–President's scheme of marginalising the Maktabi elements which were ready to throw caution to the winds and join Iraq in its 'holy' war against the West.

Bearing in mind that geopolitical realities never really offered Iran the option of insulating itself from developments around it, the final Iranian position on regional security which emerged in the course of the crisis needs a mention. A close examination reveals that it resembles very closely that of the Pahlavi regime's position on the Persian Gulf, based on the pursuit of relative supremacy. In a nutshell, President Rafsanjani endorsed the old Pahlavi doctrine of restoring to Iran the role of 'policeman' of the Persian Gulf, so as to prevent (or contain) the outbreak of any future acts of hostility. While this position of the Second Republic is not dependent on a formal alliance with the West, Iranian aims of ensuring stability in the Persian Gulf may suit long-term Western interests there. Tehran's endorsement of good-neighbourliness and co-operation with the Persian Gulf monarchies in the fields of oil exploration, trade, common defence, etc., ought to satisfy the Western powers that Iran is not seeking any longer to overthrow the regimes of their conservative Gulf Arab allies or disrupt the flow of oil from the countries of the Persian Gulf.

Despite Iran's significant diplomatic achievements during the Kuwait crisis, the war in 1991 and subsequent developments in the region forced a number of uncomfortable policy decisions on Tehran. The emergence of the now moribund '6+2' (the GCC, Egypt and Syria) Arab configuration in March 1991, which was intended to provide security for the Persian Gulf, highlighted, in Tehran's view, the Arab states' desire to 'Arabise' the Gulf region. Tehran was concerned that, in the aftermath of the anti-Iraq war, the Persian Gulf sheikhdoms were looking towards a counterweight to Iran's rising power (Hollis 1993), rather than seeking a strategy of co-operation and collective action on matters relating to the Persian Gulf as a semi-autonomous region. The fact that the accord envisaged the deployment of Egyptian and Syrian military forces in the Persian Gulf was interpreted by the Iranian leadership as an attack on Iran's legitimate interests in the Gulf and its security considerations. Iran really has had no choice in the short-term but to use persuasion as the policy instrument best suited to place it at the centre of discussion surrounding security in the Gulf, and has been using its close ties with Syria to enter the Arab discussions, but Tehran remains particularly concerned with Egypt's apparent attempts to position itself as the main guarantor of security for the GCC states and, by extension, the entire Persian Gulf region.

None of the recent regional and international developments, of course, has diminished the strategic value of the Persian Gulf region to Iran, if for no other reason than the fact that the 'backbone of the Iranian economy is its Persian Gulf oil' (Ramazani 1992: 395). The security of the Persian Gulf, and unhindered Iranian access to it, form a major element of Iranian regional policy. Generally speaking, Iranian concern for Gulf security has in turn tended to result in Iran adopting a more constructive policy on this issue at the same time as it has been keen to exploit to the full the tilt of the regional scales away from Iraq, going so far as to reach an understanding of sorts with Saudi Arabia over the future of Iraq, the islands crisis with the UAE notwithstanding. Indeed, Iran's bullish position on the status and ownership of the two Tunb and Abu Mussa islands could be viewed in this light: on the one hand Iran is seeking to reassert itself as the dominant local Gulf power and on the other it is keen to take full advantage of Iraq's absence by reordering its relations with the smaller Gulf Arab states.

In the post-Cold War environment in which the republic finds itself, and with the disappearance of a Soviet threat to the region's hydrocarbon resources, irrespective of its considerable difficulties at home, Tehran is eager to stamp its authority on the Persian Gulf region. Naturally, the pursuit of its 'national interest' here has the potential to bring Tehran into direct confrontation with the pro-Western GCC states and their Western backers. And this latter issue has been a major feature of Tehran's uneasy relations with the United States since the defeat of Iraq and the re-emergence of Iran as the latent dominant actor in this strategic waterway.

The diversity of the consequences of the 1991 war for Iran is demonstrated by a number of further developments. Foremost among these have been the internal challenges to the regime in Iraq, the role of Turkey as a bastion of the West (during and since the war as well as over the Kurdish refugee problem), and the apparent permanence of the Western military presence in the region (through bilateral security arrangements with several of the GCC states). In the case of the former, Iran chose to continue with its neutralist stance, preferring intervention through moral and humanitarian support of the anti-Saddam insurgents to any substantial direct military aid.

In view of President Rafsanjani's two primary objectives, reconstruction and rearmament, Iran had more to lose by aggravating Western and Gulf Arab fears of a return to its former policy of exporting the revolution by force than it had to gain by encouraging destabilisation of the Iraqi regime. Tehran thus chose to give moral, diplomatic and some military support to the opposition groups which had formed an anti-regime democratic front (including the Kurdish, Communist, the Al-Dawa Shii party, Sunni and secular forces and personalities) in late 1990 in anticipation of President Hussein's downfall. Tehran's acceptance of the united front principle, and the participation of Al-Dawa and other Iranian-supported Iraqi Shii organisations (such as the Tehran-based Supreme Council for the Islamic Revolution in Iraq) in the front were also significant in that they signalled a departure from an old policy. Far from acting in a sectarian and divisive fashion, Iran was lending its support to the vision of a pluralist and democratic Iraq which in fact neither promised a dominant role for the Shii forces in any future government nor immediately advanced the strategic cause of the First Republic: the establishment of an Islamic republic in Iraq.

Meanwhile, Turkey lent its services to the West as an extension of the former's military arm in the Persian Gulf region, both as a base for military action and as a partner in direct intervention. Although this manifested itself in an anti-Iraq form, the example was nonetheless pertinent to Iran in that should Iran appear to threaten Western interests in the Persian Gulf it might likewise be subject to Western interference in its internal affairs via Turkey. Other pressures since March 1991 and the Kurdish crisis also threaten to add to rather than alleviate the tensions between the two countries. Turkey's increasing contacts with the GCC states and the promotion of its role in Persian Gulf security, and some of the Turkish leaders' apparent desire to revive the former pan-Turanian empire by embracing the Turks of the former USSR in Central Asia and the Caucasus in 1991 (Turkey became the first Middle Eastern and Muslim state, on 10 November 1991, to extend diplomatic recognition to the former Soviet republic of Azerbaijan), coupled with patchy Turkish establishment support for Ankara taking control of the Ottoman *velayat* of Mosul (in effect northern Iraq), have combined to add a territorial dimension to the political friction between the two neighbouring countries.

One final observation: there is little Iran can do unilaterally to reverse the tide of Western military presence in the region. At best, it can aim to improve its relations with the Gulf Arab states so that they will never sanction the use of such force against Iran. In the meantime, Tehran can only seek to minimise the impact of that presence upon its regional prestige through co-operative and diplomatic measures. In this context, Iran's role in the continued isolation of Saddam's Iraq has considerable relevance.

Another, more recent, consequence of Operation Desert Storm has been the willingness of all relevant Arab parties to participate in the US-brokered peace process in the Arab–Israeli arena and to negotiate directly with Israel. Despite the improvements in Iran's relations with a number of European and Arab states during the Kuwait crisis, its sense of isolation in the region was compounded in the autumn of 1991 by Syria's entering into a political dialogue with its old enemy, Israel. Although the Syrian–Iranian alliance of the 1980s has so far survived many of the traumas of Syrian foreign policy reorientation towards Washington and the West's Arab allies, and although Syria finds in Iran an ally against Saddam's Iraq and Israel, the strengths of this alliance are being constantly tested whenever and wherever Tehran enters the Arab space or the arena of struggle between the *status quo* Arab states and Islamic revivalist forces.

For Iran, the Madrid conference of October 1991 evinced tangible evidence that the Islamic agenda had little or no relevance in the policies of most Arab states. This provided opportunities for Iran to explore the influence of the 'Islamic issues' in the Arab world and place itself at the heart of a new anti-Israel and anti-US coalition. The parallel Palestine conference ('International Conference on the Support of the Palestinian Islamic Revolution') held in Tehran provided a forum for the new leadership to display its radical Islamic credentials without necessarily contradicting the foreign policy imperatives of the Second Republic (Hunter 1992). As far as the Arab–Israeli conflict was concerned, Tehran could afford to talk tough while actually doing very little to prevent the Arab slide towards compromise. Iran's greatest achievement to date, however, has been to bring together an unlikely combination of anti-Madrid process Arab rejectionist forces and groups. The conference held in Tehran, for instance, was attended by representatives of 49 countries, including secular and Islamic Arab groups, officials and personalities who followed an Islamic political platform and/or opposed the US-brokered peace initiative. The terminology and recommendations of the 28 point final resolution of the conference highlight well Iran's role as an effective Islamic interlocutor with growing influence in Arab circles (for the full text see *Kayhan Havai* 30 October 1991). Representatives of Islamic and radical secular Arab and Palestinian groups continue to meet routinely in Tehran, receive some financial support from Iran and use its tribune to speak and act against the Arab states (including the PLO) which are in the Western camp, and/or favour the US-brokered peace process.

The Iranian position on the Arab–Israeli peace process carries many risks, particularly in terms of potential friction with Syria and other Arab states in favour of the Madrid discussions, but it should be recognised that opportunities also abound for Iran to use its opposition to this process as a way of maintaining direct influence in the Arab world and over the agenda of the Islamist and radical Arab forces.

The disintegration of the USSR offered further opportunities for consolidation of the Second Republic's attempts at self-advancement. Iran has been extending its influence into the Asian Muslim republics through offering economic assistance, some technical advice as well as religious guidance. The expansion of economic ties between Iran and its new northern neighbours deserves particular attention. The expansion in trade and production ties has been facilitated through the signing of a string of bilateral economic co-operation agreements since the end of the Cold War (Ehteshami 1994). The first significant agreement of this nature was signed between the IRI and Azerbaijan in August 1991, on the occasion of President Matlabov's trip to Iran – his first overseas visit as Azerbaijan's new President (*Kayhan Havai* 28 August 1991). Two months later (in October 1991) Iran signed four trade protocols with Turkmenistan worth over $130 million, again on the occasion of the Turkmani President's (Niyazov) trip to the Islamic Republic at the head of a 60-member delegation (*Kayhan Havai* 25 October 1991). Since then Iran has continued to promote trade ties and bilateral contacts with the republics of Central Asia and the Caucasus. It now has bilateral ties with all these republics and has been instrumental in expanding the ECO and the creation of the Caspian Sea grouping (see Ehteshami 1994 for details).

It should perhaps be pointed out that Iran's economic co-operation efforts have not been limited to exchanges with the Muslim republics. Two oil and trade-related agreements signed with Armenia and Ukraine are noteworthy in this context. The agreement with Armenia was reached in December 1991 (*Kayhan Havai* 11 December 1991). It is based on industrial exchanges between Iran and Armenia and on economic co-operation over oil. The agreement between Ukraine and the IRI was signed in February 1991. The two sides agreed to build an oil and a natural gas pipeline through Ukraine in order to take Iranian oil and natural gas exports to Europe. The agreement is likely to give Iran transport access to the Black Sea as well (and by extension the Mediterranean), thus enabling Iran's overland trade with Europe to bypass Turkey (which has been earning as much as $1 billion a year from its role as the land bridge between Iran and the European continent). The economic relationship between Iran and Ukraine could become significant, particularly as Ukraine seeks to lift more oil from Iran as a way of reducing the newly independent republic's dependence on oil imports from Russia. In exchange, Iran will import metal products and industrial machinery from Ukraine (*Kayhan Havai* 12 February 1991), as well as weaponry, of course.

While it was rather late in extending diplomatic recognition to these republics – formally recognising Azerbaijan, Turkmenistan, Tajikistan, Uzbekistan, Kazakhstan, Kyrghyzstan, Armenia, Georgia, Byelorussia and the Russian Federation on 25 December 1991 – Iran is clearly unwilling to forgo the advantages to be gained by closer relations, despite fierce competition for influence against Turkey and Saudi Arabia. Persian influence in Central Asia should not be underestimated. Geographical proximity, historical relations, linguistic and ethnic ties, and the appeal of Islamic Iran to many Central Asian Muslims, all help to promote and sustain Iran's interests in Central Asia (Hooglund 1994). It is perhaps telling, in this context, that the delegations of Kazakhstan and Azerbaijan were attached to the Iranian delegation attending the sixth summit of the Organisation of the Islamic Conference (December 1991) in Senegal.

IRAN: REGIONAL ACTOR OR REGIONAL POWER?

After a decade in the cold, with revolution and war detracting from its ability to assert its strategic aims in the region, Iran has since the Iran–Iraq war cease-fire, and more intensely since the Kuwait crisis, demonstrated that it is once again both willing and able to draw upon its geopolitical deposits, as well as its ideological dynamic, to resume its role as a major regional actor with ambitions. Although encouraged by circumstances, it faces at the same time a multitude of obstacles, not least outside pressures (most directly from Washington and the Clinton administration's 'dual containment' Persian Gulf security doctrine, which aims to isolate Iraq and squeeze Iran), a grave domestic economic crisis and, critically, a shortage of real power projection capabilities.

Recalling the discussion in chapter 6, Iran's major regional power status was assured by the mid-1970s, largely thanks to the close US–Iranian relationship built around the 'twin pillar' structures of the Nixon doctrine and the oil boom of the 1970s. In a relatively short period of time Tehran had managed to raise its regional profile and was increasingly influential in establishing politico-military alliances with both Arab and non-Arab states. At the same time Tehran was showing much interest in developing economic and political ties with a number of Far Eastern states, and an increasing appetite for expanded diplomatic and political influence in the Indian Ocean, specifically in the Indian subcontinent and East Africa (Cottrell 1975). The latter was to be achieved in two ways: expansion of the country's 'blue water' naval fleet and the modernisation of the air force's strategic arm, and the offer of economic assistance and financial aid (Singh 1980).

The prerequisite of much of the above was a modern and increasingly complex industrial economy. The creation of such an economic power house in under a generation was in turn predicated upon intensive use of the oil wealth as the main tool for building Iran into the fifth largest military-industrial global power. As to why Iran should want to become such an international power, this can partly be explained through the lens of geopolitics. Having tasted the power commensurate with oil wealth and having entered into a security relationship with the United States, Tehran was, in a sense, compelled to expand its regional profile. In this process, Iran was able to utilise its natural regional advantages in terms of geographical location, skilfully playing to the country's strengths and using them in turn as the rationale for the Iranian state's growing sphere of interests.

Before the revolution, therefore, Iran had already managed to assume many of the trappings of a regional power, including military and economic might, all of which were inherited by the leaders of the Islamic Republic.

While revolution and war did sap the energies of the state, the *preconditions* for a major Iranian presence in the region were never removed. The reduction in vital state energy was compensated for by the Islamic ideology of the revolutionary regime, a power source previously untapped by the Imperial regime.

With the war over and the focus of the regime shifting towards reconstruction at home and the normalisation of its foreign relations, the pendulum has slowly swung back in the direction of geopolitical assertiveness. It should not prove too surprising, therefore, that plans for the reconstruction of the economy have been accompanied by blueprints for the reconstruction of the country's military capacity and the re-equipment of the armed forces. Military reconstruction and rearmament drives in turn have accelerated the reassertion of geopolitical factors in the republic's regional policies, a complex relationship which received a boost from Iraq's military defeat in 1991 and the disappearance of the Soviet threat from Iran's northern borders.

Inevitably, as soon as Iran's foreign policy changed tempo and followed a more conventional form of interaction with other states, it became more assertive and began to conform to what I call the iron law of geopolitics, even adopting some of the main features of the policy of the Pahlavi state. Most telling have been the republic's drive towards a blue water naval capability (as the acquiring of three Kilo-class submarines illustrates), its purchasing of medium-range bombers and advanced fighters and interceptors, its acquisition of long-range SSMs, and finally its desire for an effective non-conventional weapons capability. Coupled with these military developments have been Tehran's diplomatic offensives in East Africa, the Asian subcontinent and Central Asia and other regions which were of interest to Imperial Iran.

The largely non-ideological approach to problem resolution in Iran in recent years corresponds with the ruling faction's recognition of three important realities. Firstly, the realisation that the international system is highly interdependent and that Iran is unable to function very effectively outside the given international structures for any length of time. Secondly, acceptance of the country's deep economic problems and the urgent need for reform of the entire economic system and its administrative machinery. Finally, recognition of the necessity of foreign assistance in ameliorating Iran's many economic difficulties and its military weaknesses, and its lack of investment capital. It could be argued, in a structural sense, that the pragmatic line is a result of a complex chicken-and-egg situation in which the Iranian state can develop in economic and politico-military terms only if it readjusts to the international system, and in turn such readjustment and reintegration act to impose further pressures on Iran to conform with the contours of that very (Western-dominated) system.

In terms of role conception, therefore, one can argue that Iran is poised to emerge on to the regional scene as a regional power with some influence, and that this is a natural by-product of its geopolitical situation. With the passage of time, it is clear that Iran's role performance increasingly matches its role conception. Although it has been argued that the rise of Iran to pre-eminence is a direct function of its geopolitical conditions (and advantages), the country's re-emergence as a regional power is not assured simply because of its geopolitical advantages and could be checked by a number of developments. Indeed, as has been shown, geopolitics is a double-edged sword which can cut both ways. At the domestic level, for instance, in addition to the economic, military and political problems which continue to haunt the regime, restless minorities and urban social tensions refuse to go away. Tehran's efforts to deal with these problems can serve only to sap the country's finite energies. Its ideological convictions (and revolutionary heritage) can cut both ways too, giving Tehran influence with sub-state (mainly Islamist) actors while at the same time complicating its relations with the regimes in power. Furthermore, the post-Khomeini leadership's desire to combine and gel the vitality of the regime's ideology with the state's plentiful resources as the formula for national cohesion has been fraught with contradictions.

Externally too Tehran is vulnerable. Sub-systemic rivalries have not disappeared with the Cold War and will therefore remain a feature of the West Asian strategic environment. Thus, Iran, as an interested party, cannot isolate itself from the pressures to 'enter the rat race'. There are also other pressures to consider, including the complex border problems and rising ethnic-based nationalisms on Iran's doorstep, the pervasive presence of the United States in the Middle East and the rise of a new (and rather unstable) periphery to the north of Iran.

FUTURE PROSPECTS

The constitutional reforms and change of leadership in 1989 brought to the fore a 'presidential centre', to borrow Korany and Dessouki's terminology, which was able to push through reforms of the economy and overhaul the foreign policy of the Islamic Republic at a rapid pace. The emergence of a non-charismatic and coalition-oriented Faqih (as the spiritual leader) helped to legitimise the new government's policies. A combination of factors after Iran's acceptance of SCR 598 thus facilitated the advancement of the pragmatic agenda of the reformers in Iran. The success of these reforms will of course depend on economic growth and reconstruction at home. But their success is also dependent on the survival of the current leadership and the maintenance of the existing balance of power within the ruling elite of the Second Republic. Bearing in mind the new balance of forces at the international level, without the integrationists at the helm deviations from the strategy of reform are always probable, but whether they would be reversible is not at all clear. The changes in domestic and foreign policy have acquired their own momentum, and cannot be halted overnight. The demise of the Soviet state shows the Iranian leadership the dangers inherent in half-hearted reform or sudden disruption of the process. For these reasons, none of the Maktabi factions may be willing to risk open confrontation with the government at this stage, even though they became politically active again in 1993 through resurrecting the Ruhaniyun-e Mobarez association (*Kayhan Havai* 13 October 1993).

Their chance, however, may come in the late 1990s, when Iran has to choose a new President (unless the constitution is amended for President Rafsanjani to stand for a third term). Election politics, thus, has become a main feature of political life in the Iranian Second Republic. To insure re-election in 1993, not only did Rafsanjani have to isolate the radical factions, he also had to offer material incentives (a higher standard of living, higher wages in the public sector, employment, better living conditions, more accessible luxury and essential goods, cheaper food and fuel, etc.) to the electorate. Economic reconstruction and the satisfaction of these needs depend on investment by the private sector and large-scale foreign participation in the economy, both of which depend on the continuation of the reformist policies adopted by the Rafsanjani government. Then there is the question of regional stability. The organic relationship between domestic prosperity and regional (and international) stability serves the political interests of the pragmatists as well, in that they rely on popular demand for a 'better life' to marginalise the influence of the Maktabis within the establishment. So long as they can deliver, or appear to be trying to do so, it should be possible for them to contain the challenge of the rejectionists.

Iran's economic contacts with the leading Western European countries, Japan, China, a number of the newly industrialising countries of the Third World (such as South Korea, Brazil, India, Taiwan, Turkey) and the former Comecon countries of Europe have accelerated since August 1988, and these contacts in turn have raised substantially the country's consumer and industrial goods imports, offering economic partners a rich picking ground. In addition, the government's decision in 1989 to liberalise the economy and encourage foreign direct investment in most areas of economic activity, coupled with its privatisation programme, promises to turn Iran into a high-growth economy. In as much as Iran's trade relations have a political dimension, the combination of these factors has put a premium on maintaining close diplomatic relations with the Islamic Republic. While for most of the countries listed above this has not proved problematic, the United States remains for the most part excluded from the Iranian market. Nevertheless, covert contacts continue between Tehran and Washington. This much has been evident since the Iran-Contra affair.

But direct and indirect (through the United Nations, for example) contacts in the course of the resolution of the Western hostages crisis in Lebanon show that both sides can take some steps towards establishing a structured diplomatic dialogue over matters of mutual concern, such as the future of Iraq, the security of the Gulf region, Afghanistan, and the Kurdish question. According to reports from the United States, all the key negotiations about the Western captives in Beirut were held in Iran and the representatives of the hostage-takers were provided with Iranian travel documents. It is said that Iran paid the hostage-takers an average of $1 million to $2 million for the release of each US hostage, an allegation denied by Iran. The influence of the resolution of the Lebanon hostages issue on bilateral relations and on Iran's international position was alluded to by a European diplomat at UN headquarters. Don Oberdorfer maintains that 'On December 9 [1991], shortly after the release of the last American and British hostages, the UN secretary-general issued a formal report finding that Iraq was responsible for starting the Iran–Iraq War' (*International Herald Tribune*, 20 January 1992). US qualified approval of the nature and pace of reform in the Second Republic during the Bush administration, however, has given way to a more hostile attitude towards Iran on the part of the Clinton White House. While containment remains President Clinton's main foreign policy towards Iran, his administration is fully aware that the demise of the Rafsanjani administration could not only usher in a new phase of radicalism in Iran, but also help to destabilise the vitally important Persian Gulf region.

The sea-changes in the international system since 1989, the demise of the USSR, and the emergence of NATO as the only multinational military bloc with global force projection capabilities have removed the security umbrella which many Third World countries had traditionally relied upon to resist US pressure during the Cold War. Although Iran was not a Soviet client state, it has suffered from the latter's demise. With the disintegration of the Soviet superpower Iran has lost the opportunity to manipulate the Cold War system, and the ability to play one superpower off against another as a way of affirming the country's independence. Although Tehran remains hopeful that, post-1992, the European Union may be in a position to provide a counterweight to the US as it begins the arduous task of developing a coherent foreign and security policy system independent of US interests, it is apparent that for the foreseeable future Europe will toe the American line regarding regional and North–South issues. For these reasons, pragmatists argue, in the post-bipolar international system, with the emergence of a unipolar world, it is much more advisable to make a friend of the United States than an enemy. The example of Iraq serves to illustrate the point for them.

In so far as Iran can find ways of reducing the impact of the Western-dominated and US-orchestrated 'new world order' on its own socio-economic and politico-military system, it has been emphasising the importance of multilateral regional and international organisations and agencies in providing useful channels for the Third World to participate actively in the shaping of the post-Cold War international order. Iran itself has been busy raising the country's representation in such forums. Iran's willingness to participate in the ICO meeting in Senegal in December 1991 (for the first time since the revolution) and the high level of the delegation sent to the gathering (including President Rafsanjani and his Foreign Minister), and in the population conference in Cairo in September 1994 underline Tehran's chosen policy of active international representation. But perhaps the most important multilateral organisation to Iran is the United Nations. Iran's continuing support for an active UN presence in the post-Cold War order fits in well with Tehran's assessment of the international balance of power. The emphasis on the United Nations is best illustrated by Iran's willingness to reopen the UN Information Centre in Tehran, closed down in 1980 (*Kayhan Havai* 18 December 1991).

Not having formal politico-military alliances with any state gives Iran a considerable degree of autonomy in action, but at the same time having no allies to speak of imposes certain costs on the republic. Firstly, the assertion of autonomous regional power invites counteraction from threatened rivals. Thus the more Iran rises as an autonomous regional power, the more America or Russia, for example, will consider themselves forced to counter Iranian influence with their own and that of their allies. Without an alliance of any sort to back it, Iran will face unlimited counterweights, with no party feeling constrained to weigh in on its behalf. So autonomy in this instance acts also as a limit on expansion of influence. Secondly, lack of overt politico-military allies limits the scope of Iranian power both in the Arab world and in the Caucasus and Central Asia.

Then there is the problem of single-commodity export reliance. Overexposure to the hydrocarbon sector has remained a feature of monarchical and republican Iran, and the republican regime's continuing reliance on the export of oil and natural gas means that it cannot altogether function as an autonomous actor in the region, and that it is dependent on co-operation and needs collective action if it is to secure its vital interests. The most obvious area in which an alliance might be desirable for Tehran is hydrocarbons, and there is no other ally more important in this regard than Saudi Arabia, the world's most influential oil state and OPEC's largest producer. Ultimately, the needs of the state will direct its regional policies, and in order to become a regional power Iran will need to overcome its oil dependence and will thus have to face the conundrum that the Shah faced: aiming to strengthen the regional profile of the country and having no option but to co-operate with other states in order to realise that ambition. To do this sucessfully, Tehran is more than ever reliant on the goodwill of its OPEC partners, specifically Saudi Arabia and its oil-exporting GCC partners: a situation clearly not relished by the Iranian leadership. But whether Riyadh will volunteer assistance in Iran's emergence as a regional power is an open question, more so if one takes into account Washington's anxieties and sensitivities to the spread of Iranian-style fundamentalism.

In conclusion, one can say that, in a broad sense, the orientation of the IRI's foreign policy remains Islamist-based, non-aligned and pro-South. Rajai Khorasani (former Iranian ambassador to the United Nations) has argued that certain 'inclinations' have appeared in the Islamic Republic's foreign policy since its acceptance of SCR 598, which indicate changes in the conduct of its diplomacy and not a transformation of foreign policy: 'no change has taken place in the foreign policies and strategies of their implementation, but . . . modifications have occurred in [Iran's] diplomacies' (*The Echo of Iran* March 1989: 16). The thrust of the argument in this chapter has been that indeed the change in diplomacy stemmed from Iran's worsening (military and economic) domestic situation and its regional isolation. Although, in general terms, the orientation of its foreign policy did remain consistent with the past in the earlier years of post-Khomeini Iran, nonetheless the Second Republic behaves in ways wholly at variance with the doctrines of the First Republic. In time, the orientation of Iran's policies must also change to reflect its new position and role in the world. Such change, however, entails neither Iran's becoming a pro-Western state nor its abandonment of the Islamic doctrine as its guiding principle.

Within the region, in addition to seeking better and closer ties with the moderate Arab states, it has to be remembered that Iran has also sought to maintain close relations with those other Arab states and groups commonly known as 'radical'. But the ranks of the Arab radicals are thinning fast, and this in turn complicates Iran's *rapprochement* with the Arab states. Iran's position on the FIS, for instance, led to a rupture of the warm relations which had characterised bilateral relations in the 1970s and 1980s as the Algerian government accused Iran of interference in Algeria's internal affairs by providing material support to the FIS. But other countries, like Libya and Sudan, remained sufficiently isolated from the moderate Arab camp and the West to continue to offer themselves as alternative friends of the Islamic Republic. Iran's alliance with the Islamic government of al-Bashir in Sudan since 1990 has been viewed with concern by Egypt and Saudi Arabia, which regard the Red Sea and the upper Nile regions as their spheres of influence. Reports in 1991 indicated that Sudan had been receiving economic and military assistance from Iran. President Rafsanjani's visit to Sudan, at the head of a 157 member delegation, in mid-December 1991 reaffirmed the politico-military and economic relationship between the two states. It was said at the time that Iran had been financing Sudan's recent arms purchases from China, including 18 F-7 and F-8 fighters, 160 tanks, 210 armoured personnel carriers, and an undisclosed number of heavy artillery and multiple-launch rocket systems (Lusk 1991; *Financial Times* 17 December 1991). How important these ties will prove to be to Iran's attempts to extend its influence further into the Arab world cannot be answered with ease, but the acquisition of allies and friends at all levels of the Arab system (Makinda 1993), in however eclectic a way, is the most concrete achievement of the Second Republic by comparison with the First. On the Iranian–Sudanese relationship, for instance, Abd al-Salam Sidahmed has argued that this relationship offers a mutually advantageous exchange to the two sides, whereby Sudan gains access to badly needed economic, technical and military assistance from a Muslim country, and Iran expands its influence in East Africa and at the same time provides support for a like-minded Islamic regime in the Arab world (Sidahmed 1992).

Although some global changes have demanded a re-evaluation of Iran's foreign policy, for example the need to redefine the first component of the 'neither East nor West' equation since the end of the Second World (as constituted during the Cold War), the thrust of Iran's foreign policy remains Third World-oriented. Without the Eastern bloc to balance against the West, non-aligned states such as Iran have little choice but to forge new (and less antagonistic) relationships with the remaining pole. Nominally, the orientation of the Second Republic remains similar to that advocated by the republic's founding fathers, but in practice President Rafsanjani's domestic priorities have taken precedence over long-term ideological foreign policy posturing. The achievement of these domestic objectives has indeed necessitated a restructuring of Iran's foreign policy. A corollary of national politico-military strength (economic reconstruction and rearmament) is that the leadership of the Second Republic has developed a perception of Iran's role in the region based, not on Iran being primarily the hub of an expanding Islamic revolution, ultimately to encompass its Muslim neighbours, but rather on regaining its position as a militarily powerful and politically influential player in the regional arena. Ultimately, this is at heart a secular aspiration, however 'Islamic' the dressing – or indeed the conviction – of the elite which pursues it.

Finally, although to talk of Iran becoming a major regional power as we edge towards the twenty-first century may be premature, the potential remains, as well as the will and the investment. Domestic weakness and external obstacles should not be assumed to be rigid certainties and Iran may yet emerge upon the Middle East stage as a regional power in the next century. In the words of a seasoned observer of international relations,

> So long as it steers clear of breaches of international rules which could bring outsiders down on its head, Iran . . . now has the potential to become the most influential state in the Middle East. Whether this is a good thing or bad, it is something which absolutely nobody intended and virtually nobody outside Iran likes.
>
> (Calvocoressi 1991: 300)

As we have seen, there are still many pitfalls in the way of Iran emerging as the dominant actor, but once the republic is recharged and self-confident it is difficult to see directions in which Iran may not influence the destiny of the region.

8   Security and defence strategy of the Second Republic

I was right in the past. Think what the Iraqis could do today with their torpedo boats in the Persian Gulf if we did not have the power to retaliate.
(Mohammad Reza Shah Pahlavi, June 1969)

Another policy area which underwent a major transformation in the Second Republic is security and defence. The policy changes in this field have encompassed the republic's military structures as well as a review of the country's rearmament strategy and the development of its defence industries. The previous chapter discussed the issue of Iran's rearmament drive within the context of the Second Republic's security environment and foreign policy objectives. This chapter, by contrast, will deal with the mechanisms through which these ambitions of the Second Republic leaders may be realised. In addition it builds on the discussion in previous chapters to show what, if any, might be the impact of the regional arms race and other regional realities on the security strategy of the Second Republic.

Despite the idiosyncracies of the First Islamic Republic's defence strategy, and in its conduct of the war with Iraq, a constant streak of pragmatism was visible with regard to defence strategy beneath the veneer of radicalism and rejectionism. The politico-military elite, the high-ranking military personnel and their technocratic allies in the political establishment (both clerical and non-clerical), was responsible not only for the planning and execution of the war effort on a daily basis, it also supervised the country's military procurements for the Pasdaran and the regular army on the one hand, and the republic's domestic defence production efforts on the other.

The leaders of the Second Republic, including the President and the Faqih, have been involved in the nation's defence policies since 1980, many having served on important defence-related executive and decision-making committees and bodies. Khamenei, as the former President and the Chairman of the Supreme Defence Council, for instance, was directly involved in virtually every strategic decision taken by the country's military establishment. And the former Speaker, representing Ayatollah Khomeini on the same body, initiated policy at the same time as influencing critical decisions.

The transition towards 'moderation' in foreign policy led by the pragmatists, and the fuller control of the country's military affairs by the same group, began in earnest in the mid-1980s, with the direct involvement of Hojjatoleslam Rafsanjani, culminating in his successful trips to China and North Korea in the mid-1980s. The line he championed received a further boost from Ayatollah Khomeini's decision to appoint him C-in-C on 2 June 1988, just weeks before Iran's unconditional acceptance of SCR 598. With internal security assured and the justified criticisms of the populace regarding the conduct of the war deflected (both its perpetuation and its sudden end without any tangible results for Iran), reconstruction efforts began to take on a new urgency after the death of the founder of the republic.

DEFENCE AND THE SECOND REPUBLIC

Between 1988/9 and 1991/2 defence and defence-related matters, a major priority in government expenditure proposals, were destined to absorb on average about a quarter to one-third of overall expenditures (*The Middle East Military Balance* various years; *Military Technology* various years). The Second Republic's First Five Year Development Plan made a total allocation of almost $10 billion for military-related expenditures, equivalent to $2 billion per annum (*COMET Bulletin* April 1991). As Table 25 highlights, defence and security accounted for 7.6 per cent of the total foreign exchange allocation for the plan period.

Indeed, after the cease-fire agreement, Prime Minister Moussavi repeatedly pointed out that the government would continue to implement the proportional expenditures envisaged for the 1984 to 1987 wartime budgets. According to International Monetary Fund data, defence accounted for 14.2 per cent of Iranian government expenditures in 1986, 11.8 per cent in 1987, 11.7 per cent in 1988 and 11.6 per cent in 1989 (IMF 1991). Mofid calculates that military expenditures accounted for (on average) 10.9 per cent of the country's GDP between 1980 and 1985 (Mofid 1990), and International Institute for Strategic Studies figures indicate that between 1985 and 1991 defence expenditures accounted for between 8.6 per cent and 7.1 per cent of the GDP (*The Military Balance* various years). National sources, however, put the defence budget for the 1981–8 period at about 14.4 per cent of total annual government expenditure. In money terms, the total defence budget stood at $59.4 billion for the 1981–8 period (*MEED* 31 March 1989).

Soon after the end of the war Prime Minister Moussavi emphasised that a 'fundamental duty' of his government would be 'to strengthen the defence forces' (SWB, ME/0270, 30 September 1988). Although the 1989 defence

Table 25 Major Five Year Plan import allocations, 1989/90–1994/5 ($ billion)

Industry	34.35
Commerce	19.49
Oil and petroleum products	14.73
Defence and security	9.05
Agriculture	7.10
Electricity	6.24
Roads and transport	4.30
Water resources	4.10
Mining	2.90
Health	2.05
Postal and communications	1.93
Gas	1.80
Total goods imports	112.75
Service imports	4.50
Presidential discretion fund	1.00
Total including capital account	119.15

Source: Middle East Economic Survey 11 December 1989.

Note: Figures rounded up for convenience.

budget was cut to $5.9 billion (from a high of $10 billion in 1988), reports from Tehran in May 1989 indicated that the Majlis had approved a secret budget Bill for 1989/90 in which defence spending was much higher than the announced amount (*APS Diplomat 22* 29 May/5 June 1989). According to Hojjatoleslam Rafsanjani, 'during the war more than half of the country's income was spent on the war' (*Kayhan Havai* 12 July 1989). Although the total amount fluctuated in tandem with the country's oil export revenues, the large rial funds raised domestically ensured substantial domestic investment and expenditures on local procurement of defence and defence-related goods and services.

Despite Iran's pressing economic problems, therefore, the Second Republic has been no different from its predecessor in its commitment to expenditure on procurement of and investment in the indigenous production of arms and the military infrastructure. Although in overall allocation of national resources the focus of the government has been on economic reconstruction, the defence sector continues to receive investment funds as well as resources for arms purchases from abroad, though, Iranian officials would say, as a declining proportion of general budget allocations since 1992. Indications from government sources would support the view, however, that ideally defence should have received an increasingly higher proportion of resources during the second half of the implementation of the Five Year Plan. According to the navy commander Rear-Admiral Shamkhani, as part of the

Table 26 Iran's military expenditures, 1981–91

Year	Billion rials	$ million
1981	346	12,321
1982	341	10,230
1983	340	8,523
1984	363	8,082
1985	455	9,705
1986	486	9,339
1987	459	7,679
1988	505	7,353
1989	483	5,747
1990	480	5,306
1991	644	6,125

Source: SPIRI (various years).

Five Year Plan the Iranian navy was scheduled 'to acquire sophisticated air and sea defence systems, besides submarines' (SWB, ME/0707, 8 March 1990). Vice-President Habibi has said, 'In the review of the Five Year Plan in the second half of the current [Iranian] year [March 1990–March 1991] problems of more general nature such as the [needs of the] security and defence forces will come under scrutiny [of the government]' (*Kayhan Havai* 4 September 1991). As will be shown below, however, in general the government's serious economic difficulties since 1991/2 have lowered the outlays in real terms on the defence sector.

The continuing 'no war–no peace' situation with regard to Iraq (from August 1988 until Iraq's unconditional acceptance of the 1975 Algiers Accords in August 1990, after which the UN found Iraq guilty of commencing the war with Iran in November 1991, little progress towards finalising a peace treaty had been made by the beginning of President Rafsanjani's second term of office) added urgency to the new leadership's quest for military superiority and preparedness, thus merely reinforcing the complex domestic tendencies towards the establishment of a key role for defence in Iran's national life. A number of reasons can be presented for this attitude. Firstly, the long years of war had taught the Iranian leaders the lessons of entering into a conflict unprepared and with inferior arms, especially against a militarily well equipped enemy. Military deterrence, furthermore, achieved through a well armed and equipped military machine, was seen to promise future security for the republic: 'we are working towards an army which is small but efficient', in the words of Mohammad Javad Larijani (the President's adviser on foreign relations) (*Financial Times Survey* 1993: II).

Preparedness, efficiency and firepower would become essential aspects of the IRI's post-war military doctrine, especially as it had been Iran which had shied away from entering into military alliances with powerful external actors, and not its southern neighbours. The emphasis would be on the air force. Former Defence Minister Akbar Torkan explicitly endorsed the emphasis put on the air force by the leaders of the Second Republic when he said in 1990: 'the air force has so far played the biggest role in the reconstruction of armed forces equipment' (SWB, ME/0892, 11 October 1990). The air force commander himself has underlined the need to have an effective air force and advanced air defence systems in place as the minimum guarantee of the country's security, particularly during its critical reconstruction and rebuilding period (Ziarati 1992).

The establishment of the Ministry of Defence and Armed Forces Logistics in 1989, headed by the technocrat former director of the defence industries establishment, Akbar Torkan, helped to isolate the influence of the potentially troublesome IRGC, which was known for its radicalism and its domination by Maktabis. The amalgamation of the energies and resources of the Pasdaran (after the cease-fire the reorganisation of the Pasdaran forces became a major government priority. In August and September 1988 the Pasdaran's ground forces were reorganised into 21 infantry divisions, 15 independent infantry brigades, 21 air defence brigades, three engineering divisions, and 42 armoured, artillery and chemical defence brigades; *Gulf Report* October 1988) and their Ministry (founded in 1982) with the professional armed forces was intended to strengthen the position of the pragmatists, in so far as it imposed institutional limitations on the power of the Pasdaran. Besides the important political implications of disbanding the political machinery of the 'Guardians of the Islamic Revolution' (the phrase used in reference to the IRGC) and the elimination of their independent military base amongst the Iranian power elite, the choice of a technocratic civilian to head the new Ministry indicated three major developments; experienced technocrats were chosen by the President to lead the revitalisation of the armed forces and their reorganisation, the emphasis of the new leadership was clearly on co-ordinating the domestic military production efforts of various institutions and bodies, and finally, enhancing the current capabilities of the military-industrial complex was a matter of priority.

In putting into operation these sweeping policy changes, President Rafsanjani enjoyed the confidence of the regular armed forces. And by choosing a civilian with no organic ties with either the Guards or the professional armed forces as the new Minister he effectively prevented the rise of open competition between these two forces for control of the new Ministry. In re-channelling the country's military potential towards the professional army once again he won many friends in the military but also, by ensuring that the

Guards continued to receive resources and equipment commensurate with their status, prevented both the outbreak of hostilities between these hitherto competing forces and the alienation of the Guards as a powerful force within the ranks of the FIR ruling elite.

Through constantly emphasising the importance of the Pasdaran to the security of the country the Rafsanjani administration has deflected the Maktabis' criticism of his secular attitude towards matters relating to defence. The systematic emphasis on the professionalisation of the Guards has brought with it resources, prestige and kudos for this once irregular band of revolutionary volunteers. The appointment in 1989 of Ali Shamkhani, one of the Pasdaran commanders and the former IRGC Minister, as a rear-admiral to lead the regular navy was the first instance of the Second Republic's attempts to institutionalise the role of the Guards and its personnel in the new system. This appointment was followed in January 1992 by the appointment of Brigadier General Mohammad Hussein Jalali (a well known officer of the regular armed forces), a former Minister of Defence (1985–80) and commander of the airborne forces (Havanirouz), as the commander of the Pasdaran air force (at the behest of the Pasdaran's own commander) (*Kayhan Havai* 29 January 1992). The two events combined lead one to conclude that the integration of the two armed forces of the republic and the process of 'professionalisation' of the Pasdaran by the leaders of the Second Republic has continued unabated. Indeed, these appointments illustrate the relative success of the integrative measures adopted by the new regime, and highlight the emerging fluidity between the two forces' command structures and operations, a measure that the Leader–President alliance has been insisting upon since 1989.

The announcement in early 1992 of the creation of a single office of the joint chiefs of staff (offically to be known as the General Command of the Armed Forces Joint Staffs) under Hassan Firouzabadi (another civilian and a prominent figure in the Pasdaran) offers further evidence of the moves towards the total integration of the two armed forces of the republic. This move follows the merger of the country's internal security forces in 1991 (Haeri 1992). Interestingly, Mr Firouzabadi announced that one of his first administrative tasks would be the establishment of a Supreme Council on Military Policy in order to crystallise the respective duties of the various branches of the republic's armed forces (ibid.).

The introduction of new uniforms and military ranks in the formerly 'egalitarian' Guards, similar to those of the regular armed forces, announced at the end of 1989, was another feature of the efforts to professionalise, de-revolutionise and institutionalise this force. The ranks were to be divided along four categories of soldiers, fighters, officers and commandants (*Iran Focus* January 1990). Some 21 military ranks, from private to general, were formally introduced in September 1991, which with six exceptions were all equivalent to those of the regular army (*Iran Focus* November 1991).

Far from being a secondary concern of the regime, therefore, improvements in defence, security and related military matters have been regarded as an important dimension of the country's reconstruction efforts. As Hojjatoleslam Rafsanjani was to point out prior to his election as the new President:

> we have repeatedly said that our defence structure should be strong, even though our policy is a policy of peace . . . We have chosen our path by putting emphasis on domestic military industries in order to provide for our own defence needs and ensure that we do not need to depend on others.
> (*The Echo of Iran* July–August 1989: 17)

In this context the military sector is the inevitable beneficiary of industrial reconstruction, technological absorption, expanded energy production capacity and further improvements in the country's infrastructure and other utilities. Thus as the country's general economic condition improves the opportunities for further military production and military-related research and development also multiply.

POLICY ON REARMAMENT AND ARMS PROCUREMENT

The experience of the war years has shown the leaders of the Islamic Republic that there is no shortage of international suppliers of arms, only that they may not always be able to provide the most sophisticated US-made hardware at the most reasonable price. According to Hans Maull, 'at the beginning of the conflict in 1980, Iran received major weapon systems from five countries and Iraq from three; in 1985 Iran used 17 such suppliers and Iraq 18' (Maull 1991: 127). At one time or another Iran imported arms from some 20 countries, often involving a combination of Western, communist and non-aligned Third World states. But in reality as the war dragged on so Iran's military position deteriorated. Indeed, Iran's military superiority began to evaporate soon after 1982, barely two years into the war with Iraq. Its air force, according to a careful study of the Iran–Iraq war, 'not only lost its technical edge over Iraq, the entire Iranian Air Force probably could not generate more than 60–70 sorties per day under seige conditions after 1983' (Cordesman and Wagner 1990: 478). Iran's land warfare capabilities were similarly depleted, and to a lesser degree its naval power. The army's main battle tank (MBT) force and its mechanised fighting potential were substantially reduced from the early days of the war, and by 1985 it could field only about 1,200 MBTs and only another 950 armoured personnel carriers against an Iraqi MBT force of nearly 5,000 and another 2,500 armoured vehicles. As Cordesman and Wagner note, 'Iran began the war with fewer tanks and artillery pieces than Iraq [and] this disadvantage grew throughout the war' (Cordesman and Wagner 1990: 427). By 1988 it could field only about 750 tanks and a similar number of armoured vehicles.

Appreciable improvements in the number and quality of arms in the inventories of Iraq and other Gulf Arab states merely worsened the blow of depreciation of Iran's sophisticated arms inventory. This inventory depleted at an alarming rate over the last three years of the war, making complete rearmament a necessity for the new leadership. Table 27 summarises the estimated loss of military aircraft over the 1980s and the replacement drive of the Second Republic.

Table 27 Iran's advanced air power in figures, 1978–93

Aircraft	1978	1988	1990	1991	1992	1993
F-5E/F Tiger	168	55	70	80	60	60
F-4D/E Phantom	209	45	40	69	60	60
F-14A Tomcat	80	12	15	25	20	20
P-3F Orion	6	2	2	2	2	2
C-130E/H Hercules	43	12	20	20	20	20
MiG-29 Fulcrum	0	0	14	25	30	58
Su-25 Frogfoot	0	0	0	0	7	7
Su-24 Fencer	0	0	0	0	10	20
Total	506	126	161	221	209	247

Sources: Flight International (various issues); *Jane's Sentinel* (1993); *The Military Balance* (various years); *The Middle East Military Balance* (various years).

Notes: Iraqi aircraft transferred to Iran in 1991 included: 15 Il-76 Candid; four MiG-29 Fulcrum; 12 MiG-23 (+BN/ML); 24 Mirage F-1; four Su-20; 40 Su-22; 24 Su-24; seven Su-25. A total of 130 aircraft, many of which are being incorporated into the Iranian air force. Additionally, according to Jane's data, Iran operates some 70 Chinese-supplied Xi'an F-7 (MiG-21) interceptors and 16 Shenyang F-6 (MiG-19) fighters. IISS' 1993 combat aircraft figure for the Iranian air force is 293. Iran's air force deploys 53 C-130 transport aircraft, according to the former Defence Minister, considerably more than estimated (*Financial Times Survey* 1993: VII).

Throughout the 1980s Iran was able to deploy a reasonable number of Tiger and Phantom aircraft, largely thanks to assistance from Vietnam, South Korea, Pakistan and Israel. Without the original substantial supplies of these aircraft 'cannibalisation' (using parts from some aircraft to keep others airworthy) would not have been possible, indeed the existing stocks could not have been maintained at the above-mentioned levels without substantial assistance from the outside suppliers. But financial constraints and logistical difficulties encouraged the Iranians to look for cheaper, less sophisticated and more readily available alternatives for the air force and the air wing of the IRGC. The air force commander has revealed that a programme of modern-isation and 'de-Americanisation' of the air force had been proposed in 1986 and that Soviet and Chinese substitutes had been sought for Iran's aging American-supplied military aircraft (Ziarati 1992). This assertion is consis-tent with Iranian arms imports since the mid-1980s, despite Torkan's argument that Iran's fleet of F-14s, F-5s and the F-4s provide adequate air superiority, close air support and deep strikes respectively (*Financial Times Survey* 1993), though it may well be true to say that it was necessity and not desire which dictated the pace of reorientation.

So the path was opened for the transfer of Soviet-designed aircraft (and tanks) to Iran, a country historically reliant on Western (particularly Ameri-can) military hardware. Thus as the 1980s wore on we find a higher proportion of Soviet/Chinese weapons in Iran's military inventory. Towards the end of the war Iran possessed over 50 F-7 (MiG-21 equivalent) and 12 F-6 (MiG-19 equivalent) fighters and interceptors, all of which had arrived from China, North Korea and to a lesser extent Vietnam (*SPIRI* 1986, 1987; *Flight International* 1986, 1987), in addition to some 260 T-59 main battle banks and surface-to-air missiles from China (*Defence and Foreign Affairs Weekly* 1 May 1985 and 11 August 1986).

The Iran–Iraq cease-fire has had a direct impact on Iran's procurement policy, for so long as the path to Iran's real requirements, advanced Western hardware, remained blocked Iran had no choice but to look eastwards and towards China, the former USSR and the Warsaw Pact countries. Although France, amongst the Western countries, showed willingness to supply Iran with the sophisticated air and naval firepower it required, the fact that the Iranian armed forces had had little, if any, familiarity with French military hardware militated against any meaningful deals being struck. Furthermore, the fact that Iran's rebuilding of its armed forces did not start with a 'clean slate' meant that the armed forces could not adapt quickly enough to new systems without sacrificing efficiency and their limited (expert) human and capital resources.

On the other hand, the effective Iraqi use of French-made weapons and support systems against Iranian targets on land and at sea during the war did act as a sufficiently strong 'demonstrator effect' for Tehran to view more seriously the sophisticated French-built arms. In the last analysis, though, Tehran's immediate evaluation of France's role in the Iran–Iraq war, as one of Iraq's main arms suppliers, was so critical that little negotiating room for the Second Republic's politico-military leaders remained. Although after the war the Iranian leadership seemed to prefer avoiding military contacts with a country that had consistently supplied the enemy throughout the war years, since 1991 – particularly in view of Iran's possession of 24 Iraqi Mirage F-1 combat aircraft – Paris and Tehran have tried to open a dialogue on the possibilities of developing military ties, starting with French assistance in assimilating the Iraqi F-1s into the Iranian air force.

The 1989 all-encompassing $15 billion Iranian–Soviet trade and investment agreement which is known to have contained a $2 billion to $4 billion arms transfer and military assistance component is an indication that the Soviet Union, right up to its eventual collapse, was vigorously pursuing its 'non-ideological' arms transfer policy with the Islamic Republic. Perhaps more important still, the deal showed that Iran's inaccessibility to Western suppliers of advanced defence equipment had created the natural environment for both sides to capitalise on each other's needs, thus inaugurating a mutually advantageous agreement between the two neighbouring countries. Haeri has stated that the 1989 arms deal was worth $6 billion. Although this may be a slight exaggeration his report that Iran has held extensive discussions at the highest level with Moscow regarding the possible purchase of the latest Soviet fighter aircraft, the MiG-31 (priced at $40 million each), for the Iranian air force (Haeri 1991) is most interesting and consistent with Western intelligence and Russian military reports. If it is true, then we would be witnessing the rise of a new post-Cold War military relationship between two geopolitical giants in West Asia, perhaps of the sort which has existed between Moscow and New Delhi for some years now. It is difficult to foresee whether this relationship will be a lasting one and can develop into an 'alliance', particularly as the new Russian political elite is itself unsure of its historical destiny, with the struggle between the 'Atlanticists', the nationalists and the ultra-nationalists continuing unabated. But it is worth pointing out in passing that if the essentially trade ties between Iran and Russia do develop a strategic dimension, which is quite possible and consistent with the national interests of both states, the entire balance of power in West Asia and in the Persian Gulf region is likely to be dramatically altered.

Since 1990 the Iranian air force has been taking delivery of its Soviet combat aircraft. The early deliveries mainly comprised the MiG-29 multi-role aircraft, but by 1992 the air force had ordered or had begun taking delivery of other Soviet/Russian-built combat aircraft (*Jane's Sentinel* 1993; *SPIRI* 1993), and additionally had embarked upon integrating some of the Iraqi aircraft into its own force structures (Cordesman 1993). The $2 billion additional orders (said to have been placed in 1992, which have remained unconfirmed and are likely to have been cancelled or postponed, according to *Flight International*) included 12 Tu-22M strategic bombers (either from Russia or Ukraine), 24 MiG-31s, 24 MiG-27s, two Ilyushin-76 AEW aircraft, and 48 additional MiG-29s. If these orders were to be realised, Iran would indeed be creating a formidable air force with sophisticated deep strike, interdiction, air defence, early warning and heavy bomber capabilities. In addition to the 130 Iraqi aircraft and its own force of some 237, if the 1992 orders were to be delivered, the Iranian air force would once again be one of the largest and best equipped in the Middle East, with some 477 military aircraft (excluding the Chinese-supplied F-6 and F-7 combat aircraft). In a related field, air defence, it should be noted also that the Guards have already taken possession of the advanced Soviet-made SAM-6 surface-to-air missiles which were part of the 1989 arms deal (SWB, ME/0958, 31 December 1990), and are scheduled to receive more air defence equipment from Russisa (Chubin 1994). So these agreements allow Iranian forces access to the latest and most advanced Russian hardware.

Iran's familiarity with a variety of Soviet weapons (largely through China, North Korea, Vietnam, Syria and Libya) made a comprehensive arms deal between Moscow and Tehran logical; the attractive barter arrangements embedded in any such deal made it an imperative for both sides. Up to this point (i.e. between 1982 and 1989) the Soviet Union had accounted for less than 1 per cent of arms sold to Iran, compared with 33 per cent from other Warsaw Pact states, 25 per cent from China, and a further 42 per cent from other states of Europe and the Third World (Grimmett 1990). With this deal the Soviet Union launched itself as one of the Second Republic's main arms suppliers and military partners. The latter point is particularly important, as reports began circulating in 1991 and 1992 that the Russian Federation had shown a willingness to offer Iran immediate assistance in maintaining and operating the Soviet-supplied Iraqi aircraft now in Iran (*The Independent* 13 January 1992; *Issues* November 1991).

But at what expense were the two countries prepared to establish extensive military ties with each other? The Soviet Union could not afford to alienate Iraq, its long-time Gulf Arab ally and largest arms purchaser, and Iran was in no position to turn its back on China, the country's key military ally during the war years. The Kuwait crisis and Moscow's role in isolating Iraq effectively ended the Moscow–Baghdad alliance, however, and removed pressures on the Soviet Union not to sell arms to Iran. Iran for its part was able to balance its military ties with both China and the Soviet Union, partly thanks to improvements in relations between Moscow and Beijing after 1989, and to continue to buy arms and military technology from China (*Newsweek* 18 November 1991). It was reported in October 1990 that Iran had negotiated a new arms deal with China which included the sale of F-8 Finback fighters to Iran, as well as the supply of a variety of tactical missiles and modern T-80 and T-89 MBTs (*Nimrooz* 26 October 1990). The Sino–Iranian military relationship is particularly significant, having blossomed in the mid-1980s. The arrangements would allow Iran to satisfy its immediate military requirements from the PRC while the latter acquired hard currency and cheap oil for its trouble. Table 28 shows that Iran was China's largest arms customer in the world in the 1986–90 period. Iranian arms imports from China and the Soviet Union are certainly crucial to the rearmament and modernisation of the armed forces. The story does not end there, however. Iran is anxious to enter into viable military relations with Western European countries, as well as Third World arms manufacturers, such as Indonesia, Brazil and India.

Table 28 China's arms trade with Iran and the Third World, 1986–90 ($ million)

Country	From China	Total arms imports
Afghanistan	53	5,742
Algeria	54	930
Bangladesh	298	383
Chile	1	695
Egypt	89	4,717
Iran	1,488	2,913
Iraq	988	10,314
Kampuchea	17	236
North Korea	494	4,900
Laos	2	112
Myanmar	139	159
Nepal	2	9
Pakistan	1,202	2,693
Saudi Arabia	1,404	10,838
Sierra Leone	9	9
Sri Lanka	85	234
Sudan	47	189
Thailand	868	2,325
Yemen AR	35	63
Zaire	9	28
Zimbabwe	238	284

Source: SPIRI (1991).

In this light, Britain's decision not to sell the Hawk 100 jet trainer/light fighter to Iraq in August 1989 may have helped the UK's military trade prospects with Iran in two ways. Firstly, Iran did view the decision favourably, interpreting it as a sign of British willingness to transfer sophisticated firepower to Iran when the hostilities eventually cease, even at the expense of losing a lucrative contract with Iran's regional competitor. Revelations since about Britain's undeclared tilt towards Iraq after 1989 and the Rushdie affair notwithstanding, both Tehran and London view the prospects for some military contacts in the second half of the 1990s as promising.

Secondly, isolating Iraq in the Persian Gulf was also interpreted by all concerned that Britain might be willing to support the creation of an axis not too dissimilar to the order that existed in the Persian Gulf before the Iranian revolution, hence naturally attributing to Iran (in addition to the GCC states) a prominent profile in the alliance of the moderate forces in the region. Past experience has shown that such a 'respectable' profile is usually accompanied by major arms transfers to the favoured country. Saudi Arabia is a good example! Thus Britain could well have been extending a carrot to Tehran in the best and most visible way possible: the prize for 'moderation' in the IRI's regional policy could equal freer access to Western arms – at the expense of Iraq. Tehran is fully aware that Britain could play a key role in the rebuilding of the Iranian armed forces. In addition, before 1990, the monopolisation of the Iraqi market by France and the Soviet Union on the one hand, and the intense competition amongst the Western defence manufacturers for the GCC markets, on the other, made the huge 'untapped' Iranian market an engaging proposition. Since 1991 access to the Iranian defence market has increasingly been seen as vital by many Western defence contractors, including British ones.

When relations do improve, Iranian sources have said that they will be looking closely at modernisation packages for Iran's British-supplied Chieftains, and at purchases of the Challanger MBT for its ground forces; the Pavania Tornado and BAe Hawk jet trainers and modernised Jaguar fighters for the air force; British-built frigates and minesweepers for the navy, and advanced missile systems for air and naval defence. According to Arab sources, in 1991 an Anglo–Iranian arms deal was already in the offing. Kuwait's *Sawt al-Kuwait* announced that 'reliable reports' from London had spoken of an agreement which would enable Iran to purchase British-made 'modern military equipment and electronic components' (*Mideast Mirror* 10 December 1991). The same source also revealed possible British sales to the Iranian defence and heavy industries of technologies and equipment which could help to develop further Iran's defence industries. The discussions apparently took place during a low-key visit to London in December 1991 of Iran's Military Procurement Bureau chief, Mohsen Rafiq-Doost (the former IRGC Minister). Iran has not denied these reports. Iranian opposition circles have maintained for some time that the British firm Vickers has signed a secret agreement with Tehran for the supply of Challenger tanks to Iran (*Kayhan*, London, 3 October 1991).

Meanwhile, to compensate for its lack of direct access to Western suppliers, Tehran has been trying hard to gain such access through secondary channels: Pakistan, Turkey, Israel, South Korea and Taiwan. There are strong indications that of these contacts Tehran has been able to create military ties (maintenance, servicing and/or manufacturing assistance) with Pakistan, probably Israel, South Korea, India, Taiwan and China. Pakistan is to help primarily in providing advanced military (including pilot) training and servicing advice, as well as assistance in aspects of defence production through joint ventures (*MEED* 11 August 1989). According to Western defence analysts, Israel and South Korea may have been approached to provide assistance in overhaul and modernisation techniques, and know-how and technology for the aging US-made weapons in Iran's inventory. Taiwan is said to be willing to offer advice and assistance in the modernisation of the F-5 Tiger fighter and to provide some missile systems, and China has apparently agreed to establish assembly plants for the production of F-6 and F-7 fighters, and of surface-to-surface missiles, and to transfer to Iran any relevant know-how gained through its contacts with the US arms manufacturers.

In sum, therefore, we can say that Iran is pursuing a multi-layered arms procurement strategy. Firstly, to purchase (and seek limited production rights for) sophisticated Soviet-made weapons from the former USSR and Moscow's former Warsaw Pact allies, and standard Chinese-made and improved (Soviet-designed) military hardware from China. Purchases from these sources have included military aircraft, tanks and armoured vehicles, artillery and multiple launch rocket systems, air-to-air, air-to-surface, surface-to-air and surface-to-surface missiles, munitions, electronic warfare equipment, submarines and airborne early warning platforms. The significance of this 'Eastern' option for the Iranian rearmament drive is illustrated by Table 29.

Table 29 Iranian arms transfer agreements with China and the USSR, 1983–91 ($ million)

Period	China	USSR	Total
1983–6	1,845	10	8,940
1983–90	4,880	2,755	18,930
1988–91	4,500	4,800	19,800

Sources: Grimmett (1991); CRS (1992).

Note: SPIRI's figure for actual Iranian major arms imports for 1988–92 amounts to $3.6 billion (*SPIRI* 1993).

Military relations with the Ukraine have followed a similar pattern, where oil-for-arms deals have been a feature of ties between the two countries. In May 1992 opposition sources abroad spoke of a secret $5 billion three-year arms deal (*Kayhan*, London, 7 May 1992) and unconfirmed reports in May 1993 spoke of a large Iranian–Ukrainian deal which involved the delivery of eight supersonic Sunburst cruise missiles and as many as 50 MiG-29s, 200 T-72 MBTs and a number of S-300 air defence systems to the Iranian armed forces (*The Observer* 9 May 1993). In early 1993 Ukraine put to public tender a bewildering array of hardware at rock-bottom prices, expecting to raise hard currency from such potential customers as Iran. The list included: MiG-27s at $16 million each, Su-25s and Su-27s at $11 million and $31 million each respectively, T-80 MBTs for around $2 million per tank, Kilo-class submarines for $130 million each and an assortment of air defence missile batteries (*Military Technology* March 1993).

Secondly, Tehran has been seeking ways of modernising its US- and Chinese-made weapons from Third World users of similar equipment. Thirdly, it has attempted to purchase arms from the leading Third World arms manufacturing states such as Brazil (Iran ordered 55 EMB-312 Tucano fighter trainers from Brazil in 1988) (*SPIRI* 1990) and India (re-modernisation of Iran's aging tank force and guns). More recently Iran has shown interest in purchasing 40 Italian/Brazilian-made AMX ground attack jets from Brazil in addition to an unspecified number of the Brazilian-made Engesa EE-71 MBTs (equipped with a 120 mm cannon) at a cost of $1 million each (*MEED* 2 August 1991). Finally, Iran would like to gain access to Western advanced weapons and parts (excluding unfamiliar systems such as Swedish ones) manufactured in Europe or the United States. As the above analysis has shown, however, while the first three objectives outlined earlier may already have been fulfilled, it is the last, and probably the most important, aspect that remains unsatisfied. As the former Defence Minister himself made clear in early 1993: 'The first priority is spare parts, the second priority is spare parts, and the third priority is spare parts' (*Financial Times Survey* 1993: VII).

THE DOMESTIC ARMS INDUSTRY

The Islamic Republic is poised to become a player in the 'third tier' group of arms manufacturing countries in the world (Anthony 1993), helped in this endeavour by its post-1989 economic liberalisation policies and its extensive efforts to acquire Western military know-how and 'dual use' technologies. If successful, by the end of the twentieth century it could be joining the ranks of such prominent Third World arms producers as Turkey and the 'third tier' countries of Israel, Brazil, South Korea, Taiwan, South Africa, Pakistan, India, Egypt, Indonesia, Singapore, Chile and Argentina.

Modern arms production in Iran began in earnest after the 1973 oil price rises. Soon various aspects of the assembly and production expertise of US and European (including Israeli) defence manufacturers were transferred to Iran. The revolution, however, prevented the completion of many of the projects under way, and caused a collapse in the carefully planned Iranian military-industrial complex. Thus the Islamic Republic inherited a defence procurement and production strategy which was based on the expertise of expatriate labour, technology and military personnel. In this sense, the new regime's military-industrial complex remained a hostage of the pre-1979 arrangements concluded between the Shah and his closest allies in the West. Hence the country's domestic arms production potential was neglected for some time, to receive serious attention only after the start of the war with Iraq, and in the course of the rapid depletion of the army's arsenal of Western-made weapons and support systems, capped by the difficulty of obtaining replacements cheaply and easily. So successful was its arms production drive that by the late 1980s Iran had an estimated 240 operational arms production factories in addition to some 12,000 privately owned work-shops engaged in research and the production of defence-related equipment (Ehteshami 1990). In terms of employment in the military-industrial complex, Iran occupied one of the leading positions in the Third World in the early 1990s (see Table 30) and outstripped the following developed countries' arms industry employment: Sweden and other Scandinavian countries, Belgium, Switzerland and Austria (Wulf 1993).

Table 30 Selected Third World arms industry employment, 1990–2

Country	Employees	Country	Employees
India	250,000	South Korea	40,000
Egypt	75,000	Turkey	25,000
Israel	60,000	Indonesia	25,000
North Korea	55,000	Singapore	20,000
Pakistan	50,000	Argentina	20,000
Iran	45,000	Chile	10,000
Brazil	40,000	Thailand	5,000
Taiwan	40,000	Malaysia	5,000

Source: Wulf (1993).

In its quest for arms-making capacity, the Islamic regime adopted a two-pronged strategy: firstly, it set about rejuvenating the military-industrial processes already established by the Shah; secondly, it proceeded to import lower-level technology and expertise for producing less sophisticated, stand-ard weapon systems. Then Defence Minister Torkan pointed out that 'Transfer of technology is the basis of our work and at present we have several contacts for expansion of defence industries and all foreign purchases are serving this purpose' (SWB, ME/0610, 10 November 1989).

The warm relations between the Islamic Republic and the two East Asian communist powers, China and North Korea, resulted in the application of precisely this formula. The most dramatic example of lower-level technology weapons produced locally is in the field of SSM development and production. China is known to have helped in the development of the Oghab system and assisted in the establishment of a Scud-B production line in Iran (Hearings 1989; Navias 1990), and North Korea has been credited with having helped Iran in its efforts to develop Scud-type missiles, including the long-range Scud-C, and having offered co-production of the Nodong-1 missile (*CAABU Bulletin* 1 May 1993). The Nodong series is capable of delivering nuclear, biological and chemical warheads. Besides the modifications of the Soviet-made Scud-B and Frog-7 SSMs, the Iranian defence establishment has developed and produced a number of other missile and multiple-launch rocket systems which include the Oghab, the Nazeat, the Shahin (1 and 2), and a new version of the Oghab (Karp 1989). According to one source, Iran is now capable of producing eight different rocket systems (*Defense and Armament* March 1989) and may have two further research programmes under way. Furthermore, the Iranian army claims to be already self-sufficient in the production of low-calibre ammunition, some types of artillery shells and small arms.

Table 31 Iran's rocket and SSM programmes

Designation	Weapon type
Frog-7	SSM
Scud-B	SSM
Scud-C	SSM
Nodong-1	SSM
Tondar-68	SSM
Mushak-120	SSM
Mushak-200	SSM
Nazeat	Artillery rocket
Oghab	Artillery rocket
Shahin 1 and 2	Artillery rocket
Fajr-3	Artillery rocket

Sources: Military Balance (various years); *The Middle East Military Balance 1988–89* (1989); *SPIRI* (various years); *Jane's Defence Weekly* (various issues).

By the early 1990s Western governments had become extremely concerned with Iran's military ties with China and North Korea, but were also expressing anxieties about the burgeoning contacts between Iran and the two Arab states of Libya and Syria. With the latter, both parties share an interest in acquiring modern Chinese and North Korean SSMs and may have tried to co-ordinate their efforts in this regard, and with Libya unconfirmed reports indicate that the two parties may have embarked upon a joint venture project to develop in Iran Libya's dormant German-designed missile project, the Al-Fateh, which has a potential range of 950 km (*CAABU Bulletin* 1 May 1993). Assistance in missile research and development is also said to be forthcoming from a number of European and Japanese companies, often through third parties.

Further up the technology ladder, Iran is taking advantage of the small aerospace infrastructure created by the Shah to move into the assembly and eventual production of old communist-bloc military aircraft. Pakistan's assistance here (itself a long-standing user of Chinese-made weaponry) has proved invaluable. The defence establishment's experience in carrying out repairs on the US-made F-5s, F-4s, and possibly F-14s, will have made the evaluation of projects appreciably more efficient, and the decision to move towards local assembly and eventual production that much more feasible.

The nerve centre of these efforts, the Defence Industries Organisation (DIO), supervises the activities of the Iran Aircraft Industry (IAI) and the Iran Helicopter Industry (IHI) in addition to the efforts of the ammunition and other arms production and research divisions, such as the Iran Electronics Industry (IEI). Now, of course, it also controls the activities of the military-industrial efforts of the IRGC. The changes in the defence establishment's formal power structures (i.e. the creation of the new Defence Ministry, which constitutionally controls the defence industries as well) have led to rational-isation of the defence industries, and the establishment of a new division of labour in the military-industrial activities of the Second Republic. A comprehensive plan of action has been in evidence, which – if successfully implemented in the course of the First and Second Development Plans of the Second Republic – will ensure a more uniform development of the country's military-industrial activities, eventually enabling the sectors which lag behind (the naval, for instance) to catch up.

The IAI, for example, has in operation a new facility for repairing military aircraft and aircraft engines, and the IAI and the IHI work closely in research and development of engines, airframes and materials. The concentration of the efforts of the IRGC, the Construction Crusade and the regular army in one institution has brought together the various divisions that (independently of each other on many occasions) have produced a wide array of equipment which include missiles, radar parts, ammunition, artillery pieces, guns, small arms, naval craft, midget submarines, APCs, and remotely piloted aircraft, and have managed to carry out complex repair and maintenance work on foreign-made aircraft engines, some avionics and flight equipment and airframes. As a way of illustrating the advances made in various fields of military research, Table 32 provides a partial list of the republic's military electronics programme in 1989.

Table 32 The IRI's military electronics programme, 1989

Designation	Description
Goya 630	VHF radio
MR-600	Receiver
Payam	Transceiver
SB-22	Switchboard
41D220	Antenna

Source: Jane's Military Communications (1989).

Ultimately, though, Iran's search for modern and self-generating military-industrial capacity forces it to look westwards – particularly towards Western Europe. Concomitant with large-scale weapons purchases since 1989, Iran has been demanding the transfer of military technologies and processes to augment and improve its current defence production capabilities from China, the former USSR, North Korea and Brazil. As far as its military contacts with the West are concerned, the Second Republic has looked for similar technology transfers if and when military contacts were to be restored. Offset arrangements modelled on the BAe–Saudi Arabian (Al-Yamamah I and II) and Boeing–Saudi Arabian agreements are not inconceivable, and in view of Iran's current industrial base will greatly enhance the indigenous arms-making potential of the Second Republic.

Iran's solo experiences and limited efforts in the field of arms production may have been costly in many ways and economically inefficient, but these achievements have enabled the military technocrats to zoom in on the technologies that they have missed, thus reducing somewhat the assimilation time lag involved in complex technological and advanced weapons transfers. In this context, a lasting impression of Soviet-made weaponry is likely to remain, a testimony to Iran's isolation and to the subtle changes in its diplomatic profile since the revolution, providing Iran with a valuable opportunity to expand its outward-looking economic policies and cash in on the booming international market for cheap copies and refined versions of older Soviet-designed equipment, as it tried to do at the IDEX '93 international arms fair in Abu Dhabi. Familiarity with Soviet-made equipment, of course, has reduced the dependence of the armed forces on Western (largely US-made) arms, making planning and deployment less contingent on external influences.

Finally, in the coming years, Iran may elect to abandon its selective weapons production strategy in favour of the 'global' model – research and development, and production of weapon systems and processes for all three forces and under all contingencies. The latter, however, requires a comprehensive infrastructure (in plant, laboratories and labour) as an unavoidable prerequisite, coupled with political stability, continuous capital expenditure and a pool of reliable skilled labour. Only one country, Israel, has achieved this feat in the region, but two others, Egypt and Turkey, have displayed signs of progress along the same path. Iran still has a long way to go before the current strategy of selective arms manufacture is superseded, but if the domestic economic situation allows it, being a producer of major weapon systems would be consistent with its regional status in the twenty-first century. Indeed, the army's display in April 1994 of the country's first locally produced MBT, the Palang-e Iran, is indicative of the leadership's chosen path for the future: a 'global' arms production strategy.

IRAN'S NON-CONVENTIONAL WEAPONS PROFILE

Since the Kuwait crisis and revelations about Iraq's relatively successful attempts at the development of non-conventional weapons and long-range SSMs, Western powers have shown a noticeable degree of nervousness about Iraq and a resolve to prevent the emergence of 'a second Iraq' in the Middle East (*International Herald Tribune* 28 January 1991). This resolve, partly manifested in the Clinton administration's Persian Gulf security doctrine of 'dual containment' (in other words, containing Iraq and Iran) and the West's complex strategy of resolving regional disputes by peaceful means and of isolating non-conformist regional actors, coincides with Iran's rearmament drive and its search for effective non-conventional weapons deterrence. It is no exaggeration to state that, wrongly or rightly, military developments in Iran have alarmed the West, particularly as these developments seem to be running counter to the strategic and security interests of the West in the 'new world order', thanks to Tehran's political stance on the Arab–Israeli peace process. With Iraq defeated, Syria co-opted and Libya marginalised, the pro-Western Arab regimes and Israel (the region's greatest military power and its only nuclear weapon state) have played their part in keeping the spotlight on Iran as the Middle East's most 'undesirable' state, a view not too dissimilar to that of the US State Department, which regards the Iranian Second Republic as the world's most dangerous country – 'an outlaw nation', according to Secretary of State Warren Christopher.

Inevitably, one aspect of the debate about Iran's military resurgence has been its non-conventional weapons capability, with many analysts assuming that the country is likely to become a nuclear weapon state by the turn of the century. Iran's chemical weapons capability is well established: it has large stockpiles of lethal and non-lethal chemical agents and has significant facilities for the mass production of mustard gas, phosgene gas, blood agents and even possibly nerve agents (Cordesman 1993). Its forces are said to train for chemical warfare and can deliver chemical weapons by artillery and aircraft and perhaps by SSMs. The republic's biological weapons capability is also quite substantial, according to military experts. *SPIRI* brought Iran's biological weapons research to light in 1982 but little accurate knowledge of this capability of the Iranian armed forces is available. Cordesman, however, believes that Iran has made progress in the development of anthrax and biotoxins (Cordesman 1993). Other reports suggest that Iran is already producing biological weapons at a pesticide factory (Smith 1991). It should be noted, however, that Iran is a signatory of the Geneva Protocol and the Biological Warfare Convention, as well as an ethusiastic supporter of the 1992 Chemical Weapons Convention (*Disarmament Newsletter* February/ March 1993). It has also given its unreserved support to the UN Secretary-General's 'An Agenda for Peace' proposals.

When discussing Iran's nuclear weapons programme it is worth remembering that Tehran is one of the oldest adherents of the Non-proliferation Treaty (NPT) in the region, that it has ratified the treaty and that a nuclear safeguards agreement with the International Atomic Energy Agency has been in place for many years. Although it regards the possession of nuclear weapons as un-Islamic, Tehran's interest in this capability is not well disguised, fed as it is by the region's unstable situation and the presence of a number of nuclear/potential nuclear weapon states around it: Israel, India, Pakistan, Kazakhstan, Ukraine and possibly Iraq being the most important as far as Iranian strategic thinking is concerned. The evolution of Iran's nuclear doctrine owes much to its experience of the war with Iraq, and is based on two principles: 'counter-city deterrence' and 'deterrence of outside intervention' (Dunn 1991). In the meantime Tehran continues to endorse the idea of a Middle East nuclear-free zone.

In its support of non-nuclear regional defence options Tehran has been particularly impressed by the Western countries' mobility, air power and electronic intelligence-gathering networks. The impact of Operations Desert Shield and Desert Storm on the Iraqi war machine has been noted and some of its strategic lessons learnt. For former Defence Minister Torkan, for instance, Iranian deployment of nuclear weapons would be self-defeating. He has stated clearly that Iran would be risking military defeat at the hands of the Western powers were it to deploy nuclear weapons:

> Possessing nuclear weapons today is like playing with fire for Iran because, with accurate and long-range missiles which big powers possess, these sites can be easily targeted and destroyed. Thus possessing nuclear weapons and deploying them is not in our strategic programme.
>
> (*Ettela'at* 3 March 1993)

Cordesman argues that Iran 'has long been involved in developing nuclear weapons' (Cordesman 1991: 103), and that the republic may have been seeking such a capability since the early 1980s, more concertedly since the mid-1980s. Though Iran's post-war potential (and ambitions) in the development of nuclear power and technology is a shadow of its former self compared with the pre-revolution period, since 1990 Tehran has shown a distinct interest in acquiring nuclear technology and know-how from a number of sources; but, while the Shah's regime had planned to build some 23 nuclear power stations in the country, the Rafsanjani administration has moved much more cautiously and has sought the transfer of fewer than five relatively small-scale reactors. Nonetheless, Iran may have as many as 200 scientists and some 2,000 workers conducting research in various aspects of the nuclear power chain (Cordesman 1993). A further instance of Iran's seriousness about obtaining nuclear know-how can be seen in the opening of the country's first nuclear engineering centre in 1992 and its first ever Master's degree programme in nuclear engineering, with an initial enrollment of 30 students and a teaching/research staff of 40 (SWB ME/W0220, 3 March 1992).

Since 1990 Iran's nuclear programme has adopted a two-tier strategy: to seek assistance in completing one of the two badly damaged 1,300 MW German-supplied reactors at Bushehr, and to acquire new nuclear reactors and research facilities. Reports began to surface in 1990 that Iran and the Soviet Union had entered into negotiations for the supply of a number of Soviet-designed pressurised water reactors (PWR), followed by revelations that the Islamic Republic was acquiring nuclear technology and nuclear weapon material through a secret nuclear co-operation agreement with Pakistan and China (*Nucleonics Week* 25 October 1990 and 2 May 1991). In 1991 India, Cuba and Brazil were added to the list of Iran's potential nuclear partners and it was disclosed that Tehran intended to generate some of the country's energy needs (and operate its desalination plants) with the help of nuclear power (*International Herald Tribune* 1 December 1992). It was reported in 1992 that the republic had assigned $4.2 billion for the 1992–5 period to the completion of the Bushehr plant, the acquisition of new nuclear power stations and the transfer of nuclear technology and know-how. A number of important developments in 1992 underlie the republic's commitment to gaining access to nuclear know-how and nuclear power plants. Inevitably, Western fears have concentrated on the transfer of nuclear weapons technology to Iran, including nuclear fuel processing and bomb research.

After failing in 1991 to purchase a 10 MW nuclear research plant from India, it was revealed in 1992 that Iran had signed a nuclear co-operation agreement with Russia which included the supply and running of two 400 MW each PWR reactors and assistance in completing the construction of the ill-fated Bushehr plant. Under the 15 year co-operation agreement, conditional on non-proliferation measures, Russia also agreed to help Iran in key nuclear technology and development fields: radiological protection, nuclear safety, the production and application of radio-isotopes, and personnel training (*Nucleonics Week* 8 October 1992; *Nuclear Fuel* 12 October 1992). The agreement with Russia was followed by the signing by President Rafsanjani in September 1992 in Beijing of the agreement between Iran and China (in the aftermath of President Yang Shangkun's visit to Iran in October 1991) to build near Tehran, under IAEA safeguards, one 300 MW light-water reactor (whose completion was likely to need considerable Western technological assistance, according to Western assessments) and had agreed to furnish Iran's Atomic Energy Agency with two research reactors and other assistance in the field of nuclear technology and materials (*International Herald Tribune* 3 August 1992; *Nucleonics Week* 6 August 1992). An avalanche of news about Iran's nuclear intentions surrounded the country's renewed interest in nuclear power and technology.

Reports that Iran's ultimate interest in nuclear power was linked with a clandestine nuclear weapons programme (*The New York Times* 8 April 1993) was reinforced by the news that Iran had 'imported' nuclear experts from the former Soviet Union and that it had already purchased or stolen a number of tactical nuclear warheads from former Soviet republics (reputed to be Kazakhstan and/or Tajikistan). *Al-Watan al-Arabi* reported that Iran had obtained three tactical nuclear warheads from a former Soviet republic for about $150 million (*PPNN Newsbrief* Spring 1992), while other sources alleged that two such warheads had been purchased and that the deal included the sale of four 152 mm nuclear artillery shells from Kazakhstan (*PPNN Newsbrief* Summer 1992). Some Western intelligence agencies report that Iran may have received from Central Asia two warheads for ballistic missiles, one gravity bomb and one artillery shell (*PPNN Newsbrief* First Quarter 1993). Although both parties have strongly denied these allegations, no evidence has so far been produced to support the reports, and the Director of the CIA has insisted that there has been 'no credible reporting' of any nuclear warheads having left the former Soviet Union (*PPNN Newsbrief* First Quarter 1993), Russian and US intelligence sources insist that Iran has a programme of applied nuclear research as part of its military modernisation drive.

Although reports that Iran may have an active nuclear weapons programme give cause for alarm, it is not at all clear that Iran is in fact following the Israeli or Iraqi lead in acquiring nuclear weapons expertise quickly. In the words of an unidentified US government nuclear expert:

> Iran has powerful political motives for developing nuclear weapons and is trying to develop a broad-based nuclear infrastructure that it hopes will give them the option for weapons if they decide to exercise it. But I don't

see in Iran the same kind of crash nuclear program that we've learned about in Iraq.

(*International Herald Tribune* 1 December 1992)

Another US official said in 1992: 'we [the United States] have not established that there are any secret nuclear facilities in Iran' (quoted by Albright and Hibbs 1992). However, evidence pointing to an active Iranian programme, stretching across the entire northern hemisphere, may be found if one pieces together data emerging from Europe and the region itself (for details see *PPNN Newsbrief* Fourth Quarter 1993).

Nonetheless, Iran continues to face many problems in its nuclear programme. Firstly, Western vigilance and direct US pressure on Iran's potential nuclear partners is proving an effective method of control: India, Brazil, Argentina and Germany have all cancelled or reneged on their agreements and China has cancelled its proposed sale of research reactors to Iran. Secondly, a formal sales contract does not automatically follow a nuclear co-operation agreement and many technical and financial obstacles need to be overcome before any meaningful technology or know-how changes hands. Thus Iran's agreements on the transfer of nuclear know-how and reactors may not bear fruit after all.

Thirdly, most nuclear and defence experts agree that even if Iran does manage to import the required technology, acquire the expertise and invest the required $1.5 billion annually it would still take it another decade to master the complex process of nuclear weapon production. Fourthly, all Iran's known nuclear research and nuclear-material production sites are under the strict supervision of the IAEA. While sceptics may argue that co-operation with the IAEA could be the very smokescreen Iran would need for its nuclear weapons research (rather like what Iraq accomplished), Tehran has been encouraging IAEA inspections of its nuclear facilities. A recent IAEA mission to Iran concluded in its report not only that it received full support from the Iranian authorities and that 'all of the facilities and sites selected by the IAEA for inclusion in the visit were accepted by the Iranian authorities', but that it found Iranian activities at these sites during the team's visit were 'consistent with the peaceful application of nuclear energy and ionizing radiation' (IAEA Press Release 14 February 1992). A follow-up visit in November 1993 by an IAEA team gained access to facilities and sites left off the list in 1992 and again found no failure of compliance (IAEA Press Release 2 December 1993). With regard to Iran's official attitude towards nuclear weapons proliferation, it should be noted that in international forums Tehran continues to express its support for an end to global nuclear testing and a renewal of the NPT as a means of preventing nuclear weapons proliferation (*Disarmament Newsletter* November 1993).

THE REGIONAL SETTING AND THE MILITARY BALANCE

Iran's regional and international isolation, its military losses during the war and the rapid increases in the quantity and quality of weapons transferred to the other Persian Gulf states, all helped to move the Gulf military balance against the republic in the 1980s. The disequilibrium in arms transfers can be summarised in the type of military hardware transferred to the other Persian Gulf states over the last decade. The Gulf Arab states began deployment of a variety of modern tanks, including the US-made M-60 A3, the French-made AMX-40, the Italian-made OF-40 Mk II, the Soviet-made T-72 and the Brazilian Engesa, and a host of sophisticated military aircraft suitable for the regional battlefields of the 1990s. These included the AWACS, the MiG-25, the MiG-29 Fulcrum, the Tornado, the Hawk 200, the Su-24, the Su-25, the Mirage F-1, the Mirage 2000, the F/A-18 Hornet, the F-15 Eagle and the F-16 Falcon (*SPIRI* various years; *The Military Balance* various years; *Defence and Foreign Affairs Weekly* various issues; *Armed Forces* various issues). By contrast, Iran's most sophisticated acquisitions only started arriving in 1989.

In terms of quality, for instance, Saudi Arabia's 100+ Tornados and F-15s are a far superior force to the entire air force of the Islamic Republic. Naturally the large number of advanced aircraft in the inventories of the Gulf Arab states has assured a long climb for Iran in the quantitative arms race as well, the summit of which it has tried to reach since 1989. In addition, the GCC states and Iraq took delivery of advanced missile systems for air defence and for their missile boats and frigates during the same period.

Elsewhere in the Middle East the arms race had more or less levelled off by 1990, with the four main players in the Levant, Syria, Jordan, Israel and Egypt, having apparently reached saturation point in terms of their arms imports. But the dip in military expenditures tended to conceal two important phenomena. Firstly, that in the 1980s these countries were purchasing some of the most advanced military hardware developed by the West and the Soviet Union, thus needing no further supplies until these systems had been incorporated into their forces and defence structures. Secondly, the general defence cuts recorded over the 1988–90 period concealed the increasing (specific) domestic component of military expenditures, not recorded as such, either because the expenditure was mainly research-oriented or because more 'creative' accounting methods were adopted, so that defence expenditure figures were moved out of the military accounts and into the civilian budget. But, as is well known, the downturn before 1990 soon gave way to an upsurge in military imports following the 1991 Gulf war.

The proliferation of SSMs in the region is a good example of the trends in deployment. This class of weapon has acquired an indigenous footing in the region, moving ahead at an alarming rate regardless of external influences.

In the Levant and North Africa, Israel, Syria, Egypt and Libya have developed domestic SSM development/production facilities with the minimum amount of fuss. In the Persian Gulf, Iran and Iraq (prior to the Kuwait crisis) had advanced well in the missile development field, posing a danger to each other as well as to other Middle Eastern and non-Middle Eastern countries. Saudi Arabia's purchases of IRBMs from China have made targets as far afield as the Central Asian republics, the Caucasus, the Mediterranean, North and East Africa and in the Indian Ocean accessible.

These new trends in the arms race are more destabilising than the conventional race in fighters, tanks and naval vessels, for not only do they have a domestic rooting, and are thus beyond the full control of the influential external forces (sometimes even the original suppliers), but the SSM forces being developed and deployed by the Middle Eastern countries put at risk countries not directly involved in the simmering conflicts of the region.

Iran's post-war rearmament drive has caused a great deal of concern in many Arab capitals, in Israel and the United States, but the exact nature of its military expenditures, its military needs and its overall expenditures and imports in relation to its neighbours has escaped detailed examination. Since 1992 military expenditures have not featured as prominently as in government plans as they had in the immediate post-war period, when opposition sources claim it had reached about one-third (about $7 billion) of the country's oil income between 1989 and 1992 (*Kayhan*, London, 22 April 1993). The drop in expenditures has been consistent with the government's assessment of Iran's security environment and the strength of its armed forces. Former Defence Minister Torkan has said in this regard, 'We don't need to purchase new weapons', stating that most of the IRI's military needs were met through orders between 1989 and 1992 (*MEED* 12 March 1993). He has also declared that Iran 'has no intention to be dragged into [an arms race] and will focus on the reconstruction of the country', thus endeavouring to keep the defence budget to no more than 3.8 per cent of GNP (*MEED* 30 April 1993). To this end, the 1992/3 defence budget was cut by $300 million by the Majlis, down to $1.2 billion (*MEED* 10 July 1992). Torkan and President Rafsanjani have claimed persistently that the country's defence budget for 1993 was no more than $850 million. Thus, it could be argued that the process of demilitarisation of the economy as part of Iran's economic reconstruction drive may have already begun, which can only mean, other things being equal, smaller military budgets. While the cuts in the defence budget may partly have been caused by Iran's deep financial crisis (in view of low oil prices since 1992 and a foreign debt of about $30 billion) and therefore could rise if and when oil prices recover, in comparison with some of its Gulf Arab neighbours its military expenditures are indeed small. To put Iran's defence budget in perspective, it might be useful to compare it with that of the country's major regional competitor, Saudi Arabia – a country whose population is a fraction of Iran's, and which had not lost much of its sophisticated arsenal in a debilitating war and certainly did not experience wars and political tensions on every border. Military and security spending accounted for 31 per cent of the 1993 Saudi budget ($16.4 billion) and totalled $14.4 billion in 1992 (out of total government expenditure of $48.2 billion; *Mideast Mirror* 5 January 1993). Saudi military orders from the United States alone between August 1990 and September 1992 amounted to $25.7 billion (*Arms Control Today* September 1992), and if we include Saudi military imports from France and the United Kingdom the figure exceeds $30 billion for the period under review. Iran's biggest known orders during this period were the 1990 $4 billion contract with Moscow (Pohling-Brown 1993) and the unfulfilled July 1992 $2.5 billion agreement with Russia, alongside a number of relatively small contracts signed with China and North Korea (*SPIRI* 1992 and 1993). *SPIRI* data for the 1988–92 period show that Iran was not by any means the biggest arms importer in the Middle East (see Table 33).

Although Iran's arms imports during 1988–92 were greater than those of the Levant powers, compared with its neighbours in the Persian Gulf region (particularly the GCC countries), they were quite small: contrast Iran's total

Table 33 Top ten Middle Eastern importers of major conventional weapon systems, 1988–92 ($ million)

Country	Total	Country	Total
Saudi Arabia	8,690	Israel	2,768
Turkey	6,167	Syria	2,618
Iraq	4,967	UAE	2,065
Iran	3,632	Kuwait	1,243
Egypt	3,295	Algeria	997

Source: SPIRI (1993).

of $3.6 billion with the GCC total of $13.5 billion (*SPIRI* 1993). Indeed, as an unidentified Tehran-based Western diplomat told *The New York Times* 'Iran is not doing more than it should be doing for its legitimate self-defense', and that 'for what Iran needs to rebuild [its armed forces] $2 billion a year is peanuts' (Sciolino 1992: 2).

Other data also support the view that the Islamic Republic is not the worst culprit in importing modern weapons into the region. The Jaffee Centre for Strategic Studies' comparison of the forces of the eight major armies of the

Middle East (those of Egypt, Iran, Iraq, Israel, Jordan, Libya, Saudi Arabia and Syria) shows that Iran has the second lowest number of MBTs (after Saudi Arabia), the second lowest number of SSMs and rocket systems (after Saudi Arabia), the second lowest number of combat aircraft (after Jordan), the second lowest number of missile craft (after Iraq) and the lowest number of submarines (after Syria and Israel) in the region (*The Middle East Military Balance 1992–1993* 1993). Only compared with its northern neighbours (Armenia, Azerbaijan and Turkmenistan) and Afghanistan do Iran's armed forces show an absolute superiority in terms of numbers and force structures (*The Military Balance 1993–1994* 1993).

One of the sticking points in Iran's rearmament drive has been its deployment of two Russian Kilo-class submarines, the largest such vessels in the region (with 2,500 tons' surface displacement). Three submarines were ordered as part of the 1989 arms package signed with the Soviet Union but only two had been deployed by the mid-1990s. The introduction of submarines into the Persian Gulf sub-region is a net escalation of the qualitative arms race there and introduces an entirely new class of weapon system into the sub-region. The deployment of submarines has been a long-time ambition of Iran, dating back to the Pahlavi period, when the Shah had planned the purchase of a number of submarines from the West, and is now consistent with Iran's ambitions and rising influence beyond its southern borders in East Africa and around the Indian Ocean. The possession of a blue water naval capability is not only important to Iran's strategic interests in the Persian Gulf (the submarines ordered in 1989 were in part an Iranian reaction to the Iraqi order for 12 Italian corvettes, which would have made Iraq's the largest Persian Gulf navy, and the presence of NATO country naval detachments in Persian Gulf waters in the second half of the 1980s), but also forms part of Tehran's post-Cold War interest in an expanded regional influence.

But the acquisition of the submarines does not make Iran's navy the best equipped or the strongest in the Persian Gulf, as, with the delivery of the first submarine to the Iranian navy, Saudi Arabia announced the second phase of its Al-Sawari contract with France (worth $4 billion) for the delivery of three more upgraded *Lafayette*-type frigates (armed with anti-ship and anti-aircraft missiles, torpedo tubes and anti-submarine warfare helicopters) (*al-Hayat* 27 October 1992). With the completion of this deal Saudi Arabia will have the most powerful navy in the Persian Gulf, with seven frigates, four US-supplied *Badr* class corvettes, nine US-supplied *Siddiq* class missile attack vessels and dozens of supply ships, torpedo boats and minesweepers, compared with an Iranian naval force (in 1993) of two submarines, three aging destroyers, five frigates, 10 missile craft and fewer than five mine warfare vessels (*The Military Balance 1993–1994* 1993).

Finally, the decline in military expenditures elsewhere in the Middle East has raised the premium on access to the rich markets of the Persian Gulf states, including Iran, encouraging further large arms transfer agreements to this part of the region. If, on the other hand, reductions in arms transfers to the Middle East were to become the trend, then Iran may well welcome a slowdown of the race and be grateful for a breathing space in its struggle to develop the country's economy. But there may be another reason for this as well, that of enhanced security. As Sadowski observes, 'Tehran may not contribute much to abetting arms control, neither is it likely to do much to hinder it, because regional arms control arrangements are likely to leave Iran more secure' (Sadowski 1993: 65). The Kuwait crisis and 1991 Persian Gulf war, coupled with the collapse of the Soviet Union as a superpower and as an independent regional actor, accelerated the arms race in the Gulf region, with Iran and Saudi Arabia (and some of its GCC allies) carrying the burden of the race. Where the race may end still depends on the policies and perceptions of those two powerful neighbours and OPEC members – in the absence of Iraq, the Gulf's dominant actors for the foreseeable future.

9 The Islamic Republic of Iran

A revolutionary alternative for the Third World?

No doubt, therefore, the Islamic Revolution in Iran stands out from all other revolutions for its origin, for the features of its struggle and for the motives behind it. Doubtless, the Revolution in this country has been a gift of God and a favour from the Invisible bestowed on this ravaged and tyrannised nation.

(Ayatollah Khomenini, *Political and Religious Testament*)

Having dealt with the mechanisms of power in the Islamic Republic and the power structures and personalities of the Second Republic, as well as the manifestation of the IRI's internal changes in the international arena, it is possible to present the conclusions of the study in the context of its wider implications. The question being raised here is twofold: can the Iranian revolutionary experience be said to have fulfilled its agenda successfully (judged by its own expectations), and can the example of the Islamic Republic of Iran be said to offer a viable alternative model of development (compared with both Western-style free-market capitalism and socialism, including its Soviet-style system) for (at least the Muslim) Third World countries?

The discussion here is not meant to deal with the role of socialism in the Third World *per se*, or the success of capitalism, nor to provide further evidence for the 'collapse of socialism in the Third World' thesis, as put forward by Christopher Clapham, amongst others (Clapham 1990). Rather, it is to try and view the Iranian model as what is claimed to be the first successful Islamic revolutionary alternative in the Third World. In addition, the attempt is made in this final chapter to demonstrate that the experience of the 'Islamic' revolution in Iran and the birth of the Islamic Republic may indeed serve as the exceptional case needed to prove the rule that at the end of the twentieth century outside capitalism (in a sociological sense) and socialism no viable alternative socio-economic system is in existence.

In this context, and in so far as gross generalisations are possible, all Third World revolutions since 1917 can be summed up as the successful fusion of the 'exploited' classes' (workers and peasants) interests with those of the middle classes and segments of the indigenous bourgeoisie. Before that date, the Constitutional revolution in Iran itself, the Chinese rebellion of 1911 and the Mexican revolution of 1913 had shown that non-socialist movements based on multi-class alliances could successfully mobilise and lead the masses. It was fashionable during the Cold War era to regard the different versions of populism (defined as 'a predominantly middle-class movement that mobilizes the lower classes, especially the urban poor, with radical rhetoric against imperialism, foreign capitalism and the political establishment'; Abrahamian 1991: 106) and 'peopleism' as proof of the spread of socialism in the Third World, observers being content in some instances to refer to the single ruling parties and their programmes of action, or their foreign relations, as sufficient evidence of socialist transformation in the late-developing countries.

Even if we were to go along with the orthodox interpretation of socialism in the Third World and loosely regard countries like Cuba, the DPRK, South Yemen, Vietnam, Ethiopia and Angola as socialist, and Iraq, Syria, Algeria, Libya, Nicaragua, Cambodia, Burma and Mozambique as socialist-oriented or socialist camp countries, we would be faced with an interesting dilemma: where to fit in the Iranian revolution of 1979 and to what tradition to ascribe the IRI model? If we were to accept Clapham's definition of socialism as 'the direct control by the state of economic production and distribution', for instance, a major faction of the clerical rulers of Iran (within the FIR camp) could well be identified as socialist. And in so far as the clergy-dominated state has come, to varying degrees, to dominate and control economic production and exchange, then Iran since the revolution could be said to be as socialist as the Sandanistas' Nicaragua! What seems to distinguish Iran from the Third World socialist revolutionary regimes, however, is precisely its anti-Marxism and anti-socialism. While the revolutionary credentials of the Islamic Republic are fairly strong, the IRI model has opened the account of non-socialist revolutionary transformations in the Third World in the late twentieth century, portraying itself as neither in the socialist tradition nor in the capitalist (i.e. Western) one. Indeed, as we have seen, its leaders have gone to great lengths to portray themselves and their model as the third international way, as distinct from the two Cold War power blocs, morally superior to both and, objectively, in opposition to them too.

To recap, the case of Iran puts on the agenda a new (revolutionary) alternative to Third World socialism(s). What I intend to discuss in this chapter is the viability of this model, an analysis of which leads one to conclude that, while the revolution was successful, the regime born of the revolution did not produce a viable, long-term, revolutionary alternative. We may then view this 'failure' in the light of the similar decline of socialism as a Third World prescription. It remains true also that not only have the socialist experiments of the twentieth century proved unable to build the new and better 'man', as prescribed by revolutionary socialism, but so too has the present day's first anti-materialist and spiritual revolution. The utopia thus still awaits the brave!

Lastly, in so far as there exists a direct relationship between political independence and economic independence, the former is usually regarded as providing the precondition for achieving the latter in post-colonial and Third World societies; and the shortest and most reliable route to political independence has been seen to be through socialism. The case of Iran illustrates that socialism is not the only route to political independence, but paradoxically it also shows that non-socialist alternatives do not necessarily lead to economic independence.

THE IRANIAN REVOLUTION IN PERSPECTIVE

Between 1975 and 1980 eight revolutionary regimes came to power in the Third World: in Angola, Ethiopia, Grenada, Mozambique, Nicaragua, Afghanistan, South Yemen and Iran. Of these, three were the product of anti-colonial struggles, three were against Western (US) supported regimes, and two were born of other internal struggles. With the exception of Iran, however, all the others can be classified as 'socialist' regimes (applying the loose definition of the term and including orientation in external matters) with close military (except for Morris Bishop's New Jewel Movement in Grenada) and politico-ideological proximity to the former Soviet Union. All displayed an appreciable measure of hostility to 'US imperialism' and all affected the balance of power in various ways in their respective regions. Although all these countries moved closer to the Non-aligned Movement, only Iran adopted an equally hostile attitude towards the Soviet Union, perceiving itself to be exercising the policy of 'positive neutralism' in the global power equation. Although Iran's revolution did have a major impact on the balance of power in the Middle East, perhaps because of a number of other reasons in the 1980s, including the nature of the IRI's interactions with the international community, the potential threat of 'Islamic fundamentalism', the gruesome Iran–Iraq war, and the general preoccupation in Western circles with the apparent expansion of Soviet influence in the Third World, the emulative potential of the Iranian 'Islamic' revolution model was stunted. This does not mean, however, that at some future date and under the right circumstances it could not offer, at the very least, inspiration to other 'Islamic' revolutions in Africa or Asia.

As to the importance and uniqueness of the Iranian revolution, let it be remembered that this has been the only major post-War revolution not indebted to Soviet political, moral and material support. Furthermore, it was a revolution which did not necessarily serve Soviet interests, as it:

1   Could have posed a serious threat to Soviet security in Central Asia.
2   Had the potential to disrupt the balance of power in the region.
3   Replaced a stable and known quantity in a strategically important country like Iran with an unstable and hostile regime.
4   Fanned the flames of 'Islamic fundamentalism' towards the Soviet Union's own Muslim population.
5   Threatened to undermine Moscow's strategy in Afghanistan.
6   Threatened to replace Soviet-sponsored Marxism–Leninism with Islamism as the ideology of liberation in the Third World (particularly in the Middle East).

Unlike other post-War revolutions, Iran's was urban-based (although the migrant peasants-turned-lumpenproletariat did play their 'historic' role in the urban protests), but like the others it was a multi-class revolution. Secondly, it is of some significance to establish that the February 1979 uprising, which came at the end of a two-year struggle to overthrow the Pahlavi regime, was a 'revolution', at least according to one criterion, as it led to a 'sweeping, fundamental change in political organisation, social structure, economic property control and the predominant myth of a social order, thus indicating a major break in the continuity of development' (Neuman 1948–9: 333). But, as we have seen, it eventually led to these things only to a limited extent, because a strong sense of continuity with the Shah's system in political organisation, social structure and economic property control was also preserved by the new elite.

As the issue of 'fundamental change' identified in the above quotation can be problematic if the definition is taken literally – the armed forces remained quite intact, for instance, the Pahlavi bureaucracy merely found itself serving new masters, functioning with new logos and portraits of Iran's new leaders on Ministry walls, and finally, over and above the expropriation of *comprador* capital by the state, personal and commercial private property remained just that: private – a wider definition of revolution may be more applicable. As far as our discussion is concerned, the definition below is more to the point, enabling us to rechannel our efforts towards an evaluation of the phenomenon itself, and to bypass for the moment the thorny issue of whether the revolution of 1979 fundamentally changed society's economic relationships and redrew the organisation of the political life of the country as well. Hagopian (1974: 1) states:

> a revolution is an acute, prolonged crisis in one or more of the traditional systems of stratification (class, status, power) of a political community,

which involves a purposive, elite-directed attempt to abolish or to reconstruct one or more of the said systems by means of an intensification of political power and recourse to violence.

The Iranian revolution's many unique characteristics, on the other hand, have left their mark on the founding structures of the new republic. Indeed, many of these unique characteristics are at the heart of the identifying features of the new political system: the revolution was civilian-led, the military was marginalised to the fringes of political life, a brief armed insurrection did take place at the climax but there was no guerrilla campaign playing a leading part in the revolution. In addition to the above, this was the first revolution not indebted to European ideologies and to have survived without a great power protector: the revolutionary movement was religious-based and clergy-led, it allowed a greater degree of expression within the revolutionary current than other revolutions, there existed no vanguard or ruling party to lead and direct the masses, and ultimately, for the first time in modern history, the leaders of the revolution took ultimate sovereignty away from the 'people'. Thus, far from being 'a potent source of counter-revolutionary activity' (Hagopian 1974: 343), religion served the people as the main force for, and the protector of, their liberation:

> The noble people should be aware that all our victories have been attained by the will of God Almighty, as manifested in the transformation that has occurred throughout our country, together with the spirit of belief and Islam commitment and cooperation that motivate the overwhelming majority of our people . . . But if we deviate from the sacred ordinances of Islam . . . it is to be feared that God Almighty will withdraw his grace from us.
>
> (Khomeini 1991: 287)

The religious basis of the revolutionary movement and regime is borne out by the form the republic took. Article 56 of the 1979 Islamic constitution states that absolute sovereignty over the world and man belongs to God, and it is he who has placed man in charge of his social destiny (Business International 1991: 166). Ayatollah Khomeini himself, in a detailed interview after the revolution's victory (2 January 1980) stated that 'the sole determining principle in a government based on Towhid is divine law, but that is the expression of divine will, not the product of the human mind' (Khomeini 1981: 330). So freedom as an ideal gained expression only through fulfilling God's will and not as an inherent right of mankind. In the last analysis, therefore, the leaders of the Islamic Republic regard their revolution as distinct (and superior) to history's capitalist and socialist revolutions, and certainly original so far as the rest of the Middle East is concerned. The

Iranian revolution, its leaders argued, was a manifestation of divine law and justice while all the other modern revolutions were products of man's this-worldly aspirations.

THE NUANCES OF THE IRANIAN MODEL

As already mentioned, the clergy-dominated Islamic Republic has consistently portrayed its model as the only viable 'progressive' alternative to both (Western-style) capitalism and socialism. High on the agenda of IRI rulers have been such concepts as social justice, divine law, economic self-sufficiency, political integrity, an independent foreign policy and strict non-alignment. In practice, however, it has been seen that the Iranian model has not only failed to reach its more modest aims of economic diversification and reform but has been singularly incapable of universalising the Islamic Republic's alternative model.

Whether the shortcomings of the IRI experience signify the failure of the ideal-type model propagated by the ruling factions of the Shii clergy, or whether it provides further evidence for those advocating comprehensive delinking from the international capitalist system of production (if not also exchange) remains to be seen. The shortcomings of the Iranian experience, however, do seem to offer ammunition to all those who argue that non-socialist alternatives to capitalism (as a mode of production) are essentially class compromises doomed to failure, and that there is no real alternative to socialist transformation. To provide the perspective for understanding the Iranian revolutionary regime, therefore, it is proposed to scrutinise the IRI model in the four aspects of the revolutionary regime most relevant to its existence: foreign policy and revolutionary internationalism; economic policy; foreign trade regime; domestic politics.

In great anti-colonial spirit, Article 152 of the 1979 constitution declares that the IRI is against any form of domination. It rejects 'all forms of domination; both the exertion of it and submission to it', and stands for 'the preservation of the rights of Muslims, non-alignment with respect to the hegemonist superpowers, and the maintenance of mutually peaceful relations with all non-belligerent states'. Article 154 states that Tehran 'supports the just struggles of the oppressed against the oppressors in every corner of the globe'. From this standpoint emerged republican Iran's slogan 'neither East nor West' as its guiding thread in dealing with the outside world.

Taken in their totality, the two strands of Iranian foreign policy, 'positive neutralism' and 'neither East nor West', meant that Iran pursued a 'global' strategy which aimed to (a) isolate the two superpowers, particularly in the Third World; (b) extend and develop economic ties with the 'Second World'; and, (c) promote South–South ties in all spheres of life (economic, political, cultural and military). From the beginning, though, priority was given to the Islamic countries as the IRI's natural constituency. By and large the emphasis was consistently on Islam (and Islamic ethics) as the main component of the IRI's foreign policy:

> The school of capitalism . . . has revealed its detestable face and its filthy core in scandals, in crimes, in unreliability, in corruption, in that dangerous illness AIDS, and suchlike illnesses which have created such tragedies in the world and which have truly horrified the West. Marxism and Communism too – which kept raising a hue and cry, saying: You, who have become tired of the capitalist order, come under our banner – has itself declared its own bankruptcy . . . The words of Lenin and Stalin have all been thrown into the dustbin of history . . . The school which can really run the world is the school of Islam. We must support Islam; we must support it in the world. Now that those two structures are moving towards destruction . . . we must pay attention to the structure which has been designed by the Prophet of God.
>
> (Ayatollah Imami Kashani's Friday prayer sermon, SWB, ME/0600, 3 October 1989)

Despite the emphasis on Islam as the 'third new international way of social transformation', the IRI's classification of the (pre-1989) world is not too dissimilar to that of the People's Republic of China's – a 'First World' (the superpowers) is recognised, a Second World ('Lesser Satans') in close proximity to the First is said to exist, and finally an oppressed 'Third World' which makes up much of humanity is seen as the republic's potential ally. The main difference in the two categorisations, however, arises over the Third World. The Islamic Republic fragmented the Third World grouping into two camps; Islamic countries/movements and non-Islamic ones. This delineation has had a direct impact on the IRI's foreign policy behaviour. Certainly the republic has maintained satisfactory relations with both the 'non-capitalist/state socialist-oriented' Third World states and the myriad of capitalist and pro-Western Third World states, but it was singularly unsuccessful in bringing about a united 'Islamic front' in international terms. Indeed, if anything, the most divisive impact of the new republic's foreign policy was its position *vis-à-vis* the Islamic countries of the Middle East. By emphasising Islam as a new (exclusivist) rallying point for Third World solidarity, revolutionary Iran helped in dividing the Third World along new Islamic and non-Islamic lines, thus accelerating its fragmentation in the 1980s. Additionally, through isolating some Muslism states for their 'pro-Americanness' at the same time as maintaining good and close relations with some other secular and pro-US regimes in the Muslim world, the Islamic Republic managed to erode the universalism of its message, even though, objectively, the need for a new and authentic direction for anti-imperialist struggles and South–South relations may have existed.

Despite the emphasis on the Islamic states, therefore, Tehran tried hard in the 1980s to isolate the traditionalist hereditarily ruled Arab states of the region, declaring such regimes illegitimate (ostensibly because Islam is opposed to hereditary rule). It saw some Muslim countries as the perpetuators of 'American Islam' among the *umma* (the world Muslim community). In this regard Saudi Arabia and some other Persian Gulf states came in for particularly sharp criticism. Yet Iran maintained warm, close and profitable relations with its two non-Arab Islamic neighbours, Turkey and Pakistan, despite the fact that both were the United States' politico-military allies, and were well integrated into the international capitalist division of labour. Furthermore, at the same time as flying the flag of Islam internationally, and threatening the legitimacy of the traditional Islamic states of the region, Tehran was anxious to maintain close ties with the secular and 'radical' states of the Middle East, particularly with Syria, South Yemen, Algeria and, to a lesser extent, Libya. So it could be argued that the republic's 'Islam first' strategy became redundant soon after Tehran's new rulers recognised that the country's geopolitical imperatives would not allow it to isolate itself from the existing web of regional relations.

That said, the pragmatism of the regime must not be confused with measured opportunism; it should be recognised that there is nothing new in a revolutionary regime overlooking its self-proclaimed international principles, and displaying inconsistencies in the implementation of its foreign policy. For this reason Iran's desperate search for friends in any quarter should be viewed not as a measure of its willingness to abondon its ideological principles, but rather as a justifiable attempt to minimise the impact of the isolation imposed upon its revolution by the 'East and the West'. A measure, in other words, of its pragmatism and not of its opportunism.

In more practical terms, Iran left the US-sponsored politico-military CENTO in March 1979, dismantling the US spying stations along its northern border, and proceeded with the cancellation of some $10 billion worth of weapons orders from the United States and Britain. Iran severed its relations with Israel and South Africa and opened channels of communication with the PLO, the ANC and SWAPO. Generally speaking the new Iranian leaders slowly shifted the political orientation of the country away from the United States and expanded its relations with the radical/revolutionary and Third World camp.

The republic's attitude towards the national liberation movements was part and parcel of this process of change in Iran's international relations. Compared with other revolutionary regimes, however, and despite its declared support for a number of liberation movements, the Islamic Republic's policies remained ambivalent. For example, as the regime's emphasis was on 'Islamic' liberation movements first, followed by qualified support for a number of others, the secular Palestinian national movement was sidelined and represented by Iranian leaders as a religious campaign against Israel, with the Islamic fronts as its vanguard. This Iranian policy ended up challenging the role of the PLO as the 'sole legitimate representative' of the Palestinians. In the Philippines and even in South Africa, as well as in Afghanistan, 'Islamic revolution' became the guiding principle of Tehran, at the expense of secular, leftist and, at times, nationalist forces.

All in all, the IRI was supporting some 15 'liberation' movements in the early 1990s, with priority being given to those which adhered to an Islamic ideology:

1 *Far East*: MORO Liberation Front (Philippine Muslims).
2 *West Asia*: Islamic Revolution Organisation of the Arabian Peninsula, Islamic Liberation Front of Bahrain, Hezbollah of Kuwait, Hezbollah of Lebanon, Islamic Towhid Movement of Lebanon, Al-Dawa Party of Iraq (Islamic), Islamic Action Organisation of Iraq, High Council of the Islamic Revolution of Iraq, Islamic Resistance of Occupied Palestine, Islamic Coalition Council of Afghanistan, Jama'at Islami of Afghanistan, Patriotic Union of Kurdistan (Iraq) and Kurdish Democratic Party (Iraq).
3 *Africa*: Sahara Liberation Front, SWAPO (now in government) and the ANC (now in government) (increasing support since Nelson Mandela's release from gaol).

As the above highlights, although Iran did maintain some ties with the internationally recognised liberation movements, its efforts were largely concentrated on creating and consolidating the position of the Islamic fronts and movements in the Islamic territories.

Remarkably, and despite a great deal of rhetoric, few tensions have been in evidence in Iran's relations with international organisations and many leading Western countries. The republic has remained a member of virtually all the diplomatic, social and economic international organisations joined by the Pahlavi regime. It upheld the country's membership of the 'Group of 77' Third World states, ESCAP, OPEC, ICO, UNCTAD, ISS (Institute of Statisticians), IAEA, UNESCO, UNIDO, WHO, FAO, IMF, IFC, IBRD, the NPT, even the Inter-parliamentary Union. By the early 1980s, Iran was also urging the rejuvenation and expansion of the three-state (Iran, Turkey, Pakistan) Economic Co-operation Organisation, which rekindled the old economic ties between the three countries. So, far from instigating de-linking, in both global and regional terms, from the international division of labour, Iran's revolutionary rulers remain firmly lodged in the old order, and in fact since 1989 have been striving to make up ground lost to the fast expanding economies of Asia and Latin America as a consequence of the revolution.

Perhaps the country's role in the world economy as a source of hydrocarbons has been the revolutionary regime's Achilles heel. Without such a high international economic profile its de-linking (if at all intended) might have been possible. Ironically, although one would expect that those countries with high-value and capital/finance-generating resources (like crude oil and natural gas) at their disposal to be ideally placed to embark on, and successfully complete, a de-linking process precisely because of their indigenous wealth and resources, it may well be the resource-poor states, those least integrated into the international division of labour, which are perhaps better placed to pursue a de-linking strategy because they have less to lose. Although poverty is not to be advocated as the most suitable precondition for de-linking and 'autonomous' development, the possession of internationally vital commodities such as oil can actually hamper de-linking strategies, owing to external pressures, as well as the domestic configuration of social forces. That configuration is often brought about, by and large, by the very nature of state-orchestrated exploitation of such resources and the fact that the substantial revenues also accrue to the state and those in control of the state machinery.

As regards its role in the international balance of power one would be hard put to classify Iran as a 'progressive' state by established norms, despite its apparently virulent anti-Americanism, and the general anti-Western and anti-communist rhetoric of the regime. The republic's strategies in Afghanistan, in the conduct of the Iran–Iraq war, and over the Palestinian issue (to cite but a few examples), and the nature and content of its relations with the superpowers and other major powers have objectively hampered the global 'revolutionary struggle'. Perhaps the 'Irangate' episode best testifies to the nature of this revolutionary regime, casting some doubt on the often-made assumption that all revolutionary regimes are somehow 'progressive', democratic and anti-imperialist to the last fighting person. The example of the IRI and its foreign policy behaviour should challenge our assumptions and presuppositions regarding revolutionary regimes in the Third World, even if they may appear anti-imperialist and enjoy friendly relations with a number of other radical–revolutionary regimes.

In sum, what the case of Iran illustrates is not only that non-socialist revolution is feasible in the modern world, but also that the revolutionary regime coming to power as a consequence of such a revolution can prove to be 'reactionary' by both international humanitarian and legal standards (i.e. adherence to international law, the Universal Declaration of Human Rights, etc.) as well as by the commonly recognised 'progressive' principles of the twentieth-century socialisms.

On economic strategy, 'Khod Kafai', or self-sufficiency, has been the catch phrase of the revolutionary state. The adoption of this strategy was to have reduced the country's dependence on the world (Western) economies. Taking the well-established import-substitution industrialisation strategy (ISI) of the previous regime a step further, Iran's revolutionary leaders aimed not so much to chart a new path for the country's socio-economic development, but to internalise as much as possible the essentials of a successful import-substitution industrialisation process. Following on from the ISI tradition established by the Shah's pro-Western (capitalist) regime, and also because of the shortcomings associated with revolution itself, the state came to play a central role in the republic's economic life. Close scrutiny of the 1979 constitution reveals that its drafters envisaged a mixed economy along largely social democratic, Western European lines, but with the difference that clear roles would be assigned to the public and private sectors. Constitutionally, the state was given the responsibility for the control of the 'natural monopolies', as well as direct ownership of the strategic sectors and the commanding heights of the economy.

In practice the state also dominated the republic's politico-economic system. The IRI did not greatly alter previous economic practice, with the government making the major investment decisions and having them implemented through the state-controlled enterprises. The policies of the revolutionary elite towards the Pahlavi system of economic management, state ownership and control, moreover, reflected not so much the new regime's ideological commitment to common ownership and public enterprise as a series of pragmatic and *ad hoc* responses emerging from the reality of one ruling-class coalition taking over power from another. It has been shown that in 1979 the property of over 50 of Iran's richest and most powerful families was confiscated by the new government, bringing under state control almost all the country's large modern factories, banks, insurance companies, extractive and agri-business industries. Furthermore, we saw that, effectively, the country's governing body, the Council of the Revolution, put these nationalisation moves on a more systematic basis with the passing of the law on the 'Protection and Development of Iranian Industries' in 1979. This law legitimised the role of the state in the Islamic Republic as the main decision-maker and executor of economic policy and industrial development strategy. As well as facilitating the take-over by the state of all the country's heavy and basic industries, this law brought under government control industries abandoned by royal and loyal members of the *ancien régime* in addition to establishments owing money to the banks.

The nationalisation measures also passed to the state the decision-making process regarding financing and commercial strategies. This was a notable addition to the Pahlavi regime's system of economic management. The net result of these measures was a virtual take-over of the economy by the state. But this did not mean the collectivisation and 'socialist nationalisation' of bourgeois property, or indeed the demise of private capital and the decline of the bourgeoisie.

The revolution did not, and the emerging new elite would not, abolish the capitalist state, nor even modify it to represent better the interests of the deprived and the working classes (the *mostazafin*) – as other revolutionaries claimed to be doing elsewhere in the Third World. In concrete terms, the Islamic revolutionaries' main achievement was to alter the relations of production to reflect the country's new political realities, and at the same time enhance the state's relative autonomy – particularly *vis-à-vis* the revolutionary classes – in the uninterrupted process of capitalist accumulation. An unsympathetic evaluation of the socio-economic environment of the post-Pahlavi Iran, bearing in mind the heavy burden of the war with Iraq, would regard its experiment as purely populist at best. Much of the private sector, weakened as a consequence of the expansion of the state sector, but also liberated as the pressures from the *comprador* bourgeoisie evaporated, strongly endorsed the populism of the revolutionary regime, comforting itself with the fact that the Islamic credentials of the new rulers of the state provided for the inviolability of private capital.

Despite its expanded social welfare policies, the revolutionary regime did not prohibit the growth of private capital, nor did it attempt seriously to amend the country's social structure in favour of the deprived classes. Nor in other spheres did it pursue policies deemed to be in the interests of the masses: it did not redress the societal imbalance between labour and capital, and did not institute reforms (in land holdings and industrial organisation) substantial enough to warrant mention as revolutionary transformations in Iran's socio-economic realities.

The practice of privatising many of the nationalised and confiscated industries and businesses by post-Khomeini governments, and the rejuvenation of the forgotten Tehran stock market with 47 registered companies and a trading volume of $100 million to $200 million from March 1989 to March 1990, illustrate the prospects for the 1990s. Just a decade after the revolution, the leaders of the Islamic Republic declared their readiness to hand back many, if not all, of the commercial and trading companies and manufacturing and assembly industries in their possession to the private sector. The icing on the cake of the new government's many U-turns, in retreat from the populism of the 1980s, came in the form of encouraging foreign investment in the country.

As is clear from much of President Rafsanjani's policies, far from attempting to de-link from the international capitalist system and achieve self-sufficiency in the national economy, the leaders of the republic were preparing the way to return the economy to the domestic bourgeoisie and 'friendly' international capital. To whet the appetite of the latter the government raised the limit on foreign ownership from 35 per cent (established by the Shah's regime) to 49 per cent or more, thus allowing a virtual controlling interest in a project to the foreign investor. The usual guarantees to foreign investors were also being extended by the end of the 1980s. The privatisation and liberalisation of the economy arrived amidst worsening problems for the ruled: unemployment (around 2.5 million individuals, or about one-fifth of the total work force), high inflation (between 24 and 29 per cent), a worsening maldistribution of income, increasing concentration of wealth, a deteriorating housing stock and a generally declining standard of living. Whether the economic liberalisation drive of the 1990s was a symptom of the republic's policy mistakes in the 1980s or the dawn of a new beginning for the Islamic Republic was by this time a moot point. For those investigating the outcome of the revolutionary process in Iran, however, the issue is an important one, particularly if one attempts to put the Iranian revolutionary experience in the broader context of socio-economic change in the late-industrialising countries.

During the revolution and its aftermath the revolutionaries vowed to reduce the country's dependence on foreign inputs. Part of this process involved the political decision to diversify the country's foreign trade patterns, with a new emphasis on trade ties with the Islamic countries. In practice, however, Iran remained dependent on the Western industrialised countries on two important counts: imports of consumer goods, foodstuffs, industrial goods and spare parts; and exports of raw materials, primarily crude oil.

Another stated goal of the revolutionary regime was to change fundamentally the composition of the country's exports and move away from concentration on the traditional handful of commodities. This objective too remained unfulfilled, however. The proportion of non-oil goods in Iran's total exports remained small (3.5–5.0 per cent of total) and the range of non-oil export products did not substantially change over the first decade of the Islamic Republic, remaining almost identical to those of the Pahlavi regime.

In terms of diversification of trading partners the IRI did make concerted efforts to increase commercial ties with the developing countries. In 1978 about a quarter of Iran's exports went to other developing countries and only 9.0 per cent of its imports originated from the same group (IMF 1986). By 1982 developing countries accounted for 35 per cent of Iran's exports and 31 per cent of Iran's imports (IMF 1988); at the end of the Iran–Iraq war the figures were 30 per cent and 25 per cent respectively (IMF 1989). Concessionary trade arrangements and generally mutually advantageous barter deals undoubtedly helped the consolidation of the Southward expansion of Iran's trading ties. But while the aggregate data indicate a significant trade shift towards other developing countries, the pattern of the reorientation of its foreign trading strategy can become clear only when seen in the context of Iran's major Southern trading partners. Furthermore, the full picture will emerge only within a discussion of Iran's trading relations with its traditional Western partners.

The overall picture would indicate that Tehran's Southern partners have not changed dramatically since the revolution, only that by and large the volume of trade with some of them has increased substantially. Trade with Turkey, Pakistan, Argentina, South Korea, Brazil, Singapore, Thailand, Malaysia and the PRC did improve after the revolution, for instance. But the available data show little, if any, expansion in Iran's trade with other Third World countries, even the Islamic ones. However, in the context of trade with the industrialised countries significant changes are discernible. Firstly, the republic expanded its ties with a number of Eastern European countries in the 1979–89 period, particularly with Romania, East Germany, Czechoslovakia, Hungary and the Soviet Union. For most of the 1980s, it is clear, Iran used its contacts with the CPEs of Eastern Europe firstly as an alternative (to Western) supplies of industrial goods and manufactured products; and, secondly, as leverage against the Western European countries in order to obtain maximum benefit from the latter.

Western European countries, of course, have been particularly important to the republic not only as sources of technology and know-how but also as key trading partners. In practical terms, the foreign policy strategy of 'neither East nor West' did not preclude commercial contacts with the Western or communist countries, and aimed to maintain the correct balance between the two power blocs (East and West) and sufficient distance from the great 'Satanic' powers (in practice the United States). It did not, however, manage to severe the county's trading links with the OECD countries as a whole.

As Table 34 underlines, throughout the 1980s Iran remained among the top six OECD markets in the Middle East. By 1990 Iran's imports (over \$10 billion) from the OECD were the third highest in the region (after Saudi Arabia and Turkey). Indeed, the extent of connections was such that with the economic liberalisation policies of the Rafsanjani administration Iran's imports from the OECD countries began to grow dramatically – the fastest in 1990, compared with those of the other Middle Eastern countries. Iran's imports from the OECD jumped by 72.2 per cent during 1989; Turkey's rose by 49.4 per cent. In 1990, 76.2 per cent of Iran's imports originated from the industrialised world, higher than the figure for Egypt (76.0 per cent) and more or less equivalent to Saudi Arabia's (76.6 per cent) (*COMET Bulletin* 1992). The pace of change was such that the OECD countries doubled their exports to Iran between 1989 and 1991, matching the peak 1978 levels in real terms (*COMET Bulletin* September 1992).

Table 34 Total OECD exports to selected Middle Eastern countries ($ billion)

Year	Saudi Arabia	Iran	Egypt	Algeria	Iraq
1977	12.2	12.1	3.9	6.0	3.7
1978	16.6	15.4	4.6	6.6	4.3
1979	19.8	5.9	6.0	6.9	6.9
1980	23.3	7.6	8.3	8.8	10.0
1981	27.4	8.0	9.2	8.7	14.3
1982	31.3	6.4	9.9	8.3	14.8
1983	30.3	12.2	9.9	8.2	7.1
1984	24.9	9.7	10.3	8.0	6.4
1985	18.9	7.2	9.3	7.3	7.0
1987	17.7	6.0	8.2	5.8	4.5
1988	17.8	5.6	8.2	6.3	6.1
1990	19.3	10.5	9.2	8.5	4.4
1991	25.2	15.4	9.6	7.4	0.6
1992	27.5	16.0	9.3	6.8	0.4

Sources: OECD (various years); *COMET Bulletin* (various issues).

Note: Figures rounded up for convenience.

Although Iran's total imports from the OECD countries did drop in the earlier years of the republican regime, since the mid-1980s on average about 8.5 per cent of the OECD's total Middle East exports have gone to Iran (OECD various years). Over the same period, the composition of Iran's OECD partners has changed too, reflecting by and large Iran's political preferences. As the data for the mid-1980s reveals, on balance the greatest loser from Iran's international trade strategy was the United States, and the overall beneficiaries, Japan, the FRG and the smaller OECD countries. By the second half of the 1980s the smaller OECD countries accounted for over one-third of Iran's OECD imports, yet still much of Iran's trade remained with the leading capitalist industrialised countries. Moreover, this pattern has been strengthened by the Rafsanjani administration's economic reform policies. In 1991, for instance, German exporters accounted for 26.5 per cent of Iranian imports and Japan's market share stood at 16.1 per cent of Iran's imports, followed by Italy (11.9 per cent), Britain (5.9 per cent), France (5.8 per cent) and the United States (3.4 per cent) (*COMET Bulletin* September 1992). Together these six countries accounted for 70 per cent of Iran's total imports in 1991.

A glance at the aggregate data would show that while Iran did manage (for a time) to reduce its export dependence on the largest OECD countries, a substantial proportion of its imports (foodstuffs as well as manufactured goods, spare parts and technical services) continued to originate in these Western industrialised economies.

Table 35 OECD market shares in Iran in the mid-1980s (%)

Year	USA	Japan	France	FRG	Italy	UK	Other OECD
1984	1.7	17.5	1.9	23.1	9.8	9.7	36.4
1986	0.5	17.3	1.2	22.5	9.8	8.8	39.7

Source: Calculated from OECD (various years).

Note: The downturn in trade occurred after 1986, reflecting the collapse of the oil price and Iran's inability to import all the consumer goods and industrial products that local industry required.

Overall, and as Table 36 demonstrates, the OECD countries continued to maintain their leading role in Iran. This pattern was already apparent in 1981:

[the] picture of the political structure [in post-revolution Iran] indicates that the major socio-political elements in Iran will continue to trade with the West. Having followed capitalist routes to development, they have no choice but to continue [with the] traditional trading relationships and indeed are happy to do so.

(Nassoori 1981: 13)

The data in Table 36 leave one in little doubt, however, that by the late 1980s Iran had been relatively successful in finding alternative export outlets. A substantial proportion of Iran's exports in the late 1980s went to the

Table 36 Patterns of Iran's trade, selected years (%)

	1977		1980		1983		1985		1987		1988	
	E	I	E	I	E	I	E	I	E	I	E	I
OECD	78	86	65	66	67	65	58	61	65	66	58	61
EC	36	43	32	42	39	38	35	38	36	41	41	39
Other OECD	42	43	33	24	26	27	23	23	29	25	17	22
LDCs	22	11	34	25	33	29	42	32	35	27	42	30
CMEA	–	4	–	14ᵃ	–	7ᵇ	–	5	–	5	–	9

Source: IMF (various years).

Notes: Figures rounded up for convenience. (a) Data for 1981. (b) Data for 1984. *E* exports, *I* imports.

developing countries, compared with only 22 per cent ten years earlier. In terms of imports also, the gains for the South are quite impressive. The proportion of Iran's imports from the developing countries jumped from 11 per cent in 1977 to some 30 per cent in the late 1980s.

A comparison of the changes in the IRI's trade relations with two countries, Brazil and the United States, may prove instructive in highlighting the impact of Iran's new outlook on its trade policies. Before the revolution, the United States was Iran's main trading partner, but by 1988 Iran's total trade with the United States stood at only $88 million, just under one-sixth of Brazil's total trade figure ($517 million) with the Islamic Republic (IMF 1989). Furthermore, between 1985 and 1989 Iran's imports from Brazil were on average four times those from the US (ibid.). One of the most striking features of Table 37 is that some ten years after the revolution, and despite Iran's professed desire to expand its economic ties with the Muslim world, Turkey (itself a close US ally and member of NATO) was the only Islamic country which appeared on the list of the Islamic Republic's main trading partners.

Table 37 Iran's main trading partners, 1989

IRI's exports to	% of total	IRI's imports from	% of total
India	16.4	West Germany (EC)	15.4
Japan	12.1	Japan	10.5
Benelux (EC)	7.3	Turkey	7.0
France (EC)	7.0	Italy (EC)	6.4
Netherlands (EC)	7.0	United Kingdom (EC)	4.8
Spain (EC)	5.6	France (EC)	4.1
Romania	5.6	Romania	3.8
Italy (EC)	5.5	India	3.7
Turkey	4.5	Brazil	3.3
West Germany (EC)	4.3	Australia	3.0
Proportion of total	75.3	Proportion of total	62.0

Source: Calculated from IMF (1988 and 1989 editions).

Looking through other important features of the Iranian economy, one is struck by how unrevolutionary post-Pahlavi economic policy has been, contrary to the stated aims of the revolution's leaders. One important indicator in this regard is the imports-to-GDP ratio (calculated by dividing total non-military imports by the country's gross national product), which shows an economy's import dependence. In Iran the figure has not been substantially reduced since the revolution and has continued to hover around the 12–15 per cent figure, lower than the 18 per cent average for the 1973–7 period, but still very high considering the general lowering of imports for a time after the revolution.

Other data for the 1979–85 period indicate that the level of consumer goods imports was not reduced either. In fact, as a proportion of total imports they rose from an annual average of 17 per cent during the 1970s ('the decade of opulence') to about 26 per cent during the first five years after the revolution (Mofid 1987). Thus one of the cornerstones of the revolution had been overturned: the desire to move away from consumerism and dependence on consumer goods imports had not been realised. Particularly important in this context were the significant increases in Iran's food imports, costing on average between $2.5 billion to $3.0 billion in annual imports. In addition, intermediate products have continued to account for over 50 per cent of the country's total non-military imports in the years following the revolution, a figure almost identical to that of the 1970s (Central Bank of Iran various years).

One area, that of capital goods imports, did register a decline following the revolution, although this could easily be accounted for by the departure of the *comprador* class after the revolution and the nationalisation of its property (hence the loss of access to imported capital goods), the trade embargo imposed by the United States against Iran, and the general run-down of the country's manufacturing outlets. All in all, the share of capital goods in Iran's total imports declined from 28 per cent in 1978 to about 20 per cent in the mid-1980s (ibid.): a figure which was set to rise in the reconstruction phase.

Again it may not be too unreasonable to claim that the war economy of the 1980s imposed severe restrictions on Iran's revolutionary plans, forcing the leadership to settle for compromises. On food imports, for instance, it would be perfectly true to state that Iran's situation worsened after the revolution, owing to a number of independent factors: high population growth rates (of over 3 per cent per annum), lack of investment in agriculture, absentee landlordism and neglect of agricultural land, rapid permanent migration to the cities and war damage to some of the country's fertile areas. Some of these problems, however, could have been alleviated by proper planning on the one hand, and the implementation of a comprehensive land reform policy to transfer land to co-operatives and landless peasants on the other.

On the broader economic front, consumption patterns did not change sufficiently to usher in an era of revolutionary transformation. Luxury goods were harder to come by, certainly, but largely as a consequence of import restrictions imposed by the populist government. The reasons for this, however, may have been rather less ideological than was previously thought. The shortages of foreign currency, the diversification of resources away from the civilian sector in order to meet the demands of the war effort and, last but not least, the need to proceed with the old strategy of import-substitution industrialisation, all affected the revolutionary state's domestic economic policies and its international economic relations. But, on the whole, all that can be said of the regime's economic policies is that the Islamic Republic's leaders may have indisputably changed the country's position (and worsened it in the context of the New International Division of Labour) in the world economy, but evidently not its orientation.

Finally, the spirit of the anti-Shah revolution itself, and the legacy of the other revolutions this century, would certainly lead one to expect the introduction of some form of international reorientation in economic policy by Iran's new leaders, based perhaps on a partial transformation of the domestic economy. In the end the reorientation which did occur took place after Ayatollah Khomeini's death and was towards rapid reintegration into the Western-dominated capitalist world economy, and not away from it.

Democracy and political participation were the two key issues high on the agenda of the revolutionaries during the 1977–9 uprising. The people were demanding the downfall of the Shah largely because of their dissatisfaction with his autocratic and dictatorial style of government. While towards the end of his regime the Shah did eventually accept the people's demands, it was already too late to incorporate them into the existing structures. In retrospect, the rallying cry of the uprising, 'Independence, Freedom, Islamic Republic', contained within it the seeds of the confrontations which followed the overthrow of the Shah. In particular, two important limitations imposed on the meaning of the word 'freedom' caused tensions among the revolutionary forces. Freedom had two legitimate realms in the Islamic Republic: firstly, the right to organise only within its permissible structures; and secondly, freedom seen as a religious concept and not as a secular right of the people. Thus to function and to propose ideas outside the Islamic legal framework were considered illegal.

The writing, one can say, was on the wall even before the victory of the revolution. When commenting on the nature of political participation in post-Pahlavi Iran, for example, Ayatollah Khomeini pointed to legal limitations that might be placed on freedom of action and expression: 'All parties will be free to exist in Iran, except those that clearly oppose the interests of the people, and the elections will also be free. Of course, we will make our recommendations to the people, which they may or may not follow' (Khomeini 1991: 324).

As the undisputed leader of the revolution Ayatollah Khomeini also became the republic's supreme constitutional leader and jurist. It soon became unlikely that his 'recommendations' would not be followed by the populace – or that any individual or group could offer an alternative to the theocracy's programme without violating its own constitutional right to freedom of expression, let alone action. More alarming still was the regime's attitude towards the notion of democracy. Ayatollah Khomeini summed up the theocratic elite's position on the question of democracy as follows:

> But as for 'democratic', that is a concept that has constantly changed its guise throughout history. In the West it means one thing, and in the East, another. We don't understand any of it. And why should something we don't understand appear on the ballot forms for us to vote on?
>
> Even apart from this . . . to juxtapose 'democratic' and 'Islamic' is an insult to Islam. Because when you place the word 'democratic' in front of 'Islamic' it means that Islam is lacking in the alleged virtues of democracy, although Islam is, in fact, superior to all forms of democracy.
>
> (Khomeini 1991: 337–8)

So the demarcation lines were drawn and the Islamic Republic came to replace one form of absolutism with another.

Other Third World leaders, populist and radical revolutionary alike, have used similar tactics and excuses to abolish opposition to their rule. The uniqueness of the Iranian case is perhaps its profound ideological opposition to Western democratic principles and its claim to absolutism as the will of God. This follows from the earlier discussion regarding sovereignty; if the people have no sovereignty and sovereignty is said to belong only to God, then it stands to reason that his representatives on earth – the clerics – should have absolute control over the state and society alike. This is precisely the basis of Ayatollah Khomeini's Faqih principle. Indeed, as events in Iran since the revolution have shown, it is only a short step from prohibition to suppression. Hence both liberal and leftist forces came under attack and their organisations were declared illegal. In fact at the time of the emergence of the Second Republic only one opposition organisation, Mehdi Bazargan's Freedom Movement, was tolerated.

What is striking, moreover, is the commensurate increase in the political power of the clergy in tandem with the demise of the country's other revolutionary and democratic forces. The coercive force of the state machinery was utilised not only to increase the power of the clerical elite within the system, but also against the ethnic and national minorities, which had risen to demand their due from the revolution. In a more structural way, it was also used to consolidate the new government's control over the country. The clerics' eventual near-monopolisation of power brought with it resort to control mechanisms similar to those developed under the Shah's long rule, and the utilisation of the machinery of the old regime in turn meant that the clerics did not need to develop a parallel political structure of their own to consolidate their power. It is worth noting therefore that the clerical heirs of the revolution did not gain power as a consequence of the efficiency of their vanguard party or their domination of any anti-Shah popular front organisation. Beyond belonging to the same 'professional club' the clerics had very little in common with each other, only common priorities against other groups. Thus their 'revolutionary' party, the Islamic Republic Party, was formed only after the victory of the revolution (the reverse of the accepted norm and revolutionary conventional wisdom), and only began serving the regime after its victory by its efforts to keep the corridors of power clear of the clerical coalition's opponents.

The revolution also provided the clerics with a golden opportunity to reverse the trend of history by putting an end to the nationalisation of Islam, and to proceed with the Islamisation of the nation. Even the country's regular elections came to serve the purpose of this Islamisation process. All candidates to the Majlis, for instance, have had to declare their allegiance to the Islamic Republic and put forward their Islamic credentials before being allowed to stand for contested elections. Many hopefuls were denied participation in elections as candidates because they failed to satisfy the Islamic requirements of the regime. Those who passed the first hurdle were then subjected to a lengthy and bureaucratic process of investigation and vetting before their candidature could be confirmed. This involved process served two main purposes. Firstly, it ensured that no 'undesirables' could ever be elected to serve the Islamic Republic. In addition, the complex nature of the electoral procedures acted as a deterrent against opposition groups trying to enter and influence the system of government. Secondly, the vetting process attempted to maintain not only uniformity of style of debate surrounding national issues, but also the very content of such debates.

It was through such mechanisms that the founders of the theocracy maintained and exercised control over the affairs of the Islamic Republic. Political *yekdastegi* (loosely translated as 'purity') in the Islamic Republic was thus ensured. *Yekparchegi* (loosely translated as 'uniformity'), however, proved to be an unattainable goal during the life of the First Republic. In post-Khomeini Iran, too, we have seen that the same emphasis on *yekparchegi* has brought to the pinnacle of power those clerical figures who had tried hard to make the Islamic Republic system function.

As a way of arriving at an overall conclusion, therefore, it is appropriate to ask what then has been the contribution of the Iranian revolution and the IRI model to the historical debate about social transformation in the Third World? Has it indeed served to challenge the accepted models?

CONCLUSION

Though not exclusively, the intention in this chapter was to question to some extent some of the conventional wisdoms of the revolution paradigm as a way of arriving at a more formal understanding of the revolution in Iran. The fact that the Iranian revolution did not adopt socialist ideals and terminology, in fact went out of its way to denounce them, and the fact that it was not led by the 'oppressed' classes, has enabled us to examine it as a 'political' rather than a 'social' revolution: 'viewing political revolution as entry into the ruling class of new recruits who expel a corrupt and restrictive political class, and social revolution as the wholesale replacement of the ruling class' (Guido Dorso's definition, quoted by Hagopian 1974: 105).

Taken in the context of the earlier discussion regarding a workable definition of what constitutes a revolution, the characterisation of the Iranian revolution as a political revolution is not intended to belittle the impact of the 'inheritor' regime on the economic and social life of the country. If anything the above analysis will have shown the very real ways in which a new political elite has set about 're-engineering' the socio-economic system. By classifying the Iranian revolution as political, one is enabled to draw attention to the peripheral impact of the revolution on the prevailing class system, for instance, or focus on its limited impact on the overall orientation of the economy.

The four features of the Iranian case chosen for further comment in this concluding chapter have brought to the fore the endemic difficulties, in analytical terms, of dealing with the process of change – whether political, social or economic – in the modern world. In the late-developing countries such change has usually been socialist-indexed, but the case of Iran (amongst others) illustrates that the change need not be exclusively socialist. The Iranian case also shows, however, that without a social revolution, although the regime (and the accompanying political system) may change, society as a whole will not be transformed so as to justify the label of 'social' revolution. More precisely, in the case of Iran, its revolutionary alternative, far from being a universal alternative, quickly degenerated into an exclusivist model stemming from the religious (Shii) tradition of the country and the revolutionary leadership's concept of an Islamic state. It is not always recognised that by emphasising the 'Islamic' nature of the revolution its catchment area was immediately reduced to the Muslim countries, and then only to those where Shia groups prevailed. It could be maintained therefore that the revolution is on its own admission exclusivist and not universalist. But that does not reduce its relevance, or indeed its impact on the region.

Therefore, almost a century since Iran's much praised constitutional revolution, when it comes to analysing a revolutionary situation we are perhaps none the wiser. In 1908 a prominent Iranian socialist (Arshavir Chalangarian) wrote to Karl Kautsky seeking his advice.

> As you may know there are two views among us concerning the nature of the movement in our country. According to the first, the Iranian revolution has no progressive content. This view contends that the thrust of the movement is against foreign capital, which is the only factor that can help develop the economy . . . By contrast, those who support the second view claim that the movement is progressive because it is aimed against the feudal order, and because it is a movement of the masses . . . We hope that you will be in a position to answer the following theoretical and scientific questions . . . (1) What in your view is the character of the Iranian revolution? Is it retrogressive? (2) How should Social Democrats participate in a democratic and progressive movement? What if the movement is reactionary?
>
> (Riddell 1986: 61)

The thrust of these arguments is still with us, and the questions remain equally pertinent to both the Iranian 'Islamic' and the many Third World 'socialist' revolutions alike. In the Iranian context it is vital to appreciate that the IRI model could be regarded as less than successful, above all because it has been singularly unable to achieve the harmony and social reconciliation demanded by the anti-Shah revolutionary movement. That this failure could well be a reflection on Iranian society itself must be highlighted. Ian Roxborough notes that the 'weakness of any domestic bourgeoisie in [the late-developing] countries has enabled the elites which have come to occupy state power to transform themselves into new dominant classes' (Roxborough 1986: 142). In post-revolutionary Iran the *ulama* cannot be said to have become a new 'class' (in the Marxian sense) but have unquestionably been the dominant elite (in terms of control of political power). By the virtue of this dominant position they have been able to extend their influence (and in many instances control as well) to almost all aspects of life in Iranian society, and secure a privileged position for the merchant bourgeoisie which traditionally congregates around the bazaar.

This phenomenon, the emergence of a new political elite, can be said to have emerged, as Roxborough suggests, because of the weakness of the remaining domestic bourgeoisie in post-Pahlavi Iran. But, as we have seen, the elite that took over the reins of power was not homogenous, and indeed while the form of the ruling elite may have remained more or less the same after the summer of 1989 and the death of the first Faqih the shape of the elite, and the content of its policies, have been very different from the original – limited – agenda of the First Republic.

Secondly, many of the individuals leading the Second Republic were products of the Islamic Republican system which emerged under the guidance of the leader of the revolution, Ayatollah Khomeini. As we saw in earlier chapters, the very policies of the Second Republic have been designed to strengthen the presence and role of the domestic bourgeoisie, to the extent of inviting back to the Iranian market the exiled *comprador* classes which had been closely associated with the old, pro-Western, Pahlavi regime. The new elite which had come to occupy state power by 1979–80 thus not only proved unable to transform itself into a new class in the first phase of the revolutionary experience but has shown great enthusiasm in the Islamic regime's second phase for rejuvenating the social classes which can enhance the capitalist economy of Iran. The Iranian elite, thus, can be said to be undertaking a 'passive revolution' in the 1990s, to adopt a term used by Gramsci. This process has been defined by Roxborough as 'any attempt by an elite other than the bourgeoisie to use its control of the state to oversee an attempt at rapid economic development [in the case of Iran, economic reconstruction] in which, by and large, bourgeois property is not totally expropriated' (ibid.: 143). The passive revolution in Iran has necessarily required the return of the expropriated bourgeois property to its original and new class of potential private owners. This strategy of the Iranian government has been motivated not only by domestic difficulties in dealing with the task of reconstruction but also by Iran's inability to recover its former position in the international division of labour without the support of Western capital.

In the context of the new international division of labour, a semi-industrialised or semi-peripheral country like Iran could not survive long without external inputs for its 'dependent' industries; the rejuvenation of these same industries was essential if recovery was to take place in the domestic economy. Recovery in turn could secure the political power of the 'Islamic' elite and minimise the threat to its position from below. In addition, without the transformation of the country's productive structures effected by the Pahlavi regime after the revolution, to recover economically at home had always meant the recovery of Iran's role as an emerging newly industrialising country in West Asia. The organic linkage between the two realms of indigenous and exogenous, and the combination of the two dealing with the economic difficulties of the country, have practically determined the policy agenda of the post-Khomeini leadership. In order to avoid becoming what Gordon White has called a 'Catch 22' state ('a pervasive state is established in the initial stages of industrialisation for defensible . . . reasons but then outstays its historical welcome as a bastion of economic irrationality and political authoritarianism' (White 1984: 115), the Islamic Republic's leaders, never having encouraged departure from the international capitalist system in any meaningful sense, seem to have had little choice but substantially to open up to that same global system again.

Outside the Iranian case, it is all the more urgent to ask, with the long established prevailing models of revolutionary transformation crumbling before our eyes, where should we look now for alternative theoretical constructs and non-capitalist options to the international capitalist mode of production? The answers, I suspect, will continue to have much to do with the ways in which the questions are postulated.

Bibliography

NEWSPAPERS AND NEWS PERIODICALS

Abrar
al-Hayat
APS Diplomat
Aynch Eghtesad
Arab Press Service
Arabia
Armed Forces
Arms Control Today
BBC's Summary of World Broadcasts (SWB)
CAABU Bulletin
Defence and Armament
Defence and Foreign Affairs Weekly
Disarmament Newsletter
Eqtesad
Ettela'at
Ettela'at Siasi-Eghtesadi
Farhang-e-Towsee
Financial Times
Foreign Broadcast Information Service (FBIS)
Gulf Report
IAEA Press Release
International Herald Tribune
Iran Farda
Iran Focus
Iran Times (Washington, DC)
Iranian Journal of International Relations
Issues
Jane's Sentinel
Jomhouri Islami
Kar
Kayhan
Kayhan (London)
Kayhan International
Kayhan Havai

Middle East Economic Digest (MEES)
Middle East Economic Survey (MEES)
Middle East International
Mideast Mirror
Mojahed
Newsweek
Nimrooz (London)
Nuclear Fuel
Nucleonics Week
PPNN Newsbrief
Resalat
Salam
SIPRI
The Economist
The Echo of Iran
The Guardian
The Middle East
The Military Balance
The New York Times
The Times
Time
Voice of Iran

BOOKS AND REPORTS

Abrahamian, E. (1982) *Iran Between Two Revolutions*, Princeton, New Jersey: Princeton University Press.

Abrahamian, E. (1989) *Radical Islam: The Iranian Mojahedin*, London: I. B. Tauris.

Abrahamian, E. (1991) 'Khomeini: fundamentalist or populist?', *New Left Review* 186, March/April, 102–19.

Abrahamian, E. (1993) *Khomeinism: Essays on the Islamic Republic of Iran*, Berkeley: University of California Press.

Ajami, F. (1988/89) 'Iran: the impossible revolution', *Foreign Affairs* 67, 2, Winter: 135–55.

Akbari, A.A. (1990) *Jomhouri-e Eslami va Mosadereh-e Sarmayehay-e Khosoozi* (The Islamic Republic of Iran and Confiscation of Private Capital), West Germany: N.P.

Akhavi, S. (1980) *Religion and Politics in Contemporary Iran: Clergy–State Relations in the Pahlavi Period*, Albany: State University of New York Press.

Akhavi, S. (1985) 'The power structure of the Islamic Republic of Iran', in S. T. Hunter (ed.) *Internal Developments in Iran*, Washington, DC: Center for Strategic and International Studies.

Akhavi, S. (1987) 'Elite factionalism in the Islamic Republic of Iran', *The Middle East Journal* 41, 2, Spring: 181–201.

Alaolmolki, N. (1987) 'The new Iranian left', *The Middle East Journal* 41, 2, Spring: 218–33.

Alavi, H. (1979) 'The state in post-colonial societies – Pakistan and Bangladesh', in H. Goulbourne (ed.) *Politics and State in the Third World*, London: Macmillan.

Alavi, H. (1985) 'State and class under peripheral capitalism', in H. Alavi and T. Shanin (eds) *Introduction to the Sociology of 'Developing Societies'*, London: Macmillan.

Albright, D. and Hibbs, M. (1992) 'Nuclear proliferation: spot-light shifts to Iran', *The Bulletin of the Atomic Scientists* 48, 2, March: 9–11.

Algar, H. (1980) *Constitution of the Islamic Republic of Iran*, Berkeley: Mizan Press.

Algar, H. (trans.) (1991) *Islam and Revolution: Writings and Declarations of Imam Khomeini*, Syracuse: Syracuse University Press.

Amirahmadi, H. (1990) *Revolution and Economic Transition: The Iranian Experience*, Albany: State University of New York Press.

Amirahmadi, H. and Entessar, N. (eds) (1992) *Reconstruction and Regional Diplomacy in the Persian Gulf*, London: Routledge.

Amuzegar, J. (1977) *Iran: An Economic Profile*, Washington, DC: The Middle East Institute.

Amuzegar, J. (1992) 'The Iranian economy before and after the revolution', *The Middle East Journal*, 46, 3, Summer: 413–425.

Amuzegar, J. (1993) *Iran's Economy Under the Islamic Republic*, London: I. B. Tauris.

Anon. (1986) 'Iranians' letter to Kautsky', quoted in J. Riddell (ed.) *Lenin's Struggle for a Revolutionary International: Documents 1907–1916*, New York: Monad Press.

Anon. (1986) 'Public versus private in Iran: a question of ownership', *Arabia* March 1986: 66–7.

Anon. (1988) 'The Gulf War', *Gulf Report* 11, June: 16–38.

Anon. (1989) 'Imam Khomeini's message to the clergy', *The Echo of Iran* 18, 9 March: 21–4.

Anon. (1989) 'Imam Khomeini's message to the clergy', *The Echo of Iran* 19, 16 March: 21–4.

Anon. (1990) 'Inside Iran', *Mednews* 3 December: 1–2.

Anon. (1991) 'Pres. Rafsanjani's lifetime of struggle for the Islamic revolution', *Diplomat* 25 February: 12–13.

Anon. (1991) 'Iran–first five year plan', *COMET Bulletin*, 33, April: 23–32.

Anon. (1992) 'Sarmayehgozari-e kjareji, moshkel gosha ya moshkel fara?' (Foreign investment, solution or problem?) *Ayneh Eghtesad* 19, September–October: 8–14.

Anon. (1993) 'Bahsey piramoun-e sarmayehgozari-e mostagheem kjareji (a discussion on direct foreign investment), *Ettela'at Siasi-Eghtesadi* 7, 5–6, February–March: 58–69.

Anon. (1993) 'Libyan missile design "transferred to Iran"', *CAABU Bulletin* 9, 8, 1 May: 4.

Anthony, I. (1993) 'The "third tier" countries: production of major weapons', in H. Wulf (ed.) *Arms Industry Limited*, Oxford: Oxford University Press.

Atiqpour, M. (1979) *Naqsh Bazar va Bazariha dar Enqelab Iran* (The Role of the Bazaar and Bazaaris in the Iranian Revolution), Tehran: Naqsh-e Jahan Press.

Atkeson, E. B. (1993) *A Dynamic Net Military Assessment of the Middle East*, Carlisle Barracks, Pennsylvania: Strategic Studies Institute, US Army College.

Azimi, H. (1989) 'Neghahey be naqsh doulat dar touse'e eqtesadi' (An examination of the role of government in economic development), *Ettela'at Siasi–Eghtesadi* 4, 1, October: 38–42.

Azimi, H. (1992) 'Eqtesad-e Iran, bohranha va cheshmandazha' (Iran's economy, crises and prospects), *Iran Farda* 1, 4, November–December: 8–16.

Bailey, K. C. (1991) 'Reversing missile proliferation', *Orbis* 35, 1, Winter: 5–14.

Bakhash, S. (1989) 'After the Gulf war I: Iran's home front', *The World Today* March: 46–9.

Bakhash, S. (1993) 'Iranian politics since the Gulf war', in R. B. Satloff (ed.) *The Politics of Change in the Middle East*, Boulder, Colorado: Westview Press.

Baresieh-e Siasy-ijtemayi-e Rejeem-e Jomhouri Eslami Iran (A Political, Social and Economic Investigation of the Islamic Republican Regime in Iran) (N.D.), London: Socialist Publications.

Barthel, G. (ed.) (1983) *Iran: From Monarchy to Republic*, Berlin: Akademie-Verlag.

Behrooz, M. (1991) 'Factionalism in Iran under Khomeini', *Middle Eastern Studies* 27, 4, October: 597–614.

Behrouz, J. (1989) 'Imam Khomeini's predictions on post-Khomeini Iran', *The Echo of Iran* September: 14–18.

Bernard, C. and Khalilzad, Z. (1984) *'The Government of God': Iran's Islamic Republic*, New York: Columbia University Press.

Bertsch, G. K., Clark, R. P., and Wood, D. M. (1978) *Comparing Political Systems: Power and Policy in Three Worlds*, New York: John Wiley and Sons.

Bill, J. (1982) 'Power and religion in revolutionary Iran', *The Middle East Journal* 36, 1, Winter: 22–47.

Borderas, A. (1993) 'Fundamentalist tendencies and the future of democracy in North Africa', *Civilian Affairs Committee, North Atlantic Assembly*: 1–17.

Bromley, S. (1994) *Rethinking Middle East Politics: State Formation and Development*, Oxford: Polity Press.

Business International Ltd (1991) *Iran: A Manual for Foreign Business*, London: Business International Ltd.

Calabrese, J. (1990) 'Iran II: the Damascus connection', *The World Today* October: 188–90.

Calvocoressi, P. (1991) 'After Kuwait', *International Relations* X, 4, November: 287–300.

Campbell, W. R. and Darvich, D. (1984) 'Totalitarian implications of Khomeini's conception of Islamic consciousness', *Journal of South Asian and Middle Eastern Studies* VIII, 2, Winter: 43–72.

Carus, W. S. and Bermudez, J. S. (1988) 'Iran's growing missile forces', *Jane's Defence Weekly*, 23 July: 126–31.

Central Bank of Iran (Bank Markazi Iran) (1975) *Annual Report, 1974/5*, Tehran: Central Bank of Iran.

Central Bank of Iran (1980) (1359) *Annual Report and Balance Sheet 1359*, Tehran: Central Bank of Iran.

Central Bank of Iran (1988) (1367) *Annual Report and Balance Sheet 1367*, Tehran: Central Bank of Iran.

Central Bank of Iran (Bank Markazi Iran) (various years) *Annual Reports and Balance Sheets*, Tehran: Central Bank of Iran.

Chelkowski, P. J. and Pranger, R. J. (1988) *Ideology and Power in the Middle East: Essays in Honor of George Lencsowski*, Durham: Duke University Press.

Chemical Bank New York Trust Company (1964) *International Economic Survey: Iran* 141, April.

Chubin, S. (1987) *Iran and its Neighbours: The Impact of the Gulf War*, Conflict Studies 204, London: The Centre for Security and Conflict Studies.

Chubin, S. (1994) *Iran's National Security Policy: Capabilities, Intentions, and Impact*, Washington, DC: Carnegie Endowment for Peace.

Chubin, S. and Tripp, C. (1989) *Iran and Iraq at War*, London: I. B. Tauris.

Clapham, C. (1990) 'The crisis of socialist development in the Third World', paper presented at the European Consortium for Political Research Joint Sessions, Bochum, Germany, 2–7 April.

Clawson, P. (1988) 'Islamic Iran's economic politics and prospects', *The Middle East Journal* 42, 3, Summer: 371–88.

Cockcroft, J. D. (1980) 'On the ideological and class character of Iran's anti-imperialist revolution', in G. Stauth (ed.) *Iran: Capitalism and Revolution*, Germany: Verlag Breitenbach.

Committee for Middle East Trade (1982) 'Iran: some impressions of the current scene', *COMET Bulletin* 9, February: 21–30.

Committee for Middle East Trade (1991) 'Iran – first five year plan', *COMET Bulletin* 33, April: 23–32.

Committee for Middle East Trade (1992) 'Middle East trade with the world, 1990', *COMET Bulletin* 35, January: 21–3.

Cordesman, A. H. (1991) *Weapons of Mass Destruction in the Middle East*, London: Brassey's.

Cordesman, A. H. (1993) *After the Storm: The Changing Military Balance in the Middle East*, London: Mansell.

Cordesman, A. H. and Wagner A. B. (1990) *The Lessons of Modern War: The Iran–Iraq War*, London: Mansell.

Cottam, R. (1989) 'Inside revolutionary Iran', *The Middle East Journal* 43, 2, Spring: 168–89.

Cottrell, A. J. (1975) *Iran: Diplomacy in a Regional and Global Context*, Washington, DC.

CRS (1992) *Conventional Arms Transfers to the Third World, 1984–1991*, Congressional Research Service 92, Washington, DC: The Library of Congress.

Dawisha, A. (ed.) (1985) *Islam in Foreign Policy*, Cambridge: Cambridge University Press.

Deegan, H. (1993) *The Middle East and Problems of Democracy*, Buckingham: Open University Press.

Dunn, L. A. (1991) *Containing Nuclear Proliferation*, Adelphi Paper 263, London: Brassey's.

Economic Affairs Secretariat (1991) *Barresi-ye Bodjeh va Vaz'e Maliati-e Dolat 1350–67* (Investigation of the Budget and Government's Revenue Situation 1971/2–88/9), Tehran: Ministry of Economics and Financial Affairs.

Economist Intelligence Unit (1979) *Quarterly Economic Review of Iran*, 3.

Economist Intelligence Unit (1993) *Country Report Iran*, 3rd quarter, London: EIU.

Ehteshami, A. (1987) 'Succession within and without the context of the Islamic Republic of Iran', paper presented at the BRISMES Annual Conference, University of Exeter.

Ehteshami, A. (1990) 'Iran's revolution: fewer ploughshares, more swords', *Army Quarterly and Defence Journal* 120, 1, January: 41–50.

Ehteshami, A. (1991) 'Iran and the European Community', in A. Ehteshami and M. Varasteh (eds), *Iran and the International Community*, London: Routledge.

Ehteshami, A. (1992) *Political Upheaval and Socio-economic Continuity: The Case of Iran*, RUSEL Working Paper 6, University of Exeter, Department of Politics.

Ehteshami, A. (1993a) 'Iran', in T. Niblock and E. Murphy (eds) *Economic and Political Liberalization in the Middle East*, London: British Academic Press.

Ehteshami, A. (1993b) 'The Arab states and the Middle East balance of power', in J. Gow (ed.) *Iraq, the Gulf Conflict and the World Community*, London: Brassey's.

Ehteshami, A. (1994) 'New frontiers: Iran, the GCC and the CCARs', in A. Ehteshami (ed.) *From the Gulf to Central Asia: Players in the New Great Game*, Exeter: University of Exeter Press.

Entessar, N. (1992) 'The challenge of political reconstruction in Iran', in C. Bina and H. Zanganeh (eds), *Modern Capitalism and Islamic Ideology in Iran*, London: Macmillan Press.

Eshel, D. (1992) 'Arms race in the Gulf', *Military Technology* July: 62–7.

Esposito, J. L. (1992) *The Islamic Threat: Myth or Reality?*, Oxford: Oxford University Press.

Farsoun, S. K. and Mashayekhi, M. (eds) (1992) *Iran: Political Culture in the Islamic Republic*, London: Routledge.

Financial Times Survey (1985) 'Iran', 1 April.

Financial Times Survey (1993) 'Iran', 8 February.

Flight International (1986) 'World's air forces'.

Flight International (1987) 'World's air forces'.

Flight International (1993) 'World's air forces'.

Gasiorowski, M.J. (1993) 'Policy-making in a highly autonomouos state: Iran under the Shah, 1963–1978', *The Iranian Journal of International Affairs* V, 2, Summer: 440–82.

George, A. (1993) 'Fugitive endeavours', *Flight International* 17–23 February: 20.

Goulbourne, H. (ed.) (1979) *Politics and State in the Third World*, London: Macmillan.

Gow, J. (ed.) (1993) *Iraq, the Gulf Conflict and the World Community*, London: Brassey's.

Green, J. D. (1993) 'Iran's foreign policy: between enmity and conciliation', *Current History* January: 12–16.

Grimmett, R. F. (1990) *Trends in Conventional Arms Transfers to the Third World by Major Suppliers, 1982–89*, Congressional Research Service 90, Washington, DC: The Library of Congress.

Grimmett, R. F. (1991) *Conventional Arms Transfers to the Third World, 1983–1990*, Congressional Research Service 91, Washington, DC: The Library of Congress.

Group, M. (1990) *Iran's Economy: Perspectives and Prospects*, Geneva: M. Group Centre for Strategic Studies.

Gurdon, H. (1984) *Iran – The Continuing Struggle for Power*, Wisbech, Cambridgeshire: Menas Press.

Haeri, S. (1989) 'Iran goes for a clever compromise', *Middle East International* 352, 9 June: 3–4.

Haeri, S. (1991) 'Hitch in Mitterand's plan', *Middle East International* 404, 12 July: 13–14.

Haeri, S. (1992) 'Forces combined', *Middle East International* 418, 7 February: 12.

Haeri, S. (1994) 'Iran: succession conflict', *Middle East International* 466, 7 January: 13.

Haghayeghi, M. (1993) 'Politics and ideology in the Islamic Republic of Iran', *Middle Eastern Studies* 29, 1, January: 36–52.

Hagopian, M. N. (1974) *The Phenomenon of Revolution*, New York: Dodd, Mead and Co.

Haqvoroody, M. (1993) 'Siasat-e qaimatghozari-e mahsoolat-e estratejic keshavarzi dar Iran' (The pricing policy of strategic agricultural products in Iran), *Ettela'at Siasi-Eghtesadi* 7, 5–6, February–March: 96–100.

Hashim, A. (1992) *Resurgent Iran: New Defence Thinking and Growing Military*

Capabilities, prepared for the American Association for the Advancement of Science, August.

Hearings before the Subcommittee on Defense Industry and Technology of the Committee on Armed Forces Services, US Senate (1989) *Ballistic and Cruise Missile Proliferation in the Third World*, Washington, DC: US Government Printing Office.

Helfgott, L. (1976) 'Iran: capitalist formation on the periphery', *The Review of Iranian Political Economy and History* 1, 1, December: 2–24.

Heller, M. A. (1991) 'Coping with missile proliferation in the Middle East', *Orbis* 35, 1, Winter: 15–28.

Hicks, J. (1975) *The Persians*, New York: Time–Life International.

Hiro, D. (1985) *Iran under the Ayatollahs*, London: Routledge.

Hollis, R. (1993) *Gulf Security: No Consensus*, London: Royal United Services Institute for Defence Studies.

Hooglund, E. (1986) 'Social origins of the revolutionary clergy', in N. R. Keddie and E. Hooglund (eds) *The Iranian Revolution and the Islamic Republic*, Syracuse: Syracuse University Press.

Hooglund, E. (1994) 'Iran and Central Asia', in A. Ehteshami (ed.) *From the Gulf to Central Asia: Players in the New Great Game*, Exeter: University of Exeter Press.

Hunter, S. T. (ed.) (1985) *Internal Developments in Iran*, Washington, DC: Center for Strategic and International Studies.

Hunter, S. T. (1989/90) 'Post-Khomeini Iran', *Foreign Affairs* 68, 5, Winter: 133–49.

Hunter, S. T. (1990) *Iran and the World: Continuity in a Revolutionary Decade*, Bloomington: Indiana University Press.

Hunter, S. T. (1992) *Iran After Khomeini*, Westport: Praeger.

International Bank for Reconstruction and Development (IBRD) (1993) *World Debt Tables* 1993–4, Washington, DC: International Bank for Reconstruction and Development.

International Bank for Reconstruction and Development (IBRD) (1993) *World Development Report*, Oxford: Oxford University Press.

International Institute for Strategic Studies (IISS) (various years) *The Military Balance*, London: Brasseys.

International Monetary Fund (1986) *Direction of Trade Statistics*, Washington, DC: IMF.

International Monetary Fund (1988) *Direction of Trade Statistics*, Washington, DC: IMF.

International Monetary Fund (1989) *Direction of Trade Statistics*, Washington, DC: IMF.

International Monetary Fund (1990) 'Islamic Republic of Iran undergoes profound institutional, structural changes', *IMF Survey* 30 July: 226–9.

International Monetary Fund (1991a) *Government Finance Statistics Yearbook*, Washington, DC: IMF.

International Monetary Fund (1991b) *Direction of Trade Statistics*, Washington, DC: IMF.

International Monetary Fund (1992) *Direction of Trade Statistics*, Washington, DC: IMF.

Iran Research Group (1989) *Iran Yearbook '89–90*, Bonn: MB Medien and Bucher Verlagsgesellschaft mbH.

Iran Shows the Way (1976), Tehran: N.P.

Irfani, S. (1983) *Revolutionary Islam in Iran: Popular Liberation or Religious Dictatorship?*, London: Zed Press.

Irfani, S. (1986) 'Ayatollah Montazeri as Khomeini's successor', *Strategic Studies* IX, 2, Winter: 26–47.

Isenberg, D. (1993) 'Desert storm redux?', *The Middle East Journal* 47, 3, Summer: 429–43.

Ja'far, M. and Tabari, A. (1984) 'Iran: Islam and the struggle for socialism', in J. Rothschild (selector) *Forbidden Agendas: Intolerance and Defiance in the Middle East*, London: Al Saqi Books.

Jahanpour, F. (1989) 'Iran after Khomeini', *The World Today* August/September: 150–3.

Jahanpour, F. (1990) 'Iran I: Wars among the heirs', *The World Today* October: 183–7.

Jahanpour, F. (1992) *Directory of Iranian Officials*, Reading: BBC Monitoring Unit.

Jahanpour, F. (1994) 'Tehran and the Shi'ite clergy – an uneasy relationship', *Middle East International* 4 February: 19–21.

Jane's (1989) *Jane's Military Communications*, Coulsdon: Jane's Information Group.

Jansen, G. H. (1989) 'Ayatollah Khomeini: an assessment', *Middle East International* 352, 9 June: 14–15.

JCSS (various years) *The Middle East Military Balance*, Boulder, Colorado: Westview Press.

Kadhim, M. (1983) *The Political Economy of Revolutionary Iran*, Cairo: Cairo Papers in Social Science 6, 1, March.

Kamrava, M. (1992) *Revolutionary Politics*, Westport: Praeger.

Karp, A. (1989) 'Ballistic missile proliferation in the Third World', *SIPRI Yearbook 1989: World Armaments and Disarmament*, Oxford: Oxford University Press.

Karp, A. (1991a) 'Controlling ballistic missile proliferation', *Survival* XXXIII, 6, November/December: 517–30.

Karp, A. (1991b) 'Ballistic missile proliferation', *SIPRI Yearbok 1991: World Armaments and Disarmament*, Oxford: Oxford University Press.

Karsh, E., Navias, M.S. and Sabin, P. (eds) (1993) *Non-conventional Weapons Proliferation in the Middle East: Tackling the Spread of Nuclear, Chemical and Biological Capabilites*, Oxford: Clarendon Press.

Karshenas, M. (1990) *Oil, State and Industrialisation in Iran*, Cambridge: Cambridge University Press.

Keddie, N. R. and Hooglund, E. (eds) (1986) *The Iranian Revolution and the Islamic Republic*, Syracuse: Syracuse University Press.

Khomeini, R. Ayatollah (1991) *Islam and Revolution: Writings and Declarations of Imam Khomeini*, translated by H. Algar, Berkeley: Mizan Press.

Korany, B. and Hilal Dessouki, A. (eds) (1991) *The Foreign Policies of Arab States: The Challenge of Change*, Boulder, Colorado: Westview Press.

Koury, E. M. and MacDonald, C. G. (eds) (1982) *Revolution in Iran: A Reappraisal*, Hyattsville, Maryland: Institute of Middle Eastern and North African Affairs.

Lahoud, L. (1992a) 'Iran's 'disco shoe' revolution', *The Jerusalem Report* 9 April: 24–5.

Lahoud, L. (1992b) 'The Jerusalem Report interview: Abolhassan Bani-Sadr', *The Jerusalem Report* 9 April: 25–6.

Lailaz, S. (1993) 'Nazarey bar amalkard-e eqtesadi-e jomhouri-e eslami' (Review of the economic behaviour of the Islamic Republic), *Iran Farda* 1, 5, January–February 1993: 18–24.

Looney, R. (1973) *The Economic Development of Iran – A Recent Survey with Projections to 1981*, New York: Praeger.

Looney, R. (1985) 'The impact of oil revenues on the pre-revolutionary Iranian economy', *Middle Eastern Studies* 21, 1: 61–71.

Lusk, G. (1991) 'Sudan: civilians bear the brunt', *Middle East International* 415, 20 December: 11.

MacDonald, C. G. (1982) 'Iran as a political variable: patterns and prospects', in E. M. Koury and C. G. MacDonald (eds) *Revolution in Iran: A Reappraisal*, Hyattsville, Maryland: Institute of Middle Eastern and North African Affairs.

Makinda, S. M. (1993) 'Iran, Sudan and Islam', *The World Today* June: 108–11.

Malek, M. H. (1991) *Iran after Khomeini: Perpetual Crisis or Opportunity?*, Conflict Studies 237, London: Research Institute for the Study of Conflict and Terrorism.

Mann, M. (1986) 'The autonomous power of the state: its origins, mechanisms and results', in J. A. Hall (ed.) *States in History*, Oxford: Basil Blackwell.

Marlowe, J. (1962) *The Persian Gulf in the Twentieth Century*, London: Cresset Press.

Marr, P. and Lewis, W. (1993) *Riding the Tiger: The Middle East Challenge after the Cold War*, Boulder, Colorado: Westview Press.

Matsumoto, A. (1991) 'A survey of the concept "Velayat" of "Velayat-e Faqih"', in T. Kuroda and R. I. Lawless (eds) *Nature of the Islamic Community*, Tokyo: Keiso Shobo: 143–65.

Maull, H. (1991) 'The arms trade with the Middle East and North Africa', *The Middle East and North Africa 1992*, London: Europa Pubications: 122–9.

MEED Special Report (1984) 'Iran' November.

Menashri, D. (1989) 'Iran: doctrine and real-politics', in *Problems of Maintaining Peace and Security in the Gulf and Japan – Perspectives for the Middle East in the 1990's*, Tokyo: The Middle East Institute of Japan.

Menashri, D. (1990) *Iran: A Decade of War and Revolution*, New York: Holmes and Meier.

MERI Report (1985) *Iran*, London: Croom Helm.

MERIP Special Report (1992) *Arms Race or Arms Control?* 22, 4, July/August, Washington, DC: MERIP.

Middle East Contemporary Survey (various years) 'Iran', New York: Holmes and Meier.

Middle East Review (various years) 'Iran', Saffron Walden, Essex: World of Information.

Milani, M. (1992) 'The transformation of the *Velayat-e Faqih* institution: from Khomeini to Khamenei', *The Muslim World* LXXXII, 3–4, July–October: 175–90.

Milani, M. (1993) 'The evolution of the Iranian presidency: from Bani Sadr to Rafsanjani', *British Journal of Middle Eastern Studies* 20, 1: 83–97.

Military Technology (various years) *World Defence Almanac*, Bonn: Monch Publishing Group.

Miller, A. J. (1989) *Toward Armageddon: The Proliferation of Unconventional Weapons and Ballistic Missiles in the Middle East*, Kingston, Ontario: Centre for International Relations.

Moaddel, M. (1991) 'Class struggle in post-revolutionary Iran', *International Journal of Middle East Studies* 23, 3, August: 317–43.

Mofid, K. (1987) *Development Planning in Iran: From Monarchy to Islamic Republic*, Wisbech, Cambridgeshire: Menas Press.

Mofid, K. (1990) *The Economic Consequences of the Gulf War*, London: Routledge.

Moghadam, V. (1987) 'Socialism or anti-imperialism? The left and revolution in Iran', *New Left Review* 166, November/December: 5–28.

Mohtashem, E. (1993) 'An Iranian perspective', in J. Gow (ed.) *Iraq, the Gulf Conflict and the World Community*, London: Brassey's.

Mozaffari, M. (1993) 'Changes in the Iranian political system after Ayatollah Khomeini's death', *Political Studies* XLI, 4, December: 611–17.

Muller, H-G. (1983) 'Remarks on the role of the state capital sector and national private capital in the evolutionary process of capitalism in Iran up to the end of the 1970s', in G. Barthel (ed.) *Iran: From Monarchy to Republic*, Berlin: Akademie-Verlag.

Najmabadi, A. (1987) 'Depoliticisation of a rentier state: the case of Pahlavi Iran', in H. Beblawi and G. Luciani (eds) *The Rentier State*, London: Croom Helm.

Nakhjavani, S. A. (1992) 'Beh fekr nasl-e ayandeh basheem' (Let's think of the future generations), *Tazehaye Eghtessad* 28, December: 14.

Nassoori, K. (1981) 'Iran and the West', *Middle East International* 155, 31 July: 12–13.

Navias, M. (1990) *Ballistic Missile Proliferation in the Third World*, Adelphi Paper 252, London: Brassey's.

Neuman, S. (1948–9) 'The international civil war', *World Politics* 1.

Neuman, S. G. (1981) 'Arms transfers, indigenous defence production and dependency: the case of Iran', in H. Amirsadeghi (ed.) *The Security of the Persian Gulf*, London: Croom Helm.

Nonneman, G. (1988) *Development, Administration and Aid in the Middle East*, London: Routledge.

Oberdorfer, D. (1992) 'Tehran financed captors in Lebanon', *International Herald Tribune* 20 January.

Office of Economic Analysis (1983) *Baresey-e Tahavolat-e Eqtesadi Keshvar Baad Az Enqleab* (Analysis of the Transformation of the Country's Economy since the Revolution), Tehran: Central Bank of Iran.

Omid, H. (1992) 'Theocracy or democracy? The critics of "westoxification" and the politics of fundamentalism in Iran', *Third World Quarterly* 3, 4: 675–90.

Omid, H. (1994) *Islam and the Post-revolutionary State in Iran*, London: Macmillan.

Organisation for Economic Co-operation and Development (1983) *Aid from OPEC Countries*, Paris: OECD.

Organisation for Economic Co-operation and Development (1986) *Statistics of Foreign Trade, Series A*, Paris: OECD Secretariat.

Organisation for Economic Co-operation and Development (1987) *Statistics of Foreign Trade, Series A*, Paris: OECD Secretariat.

Organisation for Economic Co-operation and Development (1988) *Statistics of Foreign Trade, Series A*, Paris: OECD Secretariat.

Organisation for Economic Co-operation and Development (1991) *Statistics of Foreign Trade, Series A*, Paris: OECD Secretariat.

Organisation of Petroleum Exporting Countries (1980) *Annual Statistical Bulletin*, Vienna: OPEC.

Oxford Research Group (1993) *Strengthening the Non-proliferation Regime: 1995 and Beyond*, Current Decisions Report 13, Oxford: Oxford Research Group.

Perabo, B. (1992) *A Chronology of Iran's Nuclear Programming*, Monterey: Monterey Institute of International Studies.

Pipes, D. and Clawson, P. (1992/3) 'Ambitious Iran, troubled neighbours', *Foreign Affairs* 72, 1, : 124–41.

Piscatori, J. (ed.) (1983) *Islam in the Political Process*, Cambridge: Cambridge University Press.

Plan and Budget Ministry (1989) *The First Economic, Social, and Cultural Development Plan of the Islamic Republic of Iran 1368–1372*, Tehran: Ministry of Planning and the Budget.

Plan and Budget Organisation (1993) *Iran Statistical Yearbook March 1991–March 1992*, Tehran: Plan and Budget Organisation, Statistical Centre of Iran.

Plan and Budget Organisation (various years) *Annual Budget*.

Pohling-Brown, P. (1993) 'Sales boom expected – but careful marketing required', *International Defence Review*, February: 141–8.

Povey, T. (1986) 'Iran', *Middle East Review 1986*, Saffron Walden, Essex: World of Information.

Programme for Promoting Nuclear Non-proliferation (PPNN) Newsbrief (various issues).

Rais, R. B. (1992) 'Afghanistan and regional security after the Cold War', *Problems of Communism* May–June: 82–94.

Ramazani. R. K. (1985) 'Khumayni's Islam in Iran's foreign policy', in A. Dawisha (ed.) *Islam in Foreign Policy*, Cambridge: Cambridge University Press.

Ramazani, R. K. (1986) *Revolutionary Iran: Challenge and Response in the Middle East*, Baltimore: The Johns Hopkins University Press.

Ramazani, R. K. (1989) 'Iran's foreign policy: contending orientations', *The Middle East Journal* 43, 2, Spring: 202–17.

Ramazani, R. K. (1992) 'Iran's foreign policy: both North and South', *The Middle East Journal* 46, 3 Summer: 393–412.

Razavi, H. and Vakil, F. (1984) *The Political Environment of Economic Planning in Iran, 1971–1983: From Monarchy to Islamic Republic*, Boulder, Colorado: Westview Press.

Renner, J. (1982) 'Iranian exiles in Paris against Khomeini', *The Listener* 7 January: 9–11.

Riddell, J. (ed.) (1986) *Lenin's Struggle for a Revolutionary International: Documents 1907–1916; The Preparatory Years*, Monard Press.

Rizopoulos, N. X. (ed.) (1990) *Sea-changes: American Foreign Policy in a World Transformed*, New York: Council on Foreign Relations.

Rosenau, J. N. (1990) *Turbulence in World Politics: A Theory of Change and Continuity*, Princeton, New Jersey: Princeton University Press.

Roshandel, J. and Lotfian, S. (1993) 'Horizontal nuclear proliferation: is Iran a nuclear-capable state?' *The Iranian Journal of International Affairs* V, 1, Spring: 208–28.

Roxborough, I. (1986) *Theories of Underdevelopment*, London: Macmillan.

Roy, O. (1990) 'The Mujahidin and the future of Afghanistan', in J. L. Esposito (ed.) *The Iranian Revolution: Its Global Impact*, Miami: Florida International University Press.

Royal United Services Institute (1992) *Defence Yearbook 1992*, London: Brassey's.

Rubin, U. (1991) 'How much does missile proliferation matter?', *Orbis* 35, 1, Winter: 29–39.

Saadatmand, Y. (1993) 'State capitalism: theory and application, the case of Iran', *Critique* 3, Fall: 55–79.

Sadowski, Y. M. (1993) *Scuds or Butter? The Political Economy of Arms Control in the Middle East*, Washington, DC: The Brookings Institution.

Saffari, S. (1993) 'The legitimation of the clergy's right to rule in the Iranian constitution of 1979', *British Journal of Middle Eastern Studies* 20, 1: 64–82.

Sarabi, F. (1994) 'The post-Khomeini era in Iran: the elections of the fourth Islamic Majlis', *The Middle East Journal* 48, 1, Winter: 89–107.

Savory, R. M. (1990) 'Religious dogma and the economic and political imperatives of Iranian foreign policy', in M. Rezun (ed.) *Iran at the Crossroads: Global Relations in a Turbulent Decade*, Boulder, Colorado: Westview Press.

Schahgaldian, N. B. (1989) *The Clerical Establishment in Iran*, Santa Monica, California: Rand.

Sciolino, E. (1992) 'Counting Iran's new arms is the easy part', *The New York Times*, 26 April: 2.

Segal, D. (1988) 'The Iran–Iraq war: a military analysis', *Foreign Affairs*, 66, 5, Summer: 946–63.

Segev, S. (1988) *The Iranian Triangle: The Untold Story of Israel's Role in the Iran-Contra Affair*, New York: The Free Press.

Siavoshi, S. (1992) 'Factionalism and Iranian politics: the post-Khomeini experience', *Iranian Studies* 25, 3–4, 27–49.

Sidahmed, A. (1992) 'Tehran–Khartoum: a new axis or a warning shot?', *Middle East International* 418, 7 February: 18–19.

Singh, R. K. (1980) *Iran: Quest for Security*, New Delhi: Vikas Publishing House.

SIPRI (various years) *SIPRI Yearbook: World Armament and Disarmament*, Oxford: Oxford University Press.

Smith, J. (1991) 'Biological weapons development', *Jane's Intelligence Review*, November: 483–7.

Sreberny-Mohammadi, A. and Mohammadi, A. (1987) 'Post-revolutionary Iranian exiles: a study in impotence', *Third World Quarterly* 9, 1, January: 108–29.

Stelzer, I. (1994) 'Middle East turmoil casts cloud over oil', *The Sunday Times* 6 February: 7.

Tabari, A. (1983) 'Role of the Shi'i clergy in Iranian politics', *Khamsin* 9: 50–76.

Taylor, T. (1993) 'Sales and security in the Gulf', *International Defence Review*, February: 138–9.

The Middle East Review (various years), Saffron Walden, Essex: World of Information.

The Middle East and North Africa (various years) 'Iran', London: Europa publications.

Thiemann, E. (1983) 'Iran under the Shah regime: model of dependent capitalist industrialisation', in G. Barthel (ed.) *Iran: From Monarchy to Republic*, Berlin: Akademie-Verlag.

Thurgood, L. (1978) 'Thinking 'big' pays off in Iran', *Near East Studies* January–February: 17–20.

United Nations Commission for Refugees (1993) *State of the World's Refugees*, New York: United Nations.

Vakili-Zad, C. (1992) 'Continuity and change: the structure of power in Iran', in C. Bina and H. Zangeneh (eds) *Modern Capitalism and Islamic Ideology in Iran*, London: Macmillan.

Valibeigi, M. (1992) 'Banking and credit rationing under the Islamic Republic of Iran', *Iranian Studies* 25, 3–4, 51–65.

Vaziri, H. (1992) 'Iran's involvement in Lebanon: polarisation and radicalisation of militant Islamic movements', *Journal of South Asian and Middle Eastern Studies* XVI, 2, Winter: 1–16.

Wallerstein, I. (1979) *The Capitalist World-Economy*, Cambridge: Cambridge University Press.

Watson, B. W., George, B., Tsouras, P. and Cyr, B. L. (1993) *Military Lessons of the Gulf War*, London: Greenhill Books.

White, G. (1984) 'Developmental states and socialist industrialisation in the Third World', *The Journal of Development Studies* 21, 1, October: 97–120.

Whitely, A. (1980) *The Approach of the Islamic Republic of Iran to Economic Policy*, Bonn: Neue Gesellschaft.

Wulf, H. (1993) 'Arms industry limited: the turning point in the 1990s', in H. Wulf (ed.) *Arms Industry Limited*, Oxford: Oxford University Press.

Yaghmaian, B. (1993) 'Recent developments in the political economy of Iran: 'the triangle crisis'', in C. Bina and H. Zangeneh (eds) *Modern Capitalism and Islamic Ideology in Iran*, London: Macmillan.

Zabih, S. (1982) *Iran since the Revolution*, London: Croom Helm.

Ziarati, M. (1992) 'Iranian national security policy', *Middle East International* 422, 3 April: 18–19.

Index